GUNLORE

GUNLORE

Firearms, Folkways, and Communities

Edited by Robert Glenn Howard and Eric A. Eliason

UNIVERSITY PRESS OF MISSISSIPPI / JACKSON

The University Press of Mississippi is the scholarly publishing agency of the Mississippi Institutions of Higher Learning: Alcorn State University, Delta State University, Jackson State University, Mississippi State University, Mississippi University for Women, Mississippi Valley State University, University of Mississippi, and University of Southern Mississippi.

www.upress.state.ms.us

The University Press of Mississippi is a member of the Association of University Presses.

Copyright © 2024 by University Press of Mississippi
All rights reserved

∞

Library of Congress Control Number: 2024939090

Hardback ISBN 978-1-4968-5092-8 | Paperback ISBN 978-1-4968-5093-5

Epub single ISBN 978-1-4968-5094-2 | Epub institutional ISBN 978-1-4968-5095-9

PDF single ISBN 978-1-4968-5096-6 | PDF institutional ISBN 978-1-4968-5097-3

British Library Cataloging-in-Publication Data available

CONTENTS

Introduction. Gunlore and Gunfolks:
Defining an Old and Powerful Genre 3
ROBERT GLENN HOWARD AND ERIC A. ELIASON

Chapter 1. Young Guns:
Folklore and the Fetishization of Guns among Juveniles at
an All-Male Correctional Facility in Tucson, Arizona 41
RAYMOND SUMMERVILLE

Chapter 2. Moms Who Carry:
Femininity and Firearms in Vernacular Digital Photography. 63
ANNAMARIE O'BRIEN MOREL

Chapter 3. Between the Forest and the Freezer:
Visual Culture and Hunting Weapons in the Upper Midwest. 94
TIM FRANDY

Chapter 4. 4chan, Firearms, and Folklore 110
NOAH D. ELIASON (WITH ERIC A. ELIASON)

Chapter 5. Percussioned Flintlocks: A Nineteenth-Century
Folk Art 126
NATHAN E. BENDER

Chapter 6. NERF PUNK: The Firearm Folklife of
"Alternative History" Cosplay. 135
LONDON BRICKLEY

Chapter 7. God's Warriors: Gunlore and Identity in the
Vernacular Discourse of a Survivalist Community. 163
MEGAN L. ZAHAY

Chapter 8. A Knack for Precision:
The Art and Science of a Gun-Making Dynasty 186
SANDRA BARTLETT ATWOOD

Chapter 9. Dangerous Tools of Expression:
The Benefits and Costs of Gunlore 217
ROBERT GLENN HOWARD

Chapter 10. Gun Play as Vernacular Religious Experience 238
JAY MECHLING

Chapter 11. Symbols and Things: A Reflection on *Gunlore* 262
TOK THOMPSON

About the Contributors 277
Index 281

GUNLORE

Introduction

GUNLORE AND GUN FOLKS

Defining an Old and Powerful Genre

ROBERT GLENN HOWARD AND ERIC A. ELIASON

GUNLORE AND ITS PERVASIVENESS:
DEFINITIONS AND EXAMPLES

This volume is the first ever collection of scholarship on the topic of "gunlore," or folklore about firearms. The scope of this neologism is broad. First used in print by Robert Glenn Howard in 2019, "gunlore" refers to any folklore genre related to firearms, be it narrative, proverb, folk-speech, customs, traditions, folk art, handicraft, material culture, etc. (74). Like all expressive culture, gunlore emerges from specific communities. Folk groups with a shared interest may form around firearms for several reasons—self-protection, hunting, crime, work, sport, political or social identity signaling, historical nostalgia, the desire to creatively modify guns to look or perform more to one's liking, or even to oppose firearms' use and ownership (Hathaway 2019). Several such "gunlore" genres and "gunfolk" groups are described in this collection.

But participation in gunlore is not limited to firearms aficionados. Even those who rarely think of guns live in a gunlore-saturated society. For example, the English language's firearms-related folk speech expressions are mostly metaphorical, but contain many references to violence, so perhaps we should provide a "trigger warning" before continuing with more examples. That noted, have you ever "set your sights" on a "longshot" goal and decided to "give it a shot?" Maybe the task turned out to be as easy as "shooting fish in a barrel?" . . . if you had gotten your "ducks in a row" (for carnival air gun shooting). Perhaps you didn't want to perform an onerous task, but you "bit the bullet" and did it anyway. Or when someone "held a gun to your head," did you resist and "stick to your guns?" And if stressed because you were

3

"under the gun," did you ever "refocus" and "stay on target" to avoid "shooting yourself in the foot?" Maybe you've been warned to "keep your powder dry," or told not to go off "half-cocked," or to not be "too quick on the draw," or advised "don't take a knife to a gunfight"? Or when you took action, did you "shoot from the hip," or "pull the trigger" on a purchase decision? Perhaps you once "took a shot in the dark" but, to your surprise, you actually discovered "the smoking gun." Did you ever stand by "locked and loaded," "ride shotgun," or object to a "loaded question"? Maybe you know someone who is a "hot shot," a "big shot," a "straight shooter," or "gun shy" (a reference to a hunting dog too startled by gunfire to be useful anymore)? Did you ever take a "scattershot" approach to a problem, or enthusiastically give it "both barrels"? After a whole winter with your basement weight set working on biceps, perhaps you proudly announced your tank-topped arrival at the beach with a boisterous, "Sun's out! Guns out!" Maybe someone you know has not had children, because he is "shooting blanks"? Perhaps you once "got caught in the crossfire" between two people with "hair-trigger" tempers who were "shooting off their mouths" in an argument? Maybe after your presentation on a difficult topic, you asked the audience not to "shoot the messenger," but to go ahead and "fire away" with questions. Have you ever personally "come under fire" from some "son of a gun" who "drew a bead" on you and "leveled" a criticism at your argument? (The last two figures of speech regard aiming, referencing the small bead on a front gunsight that needs to be "leveled" with the rear sight and target.) Whether their swipe at you "hit close to the mark" or was "wide of the target," maybe you still managed to "shoot back" a good quick comeback as a "parting shot."

If you answered "yes" to any of these questions, you might realize that the "scope" (is that another one?) of firearms-related folk speech, at least occasionally, includes virtually every English speaker, regardless of their level of firearms involvement.

The antiquated nature of some gunlore folk-speech terms suggests that this pervasiveness has been the case for quite some time. "Dry powder" and "half-cocked" refer to archaic firearms technologies hundreds of years old. Likewise, "a flash in the pan"—to mean something that quickly makes a big impression then goes nowhere—has nothing to do with cooking or kitchens. In early rudimentary firearms design, "the pan" was where flint sparks were intended to ignite black powder inside the firearm's chamber to propel a projectile out the barrel. The "flash" of powder happening only "in the pan," and the bullet staying put, was a common type of "misfire" back in the day. Maybe this was because your bullet and charge combo turned out, like that uninspiring person you hired to proactively and effectively get things done, turned out to be a "damp squib"—a "squib" being a cartridge that has the benefit of being in a properly working firearm, but still does not fire because of its own internal issues. But at least a "damp squib" is not like your "short fused" (referring to the match-lock firing system that preceded flintlocks) uncle Rick, who "goes off" at the slightest provocation. Variations of "aim," "target," and "shoot" are among the most common words in gun-related folk speech and are carryover metaphors from bow-and-arrow days, long before firearms were invented.

FIREARMS' UBIQUITY, POLICY DEBATES, AND PUBLIC DISCOURSE

In the United States, not only is gun-related folk speech near ubiquitous—so are guns. In 2020, a Gallup Poll estimated that 44 percent of US households have one or more guns (Saad 2020). With the emergence of the COVID-19 pandemic, media attention on erratic weather patterns associated with climate change, an uptick in crime in some places, and a perception of increased social and economic precarity, the US saw a record number of background checks and gained five million first-time gun buyers (Eger 2020). Of these new buyers, 58 percent were African American, and 40 percent were women ("First-Time" 2020). Considered as a single group, gun owners would be one of the largest lifestyle/hobby-based subcultures in America.

While guns and gun-related folk speech are ubiquitous in US culture today, both are also a source of controversy. When President Joe Biden vowed to enact a new gun ban, he did so using a medical analogy: "Gun violence in this country is an epidemic and it is an international embarrassment." As vice president, some years before, he used a different metaphor. Speaking to the press about his attendance at a series of meetings on how to "curb gun violence," he spoke of "shooting" for a deadline and the lack of a "silver bullet" for the problem.

Why would he use seemingly gun-positive folk speech? The short answer is that our shared informal culture (our folklore) gives us lots of "ammo" to use. It's not just that we live in a gun-rich environment, it's that we humans are drawn to powerful objects and guns are powerful objects. As we attach meaning to these powerful objects, that meaning gets empowered too. If the short answer to why gunlore is so common is that it empowers our everyday expressions, then the long answer might come into better focus through the wide complexity and variety of gunlore and gun cultures documented in this book.

6 INTRODUCTION: GUNLORE AND GUNFOLKS

Before that, though, we must note that it is perhaps impossible to talk about guns in the United States without acknowledging the political tension and potential human suffering that surrounds them. This tension and potential for harm has given rise to ongoing and often impassioned public discourse. With recurring gun violence and high-profile mass shootings, this attention has encouraged a surge of new books on the topic. While more books come out and the public debate goes on, clear policy imperatives do not leap from the data quite so easily as gun-rights or gun-control advocates might like, especially on the issue of whether, or in what circumstances, the presence of firearms might foster or prevent violence from happening.

Recent years have seen several new books that present in-depth examinations of various facets of America's uniquely well-developed gun culture.[1] Historians like Michael A. Bellesiles made controversial claims about how few guns were available in the early years of the United States, that were later shown to be fabricated. Pamela Haag argued quite the opposite: that the everyday nature of guns in early American culture made them unremarkably ubiquitous. Other work, like that of Clayton E. Cramer, have shown that guns were common and essential tools in colonial America and gunsmithing was an important element of the early US economy that helped spur the industrial revolution.

Other historians have focused on how gun policy has evolved, like Samuel Cornell (2006) in *A Well-Regulated Militia*. More contemporary cultural studies have looked at different aspects of American gun culture. Noah A. Schwartz (2022) has examined the National Rifle Association's marketing techniques, while Frank Smyth has looked at its institutional history. Jennifer Carlson's (2015) work has engaged in more philosophical questions about the role of institutions in a nation of armed individuals. Other authors have considered the role guns have played in different ethnic groups in the US, such as Charles E. Cobb's (2015) look at guns' role in the US civil rights movements. Other anthologies have brought together cultural theorists from a wide range of fields to consider American gun cultures in books like *God and Guns* (Hays and Crouch 2021), *Understanding American's Gun Culture* (Fisher and Hovey 2021), and *Rhetoric and Guns* (Wilkes, Kreuter, and Skinnel 2022).

In this wealth of thoughtful writing and the discussions it encourages, it is challenging to find a way to approach the topic without appearing to take sides: as an advocate of gun rights or an advocate of gun control. As result, there is a gulf in trust and understanding between what actual contemporary gun culture is like and the fearful perceptions of people who seem to live in a world apart. Because we all do share this world (and because it is necessary and possible for us to better understand one another), this volume's focus on the expressive culture of guns from folk speech to folk art is an attempt to better understand our world. Our primary focus is on the aesthetically minded and mindfully crafted artistry of vernacular verbal, digital, and material genres of creative expression. Hence, *gunlore* rather than "gun culture" is our defining term. Instead of getting lost in politics or statistics, we seek to offer this collection of essays to help expand our understanding of the various roles firearms play, have played, and can play in our shared cultural understandings.

SOME MAJOR THEMES OF GUNLORE

The same inherent power of firearms that fills shelves of books and fuels passionate public debates has also spawned not just one, or even just a few, but many forms of folklore. Nor does that folklore exist in just one or two folk groups. In fact, the symbolic power of guns is so great, and such a wide variety of people use them for such a wide variety of purposes, that this collection can only scratch the surface of the diversity of gunlore and firearm folk groups or "gunfolk." In the vast gunlore corpus, some common and over-arching themes emerge—often expressed in traditions, proverbs, customs, folk beliefs, and legends that many gunfolk from many subgroups might recognize. Some themes are along the lines of Coke vs. Pepsi or Ford vs. Chevy consumer preference rivalries. Others are more unifying in that they undergird and form a common starting point for the practices of many, often very distinct, gunfolk groups. Some of this lore is so pervasive as to defy easy citation with a single, or even a hundred, authoritative sources. To start covering some of this immense territory, our introduction provides brief overviews of several salient issues and introduces a few of the major varieties of gunfolk groups.

AK VS. AR

A prime example of preference rivalries in gunlore, the AK-47 vs. AR-15 debate is over fifty years old and shows no signs of letting up. Variants of these Cold War icons are still the standard infantry weapons for many militaries. Former Soviet and Warsaw Pact countries have favored the Russian-designed AK rifle platform, while NATO and its allies have preferred the US designed AR platform, known in its military guise as the M-16 at its introduction in the Vietnam War era, and in a much-modified version, as the

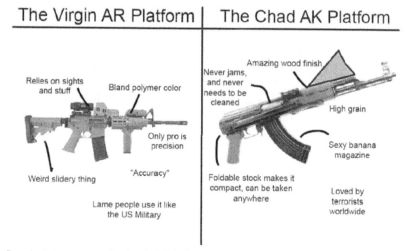

Figure I.1. An internet meme favoring the Kalashnikov.

M-4 to more recent soldiers. Variants of both rifle designs are available for sale to civilians in the United States. These weapons are, as enthusiasts will readily tell you, not "fully automatic assault weapons" but "semi-automatic modern sporting rifles." Today, these rifle types are some of the most popular types of firearms in America, and they are in common use for a range of nonmilitary purposes, perhaps most notably dealing with the economically devastating feral pig problem plaguing much of rural America (Shuppe 2018).

Which one is better? While "¿Porque no los dos?"[2] is a common answer, AK partisans prefer its reputed rugged reliability and larger bullet diameter. AR fans tout its better accuracy, range, as well as lighter weight, minimal recoil, and more compact, "easier-to-tote-more" small rounds. The orally circulated folk history follows the actual history of the Vietnam War in remembering early M-16 models as cheaply made and prone to misfires and jams. These problems were soon corrected, and today's M-16 descendant, the M-4, is a highly reliable and esteemed firearm.

But these AR improvements did not diminish the folk beliefs and legends about the AK's reliability. Perhaps the most famous story in the AK-47 narrative cycle is about Col. David Hackworth. While on patrol with his unit during the Vietnam War, Hackworth saw the buttstock of an AK-47 sticking out of the side of a riverbank. He dug the rifle out from under several feet of rock-hard dirt that, during the rainy season flooding, had once been several feet of silty mud down into which the rifle had sunk. Every moving part of the gun was absolutely caked and permeated with concrete-like filth. The colonel beat the Kalashnikov on the ground a few times, shook it off, racked back the slide to chamber around, flipped the selector to full-auto, and smoothly fired off all the magazine's remaining rounds.

"STOPPING POWER," "KNOCK BACK," AND COLT 1911 ETIOLOGICAL LEGENDS

A similar controversy of competing folk-historical anecdotes and ballistic folk beliefs has swirled around another iconic firearm, the Colt 1911 pistol originally chambered in .45 ACP.[3] Etiological legends for this still-widely popular sidearm emerge from the Moro Rebellion, or Philippine-American War, of the early twentieth century.[4] After defeating the Spanish in 1899, the US military struggled to pacify the whole archipelago, especially the southern islands of Mindanao and Jolo, where the famous General John J. Pershing would later serve as the colonial governor from 1909 to 1913. During that time, according to legend, the Moro fighters would "run amok" or come screaming down the mountainside to fall on US Army positions in a war-frenzy (Saint Martin 1999, 66–70). The soldiers on the receiving end of these fearsome assaults would blast away with their standard issue .38 caliber revolvers that repeatedly hit their targets, but failed to slow the Moros, who then sliced viciously into the American lines with their kris knives, the traditional Moro fighting weapon.

The intensity of these experiences for American soldiers caught in a complex international conflict, and these experiences' effect on American society at large, are evidenced by their contribution of two familiar elements to US culture: (1) the folk-speech phrase "running amok," a Tausug language Moro Island term referring to a frenzied state of unrestrained and chaotic violent behavior (Carr and Tan 1976, 1295–99), and (2) John Moses Browning's Colt 1911 pistol, so named for the year it entered military service.

According to the legends, US troops needed "stopping power" that their .38 revolvers were not providing. The .45 ACP rounds fired from a 1911 semi-automatic pistol had more gunpowder, a larger diameter and heavier bullet, could carry more rounds, and could be reloaded more quickly than a .38 revolver. Stories spread, and have lasted until this day, not only of the 1911's stopping power but of its rounds actually knocking Moro warriors back up the mountainside.

Eric Eliason served on Jolo island in 2005–2006 with his National Guard Special Forces unit training with Filipino Marines fighting Al-Qaeda-allied Moro insurgents, whose great-grandfathers fought General Pershing. Filipino Marines would chuckle in playful derision at their American allies' less-storied, standard issue Baretta 9mm pistols. They would say, "Look around you at these mountains. You know where you are right?" and then thumbing their own standard issue .45 ACP Colt 1911s, they would ask, "You know the story of how we got these, right?"

Folklore scholarship is replete with examples from ethnobotany, "traditional ecological knowledge," and David Hufford's experience-centered approach where the "the folk" long passed on knowledge that was only later "discovered" by science to be quite sound.[5] The folk belief of the 1911's qualitatively better "knock back power" is not one of these instances. Not even close. No pistol of any caliber can "knock back" anyone—at least on the receiving end. However, in the experience of untrained shooters with improper stances and loose grips, firing powerful handguns certainly sometimes involves perceived "knock back" of the shooter. But even the mammoth Smith and Wesson 500 cannot "knock back" attackers, despite being an ungainly wrist-wrenching behemoth with little practical use beyond perhaps personal defense in bear country and seizing the "most powerful handgun in the world" bragging rights from Dirty Harry's legendary .44 Magnum. Even rifles or shotguns cannot "knock back" or even appreciably slow the momentum of an attacker—despite Hollywood's fanciful depictions (Fackler 1998, 17–28; Duncan 2014). But since rifles are significantly more powerful than pistols, one wonders why the US troops of the 1911 etiological legends on Jolo did not use rifles?

For many of today's data- and measurement-tech–obsessed gun-geeks, talking of the 1911's ostensible "knock back power" also serves as a shibboleth. In this case, the term does not distinguish between gun culture insiders and outsiders but reveals an internal gun-culture division between those whom the "informed" consider to be out-of-date "fudds" (named after the clueless Looney Tunes character who was ever "hunting wabbits") and modern up-to-date firearms enthusiasts, serious about having the most appropriate firearms for self-defense and home protection. Such modern enthusiasts might very well even own a few 1911's for their elegant iconic design, and historical importance. Afterall, the 1911 was the America's military sidearm of two world wars, Korea, and Vietnam. But for any situation that would require a reliable, accurate pistol with sufficient capacity to get the job done, they would likely prefer something with a fifteen-or-more-round double-stack magazine and striker-fire, rather than the standard 1911's single-stack seven-round capacity and old-school hammer-fire. This particular debate over pistol choice appears in the well-known gun-culture proverb: "I show my 1911 to my friends, and my Glock to my enemies" (Howard 2019).

Both the AK vs. AR and the .45 vs. .38 debates have spawned hundreds of "myth-busters" style YouTube videos and explanatory webpages involving ballistic gel, rolling pig carcasses, and recreations of Col. Hackworth's dried out muddy riverbank. All of this enacting of folk narrative or "ostension" testifies to the importance of these two folk-debate dyads.[6]

FIREARMS SAFETY: RITUAL, CUSTOM, FOLK LAW, AND GUN GAMES

The gunlore genre with the most important impact in recent decades might be the wide diffusion and inculcation of gun safety rules. More so than "knock back," a better case for folkways being more efficacious than "official" remedies might be seen in the decline in firearms-related accidental deaths continuing over several decades.[7] Those active in gun culture over many years have witnessed, and contributed to voluntary, emergent cultural practices that appear to be a major reason for the decline (Weingarten 2017). A stable set of rules for gun safety has been widely promulgated and successfully enculturated in recent years, with a resultant reduction in firearms-related accidents. The National Rifle Association is much maligned, even by many gun owners, for its infighting, over-paid lavish living executives, ignoring minority gun-rights cases, and focus on electing Republicans over protecting gun rights for all. Nevertheless, the NRA is a powerful presence and purveyor of publications with which gunfolk have traditionally often been at least passively acquainted. Their robust and widespread training efforts deserve at least some credit for gun safety advances.

Such dramatic reductions in unintended firearm deaths could not have happened without the wide acceptance of both gun safety principals as authoritative folk law, and the emergence of a tradition of ritual practice to promulgate adherence to those laws (Renteln and Dundes, 1995; Bascom 1954, 333–49). So deep has the cultural shift among gunfolk been, that in many circles, if one speaks of an "accidental discharge" they might be firmly corrected and asked to use the more "accurate" phrase: "negligent discharge" because, according to contemporary gun culture mores, anytime anyone claims to have fired a gun "by accident" they have actually been negligent by failing to adhere to gun safety rules. In gunfolks' meta-folkloric folk-folkloristics (Eliason 2012, 58–76), it is a folk belief among many gunfolk that "anti-gunners" have a folk belief that guns can "just go off" with no human responsible. Regardless of how widespread this folk belief may, or may not, actually be among firearms' opponents, at least in gunfolk circles, the centrality of personal responsibility for firearm safety has reached near unanimous levels.

When actor Alec Baldwin claimed not to be responsible for the tragic shooting of cinematographer Halyna Hutchins on set on October 21, 2021, he stated that that he did not know the prop gun was loaded with a live round.[8] In October of 2022, Baldwin settled a wrongful death law suit out of court, and in April 2023 the criminal charges associated with the incident were dropped by the Santa Fe district attorney. At the time of the incident, however, online gunfolk were unimpressed with his explanation that seemed *not* to be a reasonable explanation, but a clear admission that Baldwin had not been following even the most basic gun safety rules even the most unseasoned of firearms users should know.

Baldwin, filming a western, was no greenhorn. So, since he failed to take personal responsibility at the level expected by many in gun culture, YouTube recreations allegedly showing the impossibility of Baldwin's mistake went into overdrive (TTAG Contributor 2021). Surely he *always* treated his gun like it was loaded, even after *always* checking to see if it was? Surely he did not point his gun at anything he did not intend to destroy? Surely he knew what was behind what he was pointing his gun at? Surely he kept his finger off the trigger until ready to fire? Surely he followed Hollywood's additional standard safety practice in filming scenes with firearms—never aiming at another actor but at a marked spot behind and to their side? Gunfolk who follow such safety rules, every time they hold a gun were baffled that the actor (a professional who has handled prop firearms many times) would not follow basic, commonly known, authoritative folk law (USCCA 2022).

In formal training settings and even in informal "plinking" sessions involving less-experienced shooters, an afternoon's shooting is likely to begin with an invocational ritual—a liturgical recitation of, and reflection on, the rules of gun safety. More seasoned shooters serve as cantors, while initiates in the congregation must all participate, even if they have done so many times before. Each rule in turn is said aloud, explained, demonstrated, and quizzed out of the potential shooters standing behind a table of same-direction parallel-placed firearms that no one is allowed to touch until their gun safety catechism is complete.

If there is a central unifying custom in the wide variety of gun cultures, the set of folk law rules of gun safety is it. Like any well-defined genre, the gun safety rules show a stability and standard sequencing of elements (Propp 1968). As with any type of lore, there are slight variants in the ways the rules

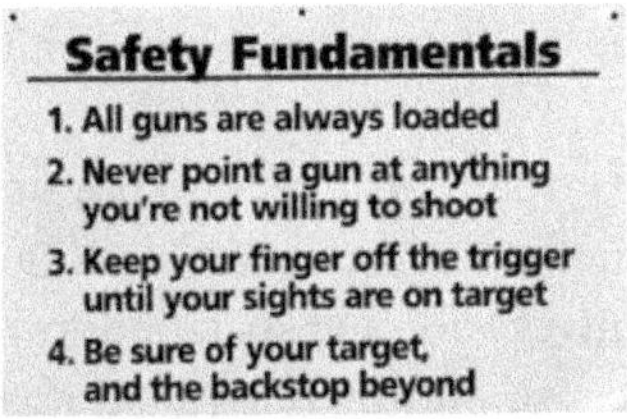

Safety Fundamentals

1. All guns are always loaded
2. Never point a gun at anything you're not willing to shoot
3. Keep your finger off the trigger until your sights are on target
4. Be sure of your target, and the backstop beyond

Figure I.2. Generic gun safety sign.

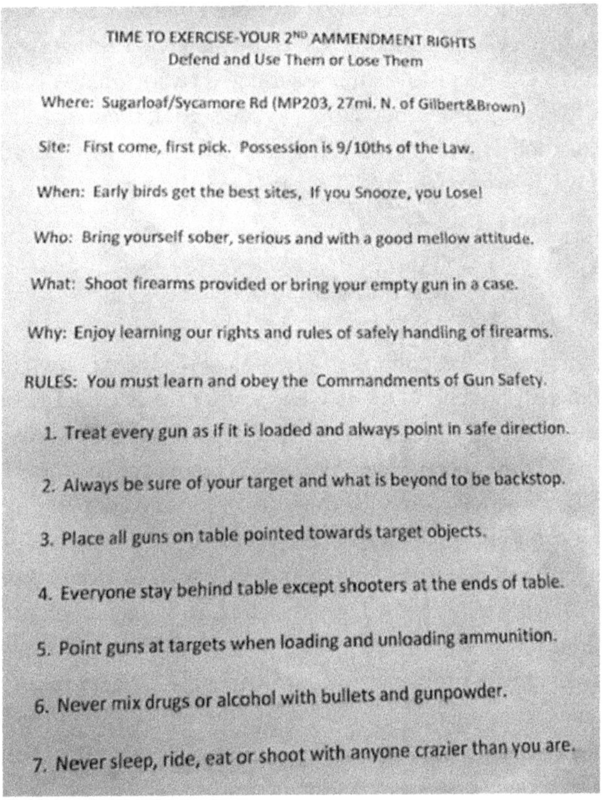

TIME TO EXERCISE-YOUR 2ᴺᴰ AMMENDMENT RIGHTS
Defend and Use Them or Lose Them

Where: Sugarloaf/Sycamore Rd (MP203, 27mi. N. of Gilbert&Brown)

Site: First come, first pick. Possession is 9/10ths of the Law.

When: Early birds get the best sites, If you Snooze, you Lose!

Who: Bring yourself sober, serious and with a good mellow attitude.

What: Shoot firearms provided or bring your empty gun in a case.

Why: Enjoy learning our rights and rules of safely handling of firearms.

RULES: You must learn and obey the Commandments of Gun Safety.

1. Treat every gun as if it is loaded and always point in safe direction.

2. Always be sure of your target and what is beyond to be backstop.

3. Place all guns on table pointed towards target objects.

4. Everyone stay behind table except shooters at the ends of table.

5. Point guns at targets when loading and unloading ammunition.

6. Never mix drugs or alcohol with bullets and gunpowder.

7. Never sleep, ride, eat or shoot with anyone crazier than you are.

Figure I.3. David Smith's oft-used handout for shooting with his children and grandchildren in Mesa, Arizona.

are numbered, worded, and organized, from fairly generic ones found and signs that can be purchased to those promoted by major institutions.

NRA gun safety rules:
ALWAYS keep the gun pointed in a safe direction.
ALWAYS keep your finger off the trigger until ready to shoot.
ALWAYS keep the gun unloaded until ready to use (NRA).

14   INTRODUCTION: GUNLORE AND GUNFOLKS

To those made by and for small groups such as families who go shooting together.

The spread of gun safety traditional practices has almost certainly pushed into even greater rarity foolhardy "gun game" traditions. Russian roulette, so well-known that narratives about, or metaphorical uses of, the term far outstrip actual occurrences of putting one round in a revolver, giving the cylinder a spin, then firing at oneself or another person. Less well-known, but similarly dangerous, "cuckoo" is rumored by today's French Foreign Legionaries to have been regularly played by their less risk-averse predecessors. Two players with pistols enter a darkened cellar. One yells, "Cuckoo!" then dives for cover. The other shoots at the sound, then takes his turn to call out "Cuckoo!" and dive away. "The game ends with either death, severe injury, or both revolvers empty" (Twigger 2017).

JOKES AND PARODIES

Researchers interested in gunlore might look at jokes circulating orally and online and discover old standbys such as, "You see the classified ad for French army surplus rifles? They are in great shape. Never fired, and only dropped once." Or back in the 1960s when Polish jokes were popular, one might hear, "In our country we play Russian roulette with a revolver. In Poland they do it with a semi-automatic." To the firearms-uninitiated, one bullet in a revolver cylinder which is spun and randomly slapped closed has a one in six chance of firing when the trigger is pulled. In a semiautomatic, if there is no malfunction or squib, and even if there is only one bullet left in the firearm, it will always fire.

Stereotypes embedded in gun jokes emerge not just in older European contexts but also in current imagery of criminal or "gangster" culture. For example, firing one's pistol perpendicular to, rather than parallel with, the shooter's torso is sometimes termed the "gangster side-grip." The side-grip was powerfully associated with Black American gang culture in the 1993 Hughes brothers' movie *Menace II Society* (Gambetta 2011). Though Marlon Brando and Clint Eastwood both seem to have foreshadowed the technique in *One-Eyed Jacks* (1961) and *The Good, the Bad and the Ugly* (1966) respectively. With popular media portrayals, the practice spread in folk culture in a variety of forms.

Rumored explanations for this technique have swirled orally and on the internet. Is it mere stylistic flourish drawing visual attention to the shooter's intention to fire? Some say it is pure Hollywood with little basis in actual criminal practice until after the release of the 1993 movie caused widespread ostension. The Hughes brothers say they witnessed the technique being used in a 1987 robbery and worked it into their movie (Palmer 2009; Lewine).[9]

Another etiological folk belief holds that the main reason the side-grip began to appear in movies was simply to avoid blocking views of actors' faces from desired camera angles. The side-grip has many gun culture haters who see it as a risky and indiscriminate violation of proper shooting technique and an affront to the serious dignity that should always accompany handling firearms. But other gun writers have claimed that it makes sense in some situations. The sideways hold is more naturally ergonomic and makes it easier to aim when a riot police officer is trying to get a sight picture through the narrow slit of his or her ballistic shield. Or, in another context, if someone is shooting from the cracked-open window of a moving car. However, usually, more of one's view of potential threats is blocked by one's hand, and regaining a site picture after firing is slower.

Brian Palmer reviewed depictions of this technique in music videos and discovered that the gesture is often not a static pose but one stage in a larger movement. The shooter at first holds the pistol properly, then slowly rotates it and lifts slightly as if to say, "I know how to hold a gun properly, but I have such contempt for you I'm going to absolutely on purpose make sure you see that I am not going to shoot you that way."

GUN PENS/FOAFS AND REGIONAL FOLKLORE

A massive potential area of investigation is "personal experience narratives" and "friend-of-a-friend stories" about interpersonal firearms use. Two separate but similar PEN/FOAF cycles can emerge from when people use guns. Depending on context and community, such narratives may portray such use as an unnecessary tragedy, preventable by stricter gun laws, or as a life-saving boon, made possible only by potential victims' ready access to guns for personal defense. One of the most common narratives of this type has two common variant classes, with divergent homiletic takeaways. One variant goes like this: "An estranged boyfriend purchases a handgun and goes to his ex-girlfriend's house and shoots her. Perhaps stricter gun laws or longer waiting periods might have prevented this." A similar but reversed narrative goes like this: "A woman learns her ex-boyfriend intends her harm, so she buys a handgun. When he arrives at her house, she uses it to prevent his attack. Perhaps stricter gun laws or longer waiting periods would have led to her death."

With annual murder rates over thirteen thousand in the United States (FBI 2019), there must be no shortage of scenarios that could spark the circulation of thousands of narratives about seemingly preventable violent encounters, or how a potential victim avoided violence by having a gun. Which of the two narrative types have you heard of, heard more of, and are more likely to believe or see as relevant to policy debates? Your answer to this may depend significantly on the set of interconnected values and folk beliefs about commonsense behaviors that are prevalent in your social circles. And what those circles are would likely be influenced by the patterns of crime and gun ownership in your area. In the United States, gun ownership is concentrated in the noncoastal West and Southeastern US where Montana has the highest rate: 66.3 guns per person and West Virginia leads the South with 58.5. New Jersey is the lowest with only 14.7 guns per person ("Gun Ownership by State" 2023). There are low-gun-ownership areas where individuals might have experienced crime and high-gun-ownership areas where crimes might be few and far between. Our personal perceptions of guns are shaped by our experiences, our communities, and our beliefs and values (Igielnik 2017; Boeck, et al. 2020, 10–22). Beyond the United States, gun ownership is largely much smaller. It has been estimated that there are 120.5 guns per person in the United States. The next highest number of guns per person is half that of the US. Nations like the Falkland Islands with 62.1 guns per person, Yemen with 52.8, Canada with 34.7, and Finland with 32.4 ("Gun Ownership by Country" 2023).

Are firearms a normal part of your local culture—owned and used recreationally often with no harm coming to yourself or anyone you know? And when guns are used in earnest, are the narratives that circulate most often about justified self-defense from a violent attacker? Or do very few people own firearms in your neighborhood except for those involved in criminal activity? And are most stories circulating about guns ones where they are used in violent crimes against innocent victims?

Regional differences may lead to differing regional folk narrative traditions, each emerging, in part, from geographically varying likelihoods of people having differing kinds of experiences with firearms. As is commonly noted in the study of narrative and folk belief, people ethnocentrically tend to see their own narrative-sustained beliefs as commonsensical and generally applicable to benighted others, who believe "crazy superstitions." Considering the vast numbers of both narrative varieties, the potential for investigation here is enormous. But little work along these lines has been done so far. So, the observations above are preliminary and exploratory in nature.

The rural/urban divide is a particularly salient differentiator in gun ownership rates and attitudes about them (Savat 2020). The recognition of cultural differences between rural and urban societies, and a preferential option for the rural, forms the very genesis of folklore as a discipline (Bennett 1993, 77–91). Alan Dundes moved us away from defining "the folk" as an undifferentiated national peasantry to "folk groups" of "any group of at least two people that share at least one thing in common." Steve Zeitlin's City Lore initiative in New York City ("Our Vision") is just one of many data points showing that ongoing urbanization has not caused folklore to disappear. Folklore is everywhere and the field's focus has appropriately shifted away from the ideal type of the peasant-filled agricultural village.[10] Gunlore, gunfolk, and gun culture are an overdue focus for folklorists, who seem well-prepared as a discipline to have something to say about this topic wherever it appears: from the rural farm to the city, to the newest internet platform.

FIREARMS MODIFICATION AND CUSTOMIZATION AS FOLK ART

The gunlore variety that most obviously meets traditional disciplinary understandings of folk art might be the metal engraving of firearms and the leatherwork of holsters. These are long-established traditions whose legacy extends back before firearms to prehistoric times, where evidence suggests that humans have always focused their creative artisanal attention on their weaponry in every culture in every era.

Often, different gunfolk subgroups prefer different aesthetics. For example, two pistols of the same design were modified for two different folk groups. One, with appeals to US veterans and World War II nostalgists with celebratory messages about World War II. A second gun of the same type is covered in ornate gold engraving with the words "I prefer to die on my feet than to live on my knees . . ." inscribed in Spanish. This pistol appeals to a rebellious and revolutionary spirit, from the swagger of the low-level cartel smuggler to the righteousness of a Marxist revolutionary—and the Norteño fashionistas seeking to imitate either.

Gunsmiths are often professional artisans that create and modify firearms for functional and aesthetic purposes; Sandi Atwood profiles her own Canadian gunsmithing family in this volume. Recent decades have witnessed a great American democratization of many of the tasks that were once more exclusively the purview of gunsmiths and their traditional master/

Figure I.4.

Figure I.5. Pistol in a stock meme.

apprentice-transmitted skillset. Have a casing ejection problem? Want to mount a scope or flashlight on your rifle? Don't like your handgrip and want an ergonomically different one? All this, and more, is all now easily accomplished by the DIY gun-owner, thanks to industry standardization and modular design. The inherent modularity of the AR-15 platform has clearly contributed to its success as the most popular rifle in America. Each gun owner can set up his or her rifle to achieve a particular purpose, be that CQB (close quarter combat), long range target shooting, home defense, or hunting. Virtually anyone can build themselves a precision instrument, a "range toy," an eye-candy "safe queen," or rugged, no-frills, knock-about field gun, or a self-deprecating joke that mocks, or takes to absurd extremes, some aspect of gun enthusiasts' proclivities.

Due to this modularity, the AR-15 platform has been called "tinker toys for grown-ups" by gun enthusiasts. The endless possibilities and the extremes to which some gun-owners go in their modifications are rich fields of harvest for internet parody makers. Try too hard to make your AR-15 or semiauto pistol look like the ones in your favorite video game, and you may be teased for not being "tactical" but "tacti-cool"—Likewise, if your "build" seems to be prioritizing a particular menacing "black gun" aesthetic by using cheap and cooler looking, rather than sturdy and function-focused, components and finishes. But, as with many epithets, "tacti-cool" has also come to be embraced by many of its intended targets, who realize they are not ashamed of their aesthetic preferences, or for letting those drive their build choices. Perhaps anyway, so long as it is clear they have successfully conveyed at least a modicum of ironic detachment.

PERSONAL DEFENSE MAXIMS FROM YOUR FIREARMS INSTRUCTOR (AND THE DALAI LAMA)

While gun-related expressions are widely popular in the English-speaking world, there is also insider lingo, sayings, proverbs, and related folk law etiquette circulating in each gun sub-culture. One of the largest of these is those who own handguns for home defense or concealed carry while out and about. Much of this lore is passed on during firearms training required by some states to get a concealed-carry permit (CCP). On why one might need their own firearm when "you can always call 911," a traditional comeback is, "When seconds count, the police are only minutes away." On the fear that one's self-defense-justified shooting might not be seen that way in court, there is the grim jury and pall bearer referencing, "Better to be judged by twelve, than carried by six."

In many jurisdictions "brandishing" a firearm is a crime. The presumption being that if a concealed-carry permit holder draws their weapon to be seen, and then puts it away without it being fired, it should not have been drawn in the first place, and the act of pulling it out was menacing and dangerous for no good reason. Others argue that if personal injury can be deterred just by demonstrating that one is armed and ready to defend oneself, is this not better than actually shooting someone?

As varying and sometimes competing maxims and unsettled mores swirl around each other in the world of defensive personal firearm use, some aspects of the concealed-carry community's folk law are clear and easily expressed in succinct, if not particularly poetic, orally relayed sayings and

> If someone has a gun
> and is trying to kill you,
> it would be reasonable
> to shoot back with your
> own gun.
>
> Dalai Lama, Seattle Times, May 15, 2001

Figure I.6. Dalai Lama Même.

proverbs. Don't ask someone whether or not they are carrying. Don't advertise in any way that you are carrying. Don't talk about it. Don't let your firearm "print" or become visible through your clothing, and do not let your concealed-carry weapon leave your person except by your own conscious choice to put it away in safe storage. The 1990s "don't ask; don't tell" US policy on "gays in the military" (as it was most often termed at that time) has been repurposed by the concealed-carry community, as has the famous line from the 1999 movie *Fight Club*, "The first rule of fight club is . . . you do not talk about fight club." For the concealed-carry community, "the first rule of CC club is you do not talk about CC club."[11]

On one of the presumed effects of the cultural spread of carrying a concealed weapon (CCW), there is, "An armed society is a polite society." This aspiration is reenforced by defensive firearms instructors who deploy many oft-shared sayings to drive this home to their students. In a discussion on the r/CCW subreddit, posters recollected their instructors' variants of lore-on-a-theme with sayings like, "You're now the nicest guy in the world." "Learn to swallow your ego, otherwise you'll end up in prison swallowing something else." "You can carry your ego or your firearm, but not both." "You can either carry a gun or a temper. Never both." "You're not allowed to be angry." "My gun is insurance against the gravest extreme. No more, no less." "Innocence, imminence, proportionality, avoidance, reasonableness." "I was taught that I'm now a loser. I will lose all arguments and never put up a fight. Always back down and retreat. Because if things escalate you're in deep shit." "Big talk is only going to needlessly escalate a confrontation and will only serve to predispose a jury against you if it comes to that. Keep your mouth shut. If someone needs shooting, shoot them. But keep your big dumb mouth closed. Save the yammering for your lawyer."

The thematic consistency of CCP instructor lore seems designed to inculcate certain behaviors and habits of mind that would supersede those that some folk beliefs hold can overtake anyone newly enamored with the power a firearm can seem to impart to its carrier. Does merely having a gun on you make you more likely to choose a violent approach to a tense situation? Not if the prevalent culture and lore of CCP instructors can turn this ostensible impulse on its head and make carrying a reason for extra restraint.

CCP instructors will often speak of the psychological devastation personal defense shooters feel when considering that they have maimed someone or taken someone's life, even if their shooting was justified. Pull a gun to stop someone from breaking into my car? Both CCP culture and the law say, "No." To protect myself or loved ones from a violent attacker? "Well, that is up to you decide, but you better consider this carefully before the heat of the moment. Be sure you can live with what you choose."

The voice of your CCP instructor talking shop and imparting wisdom showed up in popular gunlore memes of a few years ago. A wonderfully multilayered example of meta-folkloric digital folk art, one example shows an actual quote from the Dalai Lama as reported in the *Seattle Times*.

That His Holiness, a worldwide icon of peace and serenity, would say such a thing is a textbook example of the "incongruity" part of Elliott Oring's observation that underlying most humor is some sort of appropriate incongruity (Oring 2017). The meme images delve deep into the defensive shooting training community's technical insider jargon to say things that are perhaps more parody than practice. These memes imagine Dalai Lama "quotes" expressing a nugget of proverbial gunfighting folk wisdom that cleverly juxtapose with the photograph's hand gestures and facial expressions. The quotes run from "If someone has a gun and is trying to kill you, it would be reasonable to shoot back with your own gun" to "Slow down hero, you can't miss fast enough to win."

GUNFOLK

Just as this "barrage" of examples has demonstrated a vast scope and variety of gunlore, so too can a barrage of gun cultures or "gunfolk" examples demonstrate the fact that American gun culture is an array of complex, diverse, overlapping, and contradicting groups. Gunlore is even more ubiquitous than guns themselves, and to understand the roles gunlore play in the everyday lives of so many of us, we can look to these communities to understand the kinds of tools guns as symbols offer those who focus on them as important parts of their lives. Because firearms are tools (objects designed to complete a specific task), most firearms communities center around different purposes and specific kinds of activities. These activities are wildly diverse, as are the different gun cultures they spawn. We cannot easily dismiss US gun cultures with simple stereotypes. To do so would fail to capture the true nature of gunlore and, as a result, the symbolic power of the objects that have given rise to this lore. To begin to understand the communities where this lore emerges, first we have to try to describe them.

A few top-level analytic categories with subcategories under them can start to give us a sense of the diversity of gun cultures in the US today. Because individuals might well participate in several different categories, and some of the categories themselves might overlap, we have categorized these communities based on a set of five overlapping and nonexclusive sorts of communities. There are gun communities based on (1) the activities people do with their guns; (2) professions that require, or often engage, guns as tools; (3) communities focused on gender and sexuality; (4) those based on ethnic or racial identifications; and finally (5) those based on politics and advocacy.

HUNTING

Probably the biggest group of activity-based gun cultures are those emerging from hunting. Among hunters, of course, there are a huge variety of subgroups based primarily on what is being hunted, how the hunting is being done, and where and when it takes place. These groups share lore surrounding techniques, equipment, and beliefs: from building deer stands (to use with rifles that can kill at significant distances so the hunter stays in a specific place) to using camouflage to fool turkeys (who can see in color, unlike deer); and from small bird hunting with light shotgun shells for quail, grouse, pheasant, or dove where dogs are often used to flush out and retrieve the birds, to water fowl like ducks where boats and blinds to hide behind are often used as well as more powerful shotgun shells to go longer distances (Cutchins and Eliason 2009; Bronner 2008).

There is even a distinction, with attending folk beliefs and ethical positions, between those hunting edible game versus those hunting game "for sport," "trophies," or purely for recreation. Sport hunting activities can range from training dogs to chase down a bear until it is so exhausted it can only retreat up a tree where the hunter can easily shoot it at close range to, for the wealthy, big game or safari hunting in far-off locations often traveled to at significant cost.[12] After the hunt itself, of course, for each of these game animals there are traditional arts of butchering, preparing, cooking, and sometimes taxidermy for trophies, all of which are often learned of through informal face-to-face interaction.

COMPETITIVE SHOOTING

"Shooting sports" is maybe the next largest activity-based category of gun communities. Another subcategory of gun related activities that gun folks use and recognize, these tend to be competitive or self-competitive but don't typically include killing things. They are typically separated from hunting and run a range from the informal (akin to shooting pool at the bar) to the highly organized (with international organizations and professional tours).

Probably the most informal shooting sport is generally referred to as "plinking." Plinking, we think, refers to the sound a bullet makes when it hits thick steel targets. These sort of steel targets give immediate feedback, but the bullets do not leave easily identifiable holes in them. As a result, plinking steel is not very precise as would be required in bullseye shooting competitions. Even less precise, the activity of "going shooting" or even "shooting shit" generally refers to plinking where the targets offer more exciting immediate feedback like soda bottles, watermelons, old refrigerators, and the like. Especially dramatic are reactive targets or "Tannerite." These are made by mixing nineteen parts ammonium nitrate with one part powdered aluminum. This mix is completely safe and inert unless it is hit by a projectile traveling over two thousand feet per second. If so, a dramatic explosion ensues.

"Shooting targets" often refers to a somewhat less informal activity where one or more individuals shoot paper targets designed for that purpose. Most like shooting pool or playing darts, informal target shooting allows for relatively precise scoring and in that way facilitates friendly competition. This kind of shooting has its own subcategories including pistol shooting versus distance-rifle shooting, and each variety has its own equipment, techniques, skills, and challenges. Often the same scoring and targets are used in these informal activities that would be used in formal and institutional target competitions.

Following the continuum of gun-based activities from informal plinking to the increasingly formal, we can distinguish between two main types of guns sports that have formal organizations. While, of course, informal practice occurs (and even overlaps with plinking and target shooting), there are both static and moving, action, or "run and gun" sports activities that have international, national, and local levels of institutional organization.

Static shooting sports emphasize extreme precision and thus demand intense mental and small motor discipline. There are well-established clubs, specialized equipment, corporate sponsorships, college teams, and well-known competitors in "bullseye shooting." With international organizations and standardized targets and scoring, bullseye shooting typically uses small caliber firearms or even air guns to shoot at small targets where points are scored based on very small increments of highly precise shot placements. Bullseye shooting can use both rifles and handguns, but its equipment and techniques do not bear as close of a resemblance to hunting or military training as do some shooting sports.

The primary static shotgun-based sports of shooting "skeet" or "trap," for example, seem to replicate the basic skills of bird hunting. In both skeet and trap shooting, a clay "pigeon" (much like a small frisbee) is thrown with a thrower or launched by a specialized machine and the shooter is tasked with breaking the pigeon as if it were a real bird.

In addition to these static gun sports which require intense concentration and precise muscle control, formal action shooting or "run and gun" sports add the challenge of calming the muscles and mind after engaging in strenuous physical activity. In these sports, physical as well as mental fitness are of paramount importance. Well-known for its popularity in Northern Europe as well its inclusion in the winter Olympic games, the biathlon is a race that combines cross-county skiing with bullseye shooting where each competitor must ski a set distance carrying a rifle, stop and hit a number of bullseye targets, and then ski another set distance. On these courses, the faster time wins.

If a biathlon seems to have evolved out the skills of hunting in a cold environment, "practical shooting" sports evolved out of military and defensive applications of firearms. The International Defensive Pistol Association, for example, has established a range of competitions and competition standards based on defensive pistol techniques.

The "3 Gun" competitions are similar, but include pistol, rifle, and shotgun techniques that typically feature strenuous exercise followed by target shooting. Generally, these more "practical" competitions evolved out of military and law enforcement training, much as dressage horse riding competitions evolved out of cavalry training.

HISTORICAL GUN HOBBYISTS

Inhabiting the edge of the activity-based gun communities and beginning to shift into our next category, lifestyle or hobby-based communities, we can find historical gun hobbyists who come together to celebrate particular historical firearms cultures. Primary among these activities are "cowboy action shooting" competitions. These unique activities feature competitions of skills that would have been practical in the nineteenth century (or at least some

Figure I.7. SASS website, 2021.

romanticized modern idea of it) similar to how logrolling competitions and rodeo first emerged from occupational skills associated with logging and ranching. With several organizations and standardized rules, cowboy action shooting requires that competitors use nineteenth-century-style firearms, dress in nineteenth-century-style clothing, and use aliases. Cowboy action shooting competitions have a more light-hearted character to them while, at the same time, they include dedicated and serious competitors capable of astounding feats like shooting holes in coins tossed into the air.

CAS first emerged in the nineteenth century as living participants in the actual "Wild West" like General George Armstrong Custer, and the Lakota he fought, created personalities and started shows that self-consciously and flamboyantly fashioned their dress and demeanor to play up stereotypes of what iconic romantic westerners should look like in their various roles.[13] Actual Wild West participants like Buffalo Bill and Sitting Bull went on tour together in "Wild West Shows" immensely popular well into the twentieth

26 INTRODUCTION: GUNLORE AND GUNFOLKS

century, where they continued to gallop about on horseback and fire off guns. Even as such shows waned in popularity, performers for tourists in towns like Tombstone, Arizona; Dodge City, Kansas; and Ft. Worth, Texas, continued to dress like cowboys and perform feats of shooting skill. Sometimes these performers came to serve as stunt people in Western movies. In this way, today's cowboy action shooters continue a tradition of dress, single action gunslinging, and facial hair. The OG cos-players before cosplay was a thing.

Shifting away from competition as a focus but not wholly separate from the cowboy action communities, "flint and cap" clubs offer individuals another form of historical shooting activities. These clubs offer the chance to organize and attend events wearing historically appropriate clothing and firing black powder firearms as well as engaging in other historical reenactment activities, such as American Revolution reenacting, and at mountain man/fur trapper rendezvous, the latter often called "buckskinning" (Buckskinning.org). Based on particular technologies and firearms more from the eighteenth and early nineteenth centuries, these groups engage in reenactments of historical battles and other sorts of gatherings typically emphasizing American life before the Civil War era.

While there are some commercial sources for the clothing and historical equipment necessary for these sorts of activities, these communities often focus on the skills associated with crafting the objects associated with these periods in history including leather goods and similar items. Several suppliers offer muzzleloading kits that have been popular since the 1960s, and there is a devoted legion of "builders" who craft flintlock and percussion rifles, pistols, and fowling pieces based on original patterns from the seventeenth to mid-nineteenth centuries. Moreover, there is a large and active community of collectors of antique firearms that regularly hold shows and conventions. Even the skills and techniques for firing these historical guns require informal information exchange and are often created and recreated through shared activities.[14]

DIY GUN MODIFICATION

Moving away from actual shooting, to "garage," "DIY," or do it yourself gunsmithing we find another hobby-focused gun activity community as described in Sandi Atwood's chapter. While most individuals involved are not professional gunsmiths, building and modifying firearms has become a hobby for many. One of the largest of these communities focuses on modern sporting rifles. The highly modular design of AR-15-style rifles we described previously has spawned a huge community of garage gunsmiths who share knowledge and techniques for building and modifying those guns.

Other common garage gunsmith tasks include accurizing rifles and handguns through a range of techniques. Attending these techniques is a huge volume of lore about how different modifications or construction choices affect accuracy. In addition to the communities emerging from building and modifying the guns themselves, there are large communities dedicated to "reloading" or hand-loading ammunition in basement and garage workshops so they can reuse components, save money, and/or make very precise or specialized ammunition. In addition to the basic equipment and techniques related to handloading ammunition, there is a huge volume of lore shared on numerous internet discussion sites about creating effective and safe reloading.

PERSONAL DEFENSE COMMUNITIES

Annamarie O'Brien Morel's chapter in this volume examines women's voices in the concealed-carry community, and thereby profiles another activity-based group whose practice is more like a hobby than a competition. Typically, concealed weapons carriers consider what they do to be much more than a hobby. This community sees carrying a handgun as even more than a lifestyle choice, but an altruistic moral obligation that protects themselves and serves others.

For the members of this community, carrying a weapon can be a daily chore likened to brushing one's teeth. You should do it every day, but it's also a bit of a pain in the butt. Many people in this sector of the gun community see concealed carry as a moral obligation, not just some of the time, but all the time, no matter how inconvenient. Some even emphasize the importance of "home carry," meaning that they believe gun owners are obligated to have weapon on their person even in their own homes (TTAG Contributor 2020).

The moral obligation typically emerges from a sense that people who have the capacity to be armed must be ready to defend others who can't or don't choose to be. Lugging around a heavy and dangerous object all the time, that you will almost certainly never need, gets tiresome. So, the activity becomes a chore that these practitioners see as an ethical responsibility. So much so that many in this community tout the importance not just of everyday concealed carry, but also of regular shooting practice ("Concealed Carry"). Taken a step further, some individuals feel that they are morally obligated to train to be able to use larger and more powerful guns effectively, in case of an emergency.

What might be best termed "gun training communities" refers to the folk groups that have emerged around firearms courses and informal training. Both as individuals and, more often, as groups ranging from interested civilians to former and current military and law enforcement professionals, people engage in informal, semiformal, and formal military firearms training. With decades of wars prosecuted by the US military, a large population of well-trained and experienced individuals can serve both as trainers and students interested in keeping up their skills. A clear testament to this trend is the proliferation of self-defense and military training schools in the last decades, such as Front Sight in Nevada, Gunsite Academy in Arizona, and Universal Shooting Academy in Florida. At the edge of where we want to take this category, we have semiformal "militia" training both as a form of community defense and often as part of the broader "prepping" community.

PREPPERS AND POLITICS

Rounding out our survey of activity-based gun communities, these "prepping" communities inhabit the outer edge of what we can include. "Preppers" focus on preparing for a wide variety of potential collapses of human society from natural disasters to war. Firearms are only a small part of the larger adjacent prepping communities, which focus primarily on food, water, and shelter preparations. Preppers tend to view guns as necessary for both hunting and self-defense. In the gun community, these situations are typically referred to as SHTF situations (when "shit hits the fan") or an environment where a breakdown of social institutions creates a world "without rule of law" or WROL. Sometimes firearms enthusiasts even humorously refer to such potential but highly unlikely events as preparing for the "zombie apocalypse." Driven by popular media like the long running *Walking Dead* television series, gun culture here overlaps with "zombie culture" to some degree. In at least one case, at the height of pop culture's zombie infatuation, a major ammunition manufacture marketed its "Zombie Max Ammunition" in boxes depicting cartoonish zombies ("Zombie Max" 2011).

This marketing choice received mixed reviews among gun owners both because it undermined the seriousness of prepping and because it pointed to the absurd focus that some preppers put on firearms ("Legality of Zombie"). For a very few individuals, this sort of prepping overlaps with firearms training and militia communities.

Ammunition / Rifle Ammunition / 7.62x39mm Russian

Hornady Zombie Max Ammunition 7.62x39mm Box of 20

★★★★★ 6 Reviews : Write a Review : Q&A (1)　　　　　　　　　Product #: 436316

Figure I.8. "Zombie Max Ammunition" for sale at an online retailer.

In a seller of survival supplies or a health food grocery (which may be the same store), the clientele may seem drawn not so much from a representative cross section of America, but disproportionately from each end of the political spectrum. Standing in the checkout line may be a tie-dyed hippy organic farmer and a conservative Christian expecting the Millennial apocalypse, not arguing, but in friendly conversation, sharing tips about how to best set up a home off-the-grid wind or solar electrical system.

In the US's increasingly polarized political environment, it can seem that almost any opinion on virtually any topic is firmly and invariably associated with either the left or the right. Gun rights might seem not just *an* issue but one of *the* primary issues that belongs to conservative Americans, while gun control is just as predictably a progressive issue. This perception has a lot of truth to it. But individuals' personal attitudes sometimes do not line up as neatly as the loud pundits on TV and social media might like. Belief in, and practice of, the right to bear arms may be the issue, perhaps more than any other, that bleeds across the left/right divide. This is evidenced by the ubiquity of "liberal gun owners" and "progressive gun rights" internet forums, the enthusiastic response to the gunlore sessions this volume's editors organized at the American Folklore Society, fellow faculty coming out of the woodwork to tell us about their guns (remarkable as the humanities might be the most left-leaning part of academia, already one of the most left-leaning of US institutions), and gunfolk groups such as the John Brown Gun Club and its spinoff, the Puget Sound John Brown Gun Club. Their website describes the organization as an "anti-fascist, anti-racist, pro-worker community defense organization . . . [who believe] in active resistance to . . . white supremacism, sexism, bigotry, and economic exploitation."

OCCUPATIONAL GUNFOLK

While probably the majority of gun-based communities center themselves on activities as diverse as hunting, personal defense, historical reenactments, and hardcore physical competitions, other communities emerge from other forms of identity. The most obvious of these is probably that of professions that use firearms as tools. Department of Defense professions including soldiers, trainers, and civilian contractors all have their own volumes of folklore from informal techniques to humorous terms to personal experience narratives not unlike EMTs (Tangherlini 1998) or other first responders (Eliason and Tuleja 2012). While soldiers are maybe more directly associated with firearms, law enforcement personnel in the US probably interact more commonly and more regularly with firearms. Police in the US typically always carry a handgun while on duty. Like all professions, law enforcement has its own folklore (Smith, Pedersen, and Burnett 2014, 218–37).

GUN GIRLS AND "GIRLS WITH GUNS"

Less obvious than profession-based gun cultures, there are also gun communities based around personal identity markers like gender and sexuality. Of course, all kinds of people participate in all manner of shooting sports. However, some gun cultures emerge more around the association between a particular identity and guns. For example, women's gun cultures have emerged from, among other things, an emphasis on the need for women to be able to defend themselves (Blair and Hyatt 1995, 117–27). Other gun cultures have emerged around the cis-male gaze and stereotypical and sexist representations of women and guns. Going back at least as far as the 1957 exploitation film *Gun Girls*, the heterosexual male's attention has been drawn to representations of women and guns.

These representations include everything from calendars to decals and probably relate to guns' early association with male-oriented professions. Less common now, gun girl pinup posters and calendars were once common décor for male-dominated blue-collar workplaces such as automotive garages, welding shops, law enforcement, and the military.

As such professions have begun to open to women, however, women have increasingly self-represented as gun users. The fantasies generated to satisfy the male gaze and the women's self-representation as gunfolk have begun to blend. Probably the most famous recent instance of this is gun-rights activist Kaitlin Bennett's social media selfies depicting her with a variety of guns.

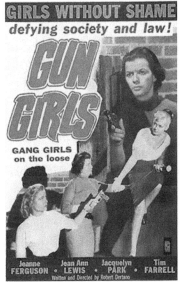

Figure I.9. Gun Girls, 1957 promotional poster. Figure I.10. 2022 Guns n Girls calendar.

Figure I.11. BBC Report on Kent State graduation photos posted on Instagram, 2018.

She gained notoriety for posting images of herself carrying her rifle on her college campus to make a political statement for gun rights. In social media, there are thousands more women self-representing as "gun girls" and often acting as influencers for gun products (Zurcher 2018).

LGBTQ+ AND ETHNICITY

Although gun cultures are rife with male-gendered elements, self-aware men's gun cultures seem less common, perhaps because guns being a "guy thing" has been such a cultural given for so long that it does not need to be highlighted. Increasingly common, however, are LGBTQ and gender nonconforming gun cultures. Most well-known among these is probably the national organization "Pink Pistols," whose slogan is "pick on someone your own caliber." Stating that "armed queers don't get bashed," the group makes its goal to "build bridges between the shooting community and other communities" with a special emphasis on communities centered on "alternative sexualities"(Palette 2019).

In addition to gender and sexuality-based gun cultures, there are gun cultures centered on ethnic and racial identifications. White supremacist gun cultures certainly do exist as profiled in Megan Zahay's contribution to this volume. There are also Black American gun cultures including those associated with popular culture harkening back to early African American music and storytelling traditions as noted in Raymond Summerville's chapter in this volume. Gun ownership carries special significance for some Black folk groups in the US because the antebellum South generally forbad enslaved people from handling guns (Cornell 2006, 29). Later, Jim Crow laws sought to limit gun ownership by Black people. In the 1960s, The Black Panthers US political organization staged armed marches to demonstrate Black rights as

Figure I.12. Malcolm X in *Ebony* magazine, September 1964. (Note his use of the gunlore custom of taping two magazines together in such a way that when one is out, they can be easily rotated 180 degrees, so the shooter can quickly keep firing with a second magazine.)

US citizens (Cobb 2015). In 1964, civil rights activist Malcolm X famously posed with a M1 Carbine military rifle for *Ebony* magazine while fearing an impending assassination attempt.

In 1967, Ronald Reagan, then governor of California, signed the Mulford Act to make carrying guns openly illegal in California specifically in response to fears about the Black Panthers and other armed African American groups demonstrating in Oakland. The Gun Control Act of 1968 (sweeping legislations that outlawed most automatic guns and dramatically regulated gun lengths and sound suppressor sales) is thought by many to have emerged from the same fears among white people (Winkler 2011). Today, there are several Black gun ownership advocacy groups, ethnically oriented gun clubs, websites, and forums.

A final category of gun cultures is those centered on advocacy and politics about guns themselves. Among these, the most common are those associated with gun control and those associated with gun rights. In both categories there are more institutional organizations like the Coalition to Stop Gun Violence and the National Rifle Association as well as more vernacular and local organizations.

"PARA-GUN" GROUPS

In addition to all these diverse and complex gun cultures, there are more untold gun-adjacent cultures. These are communities that are maybe not directly about real guns but exist with significant overlap both in terms of discourse and membership with gun-based communities. For example, there is a large EDC or "Everyday Carry" community that does include carrying guns, but guns are not necessary and often are only one part of a whole EDC tool kit that people carry to help them be prepared for all manner of emergencies. As we already noted with cowboy action shooting, LARPing or Live Action Role Playing as well as historical reenactment groups are a kind of gunfolk. This is true even for communities where firearms are not the main focus, or the firearms are fanciful and nonfunctional, such as the steampunk LARPers profiled by London Brickley in this volume.

Particularly popular in countries and jurisdictions where firearms' ownership and use are restricted, air gun communities and shooting clubs are common. Air gunners may also own firearms just as bow hunters and target archers might. All these groups are just as concerned about accuracy and effectiveness as firearms enthusiasts (and might even be the same people) regardless of which projectile-launching tool they are using. But arrow

34 INTRODUCTION: GUNLORE AND GUNFOLKS

shooting and air gun subcultures are not, obviously, predicated on firearms despite often similar goals.

Perhaps even more distant from archery are paintball and airsoft. Both are communities that outsiders might say focus on "toy guns" instead of actual firearms. These multi-layered communities, much like those associated with guns above, also spawn not only hobbyists but competitions and serious competitors. Many individuals in these communities are no doubt also members of firearms-related folk groups. However, many paintballers, especially professional associations, have gone to some length to distinguish themselves from any trappings that might seem remotely military or gun culture–esque, insisting that their paintball-shooting devices are "markers" not "guns" (Powers 2009). And at competitions, dayglow colors, rather than camouflage, are de rigueur (Paintball League). Airsoft culture has gone in the other direction with exacting replications of period and modern firearms and accessories, often used during WWII, Vietnam, or even Global War on Terror reenactment and competitive roleplay ("Airsoft").

AMERICAN GUN CULTURES

Gun cultures are highly diverse, and those cultures are not exclusive to each other or to other nongun cultures. In US gun culture today, there seem to be less distinct "cultures" but overlapping networks of association where one person generally participates in many folk groups at once. Whatever the specific nature of these associated networks, they all emerge from interest in guns. In order to render these community identities meaningful, guns are (in these cases at least) more than just tools. They are more than just inert technologies. Guns are also empowering to individuals such as those seeking to hunt game, defend themselves and others, or assert their rights.

Firearms are exciting because, for one, they go bang.[15] For many people, that bang is precisely the draw. But even for vast numbers of people who don't own guns, firearms are clearly exciting as evidenced by their pervasive presence in all forms of entertainment, from old folk songs to the latest big budget action movies. Guns grab our attention—because of their power and the excitement they impart. As such, they can mark an individual's identity as one that is empowered. When guns are used to mark our identities as citizens, women, bad-ass criminals, self-reliant outdoors people, and/ or protectors of our communities, guns do more than shoot. Guns *mean*. They are powerful tools and powerful transmitters of meaning. As a result, our entire community, our contemporary society, would do well to better understand guns and how they mean so that we can better understand each other. Like all folklore, documenting, sharing, and thinking about gunlore is a means to understand ourselves. To recognize the powerful ways gunlore means for us is to also recognize both that guns are dangerous objects and a real source of good things for many people.

Through this collection of case studies of real gunlore, we offer this volume not as the final statement on the topic or as nearly comprehensive. Instead, we offer it as evidence of the wide diversity of gunlore and gunfolk. From this diversity we can at least surmise that many people have for a very long time been empowered by "the gun"—as tool and as symbol. In the important debates about guns today, it is essential for us to add to our understandings about the symbolic power guns clearly possess. We hope the studies contained in this collection can contribute to those understandings and thus also contribute to the important public discourse about guns in the United States today and into the future.

Notes

This volume's editors wish to thank Katie E. Keene, editor-in-chief at University Press of Mississippi. She tracked us down at the 2017 American Folklore Society Annual Meeting to urge us to turn our gunlore double session into a book. In 2018, we organized a second AFS gunlore double session. Both years, presenters, respondents, and audiences were enthusiastic and engaged. These discussions provided many helpful insights and suggestions. Most chapters in this book emerged from these two AFS gunlore sessions. We also appreciate the wide variety of firearms using—and firearms opposing—communities willing to share their lore with this volume's contributors.

The editors especially wish to thank Abbie Call and the editors of Brigham Young University's Faculty Publishing Service for helping prepare this manuscript for publication.

1. See for example: Fisher and Hovey's *Understanding America's Gun Culture*, Cramer's *Lock, Stock, and Barrel: The Origins of American Gun Culture*, Haag's *The Gunning of America: Business and the Making of American Gun Culture*, Schwartz's *On Target: Gun Culture, Storytelling, and the NRA*, Hays and Crouch's *God and Guns: The Bible against American Gun Culture*, and Bellesiles's controversial *Arming America*; also add Cobb's *This Nonviolent Stuff'll Get You Killed*, Jennifer Carlson's *Citizen-Protectors*, Cornell's *Well Regulated Militia*, and Wilkes, Kreuter, and Skinnell's *Rhetoric and Guns*.

2. This Spanish rendering of "why not both?" is a common variant of the traditional follow on to the AR vs. AK question as it emerges in the "gun talk" of "gun folk." It is likely an inter-textual reference to a 1990s Taco Bell commercial that likewise encouraged a "both/and" approach over the "either/or" option in customers' taco vs. burrito purchasing dilemmas.

3. Some of these stories can be found on the website "1911 Myths & Legends," *Sight1911 .com*, accessed December 21, 2021.

36 INTRODUCTION: GUNLORE AND GUNFOLKS

4. On the history of the US/Moro conflict see Ronald K. Edgerton's *American Datu: John J. Pershing and Counterinsurgency Warfare in the Muslim Philippines, 1800–1913*.

5. On ethnobotany see Schultes and von Reis's *Ethnobotany: Evolution of a Discipline*, Davis's *One River*, and Minnis's *Ethnobotany: A Reader*. On the experience-centered approach see Hufford's *The Terror that Comes in the Night: An Experience-Centered Study of Supernatural Assault Traditions* and Walker's *Out of the Ordinary: Folklore & the Supernatural*. On traditional ecological knowledge see Berkes's *Sacred Ecology: Traditional Ecological Knowledge and Resource Management*, Ingliss's *Traditional Ecological Knowledge: Concepts and Cases*, and Toledo's "Ethnoecology: A Conceptual Framework for the Study of Indigenous Knowledge of Nature."

6. On ostension see Dégh and Vázsonyi, "Does the Word 'Dog' Bite? Ostensive Action: A Means of Legend-Telling," *Journal of Folklore Research* 20, 5–34; and Ellis, "Legend-Trips and Satanism: Adolescents' Ostensive Traditions as 'Cult' Activity." In Richardson, Best, and Bromley's (1991) *The Satanism Scare*, 279–95.

7. See for example, "Decades of Success in Reducing Firearms Accidents, Background Paper #1" SAAMI: Newton, Connecticut, 2003; Gary Kleck, *Point Blank: Guns and Violence in America*, New York: Routledge, 2005, p. 306, Table 7.1; Kurtis Lee, "Amid Rising Gun Violence, Accidental Shooting Deaths Have Plummeted. Why?" *Los Angeles Times*, 1 January 2018, https://www.latimes.com/nation/la-na-accidental-gun-deaths-20180101-story.html, accessed 4 January 2022.

8. "Alec Baldwin Told Prop Gun Was Safe & Didn't Know It Was Loaded Before Fatal Shooting, Per Affidavit," https://www.msn.com/en-us/tv/news/alec-baldwin-told-prop-gun-was-safe-and-didnt-know-it-was-loaded-before-fatal-shooting-per-affidavit/ar-AAPQWIU, accessed 15 February 2022.

9. Much of the analysis in this section is drawn from Brian Palmer, "Why Do Rappers Hold Their Guns Sideways?" *Slate*, December 14, 2009; and Edward Lewine, "Ready, Aim. No, Wait a Second. Hold That Gun Sideways," *New York Times*, 5 November 1995.

10. On William Gottfried von Herder's influence on romantic nationalism and the emergence of folklore studies as a discipline, see William A. Wilson's 1973 essay "Herder, Folklore, and Romantic Nationalism," reprinted in William A. Wilson and Jill Terry Rudy, *The Marrow of Human Experience: Essays on Folklore*, Logan: Utah State University Press, 2006, 107–23. Robert Redfield, *Tepoztlan, a Mexican Village: A Study in Folk Life*, University of Chicago Press, 1930; and *The Little Community: Peasant Society and Culture*, Chicago: University of Chicago Press, 1956.

11. Many of these maxims came out in a CCW subreddit discussion. https://www.reddit.com/r/CCW/comments/7hae8w/i_sat_on_a_trial_where_we_found_a_cc_holder/?st=JARJ2CKF&sh=b971d57b. Accessed January 4, 2022.

12. At least in American English, hunting and firearms form an overlapping Venn diagram with much hunting with guns, but also hunting-unrelated gun use and hunting without firearms. In Britain, "stalking" refers to people with rifles going after quarry, usually deer. Whereas "hunting" is done with hounds. See Eliason, *To See Them Run: Great Plains Coyote Coursing*, and "Foxhunting Folkways under Fire and the Crisis of Traditional Moral Knowledge," *Western Folklore* 63, no. 1–2: 123–67.

13. On "hyper-Indianism" and the mutually reinforcing performative clothing, adornment, and fighting styles that emerged on both sides of the West's Indian wars, see Nathaniel Philbrick, *The Last Stand: Custer, Sitting Bull, and the Battle of the Little Bighorn*, New York: Penguin, 2010. On wild west shows' emergence with actual participants while the "wild west" was still ongoing, see Frank Christianson, ed. *The Popular Frontier: Buffalo Bill's Wild West and Transnational Mass Culture*, Norman: University of Oklahoma Press, 2017.

14. For more on the cosplay that is featured at these meetups or "rendezvous," see buckskinning.org.

15. In Eric Eliason's Utah National Guard Special Forces unit there was no shortage of "gun guys." As chaplain, he often conducted suicide awareness training. In some contexts, a buddy's buying a gun might be a reason to proactively ask him if he is considering suicide. Among Green Berets, however, giving away one's guns or seeming uninterested in going to the range might actually be more troubling possible signs of suicidal depression. Nevertheless, some special operators saw too much "gun nerdiness" as all well and good for the unit armorer, but evidence of unbalanced interest in one aspect of the whole suite of soldier-craft skills. If a gun nerd asked such a soldier about the best caliber for this or that, the soldier might answer, "I pull the trigger; it goes bang." This was widely understood as shorthand for, "Dude, it is possible to be too into guns."

References

Airsoftc3. "Airsoft: Connecting the Airsoft Community." https://airsoftc3.com. Accessed January 8, 2022.

"Alec Baldwin Told Prop Gun Was Safe & Didn't Know It Was Loaded Before Fatal Shooting, Per Affidavit." https://www.msn.com/en-us/tv/news/alec-baldwin-told -prop-gun-was-safe-and-didnt-know-it-was-loaded-before-fatal-shooting-per- affidavit/ar-AAPQWIU. Accessed February 15, 2022.

Bascom, William R. 1954. "Four Functions of Folklore." *Journal of American Folklore* 67, no. 266: 333–49.

Bellesiles, Michael A. 2000. *Arming America: The Origins of a National Gun Culture*. New York: Alfred A. Knopf.

Bennett, Gillian. 1993. "Folklore Studies and the English Rural Myth." *Rural History* 4, no. 1 (April): 77–91.

Berkes, Fikret. 1999. *Sacred Ecology: Traditional Ecological Knowledge and Resource Management*. London: Taylor & Francis.

Blair, M. Elizabeth, and Eva M. Hyatt. 1995. "The Marketing of Guns to Women: Factors Influencing Gun-Related Attitudes and Gun Ownership by Women." *Journal of Public Policy and Marketing* 14, no. 1 (Spring): 117–27.

Boeck, Marissa A., Bethany Strong, and Andre Campbell. 2020. "Disparities in Firearm Injury: Consequences of Structural Violence." *Current Trauma Reports* 6, 10–22.

Bronner, Simon. 2008. *Killing Tradition: Inside Hunting and Animal Rights Controversies*. Knoxville: University of Tennessee Press.

Buckskinning. "Buckskinning.org." https://www.buckskinning.org. Accessed April 4, 2022.

Carlson, Jennifer. 2015. *Citizen-Protectors: The Everyday Politics of Guns in an Age of Decline.* Oxford: Oxford University Press.

Carr, J. E., and E. K. Tan. 1976. "In Search of the True Amok: Amok as Viewed with the Javanese Culture." *American Journal of Psychiatry* 133, no. 11: 1295–99.

City Lore. "Our Vision." https://citylore.org/about-city-lore/who-we-are. Accessed 8 January 2022.

Cobb, Charles E., Jr. 2015. *This Nonviolent Stuff'll Get You Killed: How Guns Made the Civil Rights Movement Possible.* Durham, NC: Duke University Press.

"Concealed Carry Weapons." *Reddit.* https://www.reddit.com/r/CCW/comments/875a7i/home_carry/. Accessed April 4, 2022.

Cornell, Saul. 2006. *A Well Regulated Militia: The Founding Fathers and the Origins of Gun Control in America.* Oxford: Oxford University Press.

Cramer, Clayton E. 2018. *Lock, Stock, and Barrel: The Origins of American Gun Culture.* Santa Barbara, CA: Praeger.

Cutchins, Dennis, and Eric A. Eliason. 2009. *Wild Games: Hunting and Fishing Traditions in North America.* Knoxville: University of Tennessee Press.

Davis, Wade. 1997. *One River.* New York: Simon & Schuster.

Edgerton, Ronald K. 2020. *American Datu: John J. Pershing and Counterinsurgency Warfare in the Muslim Philippines, 1800–1913.* Lexington: University of Kentucky Press.

Edward, Lewine. 1995. "Ready, Aim. No, Wait a Second. Hold That Gun Sideways." *New York Times,* November 5, 1995.

Eger, Chris. 2020. "NICS Gun Check Figures Highest on Record for Any May in History." *News* (blog), *Guns.* June 1, 2020. https://www.guns.com/news/2020/06/02/nics-gun-check-figures-highest-on-record-for-any-may-in-history.

Eliason, Eric A. 2012. "'Folk-Folkloristics': Reflections on American Soldiers' Responses to Afghan Traditional Culture." In *Warrior Ways: Explorations in Modern Military Folklore,* edited by Eric A. Eliason and Tad Tuleja, 58–76. Boulder: University Press of Colorado.

Eliason, Eric A., and Tad Tuleja. 2012. *Warrior Ways: Explorations in Modern Military Folklore.* Boulder: University Press of Colorado.

Fackler, Martin L. 1998. "Civilian Gunshot Wounds and Ballistics: Dispelling the Myths." *Medicine Clinics of North America* 16, no. 1: 17–28.

Federal Bureau of Investigation. 2019. "Expanded Homicide." *Uniform Crime Reporting.* https://worldpopulationreview.com/state-rankings/gun-ownership-by-state. Accessed April 2, 2022.

"First-Time Gun Buyers grow to Nearly 5 Million in 2020." 2020. *National Shooting Sports Foundation News,* August 24, 2020. https://www.nssf.org/articles first-time -gun-buyers-grow-to-nearly-5-million-in-2020/.

Fisher, Lisa, and Craig Hovey, eds. 2021. *Understanding America's Gun Culture.* Lanham, MD: Lexington Books.

Gambetta, Diego. 2011. *Codes of the Underworld: How Criminals Communicate.* Princeton: Princeton University Press.

Haag, Pamela. 2016. *The Gunning of America: Business and the Making of American Gun Culture.* New York: Basic Books.

Hathaway, Rosemary V. 2019. "'We Can't Even Create a Group Text, and We're Taking on the NRA': Resisting Campus Carry in West Virginia." Paper presented at the American Folklore Society annual meeting, Baltimore, MD, October 2019.

Hays, Christopher B., and C. L. Crouch. 2021. *God and Guns: The Bible against American Gun Culture.* Louisville, KY: Westminster John Knox Press.

Hornady. 2011. "Zombie Max™ Ammunition . . ." Media Center. https://press.hornady.com/release/2011/10/14/zombie-max-ammunition. Accessed 4 April 2022.

Howard, Robert Glenn. 2019. "Vernacular Authority Speaks for the Glock: Heterogeneous Volition in an Institutional Proverb." In *Digital Folkloristics*, edited by Pekka Hakamies, 73–91. Turku, Finland: Folklore Fellows' Communications.

Hufford, David. 1989. *The Terror That Comes in the Night: An Experience-Centered Study of Supernatural Assault Traditions.* Philadelphia: University of Pennsylvania Press.

Igielnik, Ruth. 2017. "Rural and Urban Gun Owners Have Different Experiences, Views on Gun Policy." *Pew Research Center,* July 10, 2017. https://www.pewresearch.org/fact tank/2017/07/10/rural-and-urban-gun-owners-have-different-experiences-views-on -gun-policy.

Ingliss, J. T. 1993. *Traditional Ecological Knowledge: Concepts and Cases.* New York: International Development Research Center.

"Legality of Zombie Max Ammo for Defense?" *Survivalist Boards.* https://www.survival istboards.com/threads/legality-of-zombie-max-ammo-for-defense.346520/#post -6464377. Accessed April 4, 2022.

MacPherson, Duncan. 2014. *Bullet Penetration: Modeling the Dynamics and Incapacitation Results from Wound Trauma.* El Segundo, CA: Ballistic Publications.

Minnis, Paul E. 2000. *Ethnobotany: A Reader.* Lincoln: University of Oklahoma Press.

"Mystery of Malcolm X." 1964. *Ebony* 19, no. 11: 38–46.

National Rifle Association. "Gun Safety Rules." https://gunsafetyrules.nra.org/.

Oring, Elliott. 2017. *Jokes and Their Relations.* Boca Raton, FL: Routledge.

Paintball League International. "Welcome to Paintball Leagues International." https://pbleagues.com. Accessed January 8, 2022.

Palette, Erin. 2019. "Why There Will Be No Gatekeeping Within the Pink Pistols." *Pink Pistols,* 13 July 2019. https://www.pinkpistols.org.

Palmer, Brian. 2019. "Why Do Rappers Hold Their Guns Sideways?" *Slate,* December 14, 2009.

Powers, Tina M. 2009. "Markers vs. Paintball Guns," *Ezine Articles* (blog). September 1, 2009 https://ezinearticles.com/?Paintball-Markers-Vs-Paintball-Guns&id=2854708.

"PROOF That Alec Baldwin LIED?! (Gun Demonstration)," USCCA. https://www.you tube.com/watch?v=IImxZbBaaSM. Accessed February 15, 2022.

Propp, Vladimir. 1968. *Morphology of the Folktale.* Austin: University of Texas Press.

Renteln, Alison Dundes, and Alan Dundes, eds. 1995. *Folk Law.* Madison: University of Wisconsin Press.

Saad, Lydia. 2020. "What Percentage of Americans Own Guns?" *Gallup,* November 13, 2020.

Saint Martin, Manual L. 1999. "Running Amok: A Modern Perspective on a Culture-Bound Syndrome." *Primary Care Companion to the Journal of Clinical Psychiatry* 1, no. 3 (June): 66–70.

Savat, Sara. 2020. "The Divide between Us: Urban Rural Political Differences Rooted in Geography." *The Source*, February 18, 2020. https://source.wustl.edu/2020/02/the-divide-between-us-urban-rural-political-differences-rooted-in-geography.

Schultes, Richards Evans, and Siri Von Reis. 1995. *Ethnobotany: Evolution of a Discipline*. Portland: Timber Press.

Schwartz, Noah S. 2022. *On Target: Gun Culture, Storytelling, and the NRA*. Toronto: University of Toronto Press.

Shuppe, Jon. 2018. "America's Rifle: Why So Many People Love the AR-15." *NBC News*, February 15, 2018. https://www.nbcnews.com/news/us-news/america-s-rifle-why-so-many-people-love-ar-15-n831171.

Smith, Robert, Sarah Pedersen, and Simon Burnett. 2014."Towards an Organizational Folklore of Policing: The Storied Nature of Policing and the Police Use of Storytelling." *Folklore* 125, no. 2 (August): 218–37.

Tangherlini, Timothy R. 1998. *Talking Trauma: Storytelling among Paramedics*. Jackson: University Press of Mississippi.

Toledo, V. M. 2002. "Ethnoecology: A Conceptual Framework for the Study of Indigenous Knowledge of Nature." In *Ethnobiology and Biocultural Diversity*, edited by John R. Stepp, Felice Wyndham, and Rebecca K. Zarger. Athens, GA: International Society of Ethnobiology.

TTAG Contributor. 2020. "Why You Need to Carry a Gun at Home . . . Even in the Shower." *The Truth About Guns* (blog). March 10, 2020. https://www.thetruthaboutguns.com/home-carry.

TTAG Contributor. 2021. "Baldwin: I'm Not Responsible for Halyna Hutchins' Death." *The Truth About Guns* (blog). December 3, 2021. https://www.thetruthaboutguns.com/baldwin-im-not-responsible-for-halyna-hutchins-death.

Twigger, Roger. 2017. "The Legend of the Legion." *Aeon*, April 10, 2017. https://aeon.co/essays/why-young-men-queue-up-to-die-in-the-french-foreign-legion.

Walker, Barbara. 1995. *Out of the Ordinary: Folklore & the Supernatural*. Logan: Utah State University Press.

Weingarten, Dean. 2017. "Fatal Firearms Accident Rate Reaches Record Low." *The Truth About Guns* (blog), 3 February 2017. https://www.thetruthaboutguns.com/fatal-firearms-accident-rate-reaches-record-low.

Wilkes, Lydia, Nate Kreuter, and Ryan Skinnel. 2022. *Rhetoric and Guns*. Logan: Utah State University Press.

Winkler, Adam. 2011."The Secret History of Guns." *The Atlantic*, September 2011. https://www.theatlantic.com/magazine/archive/2011/09/the-secret-history-of-guns/308608.

World Population Review. "Gun Ownership by Country 2023." https://worldpopulationreview.com/country-rankings/gun-ownership-by-country.

Zurcher, Anthony. 2018."Kaitlin Bennet: Why She Wore a Rifle for Graduation Photos." *BBC*, May 17, 2018. https://www.bbc.com/news/world-us-canada-44158099###IT.

Chapter 1

YOUNG GUNS

Folklore and the Fetishization of Guns among Juveniles at an All-Male Correctional Facility in Tucson, Arizona

RAYMOND SUMMERVILLE

Folklore, guns, fetishism, and male juveniles are topics that, together, seem to overextend the very possibilities of interdisciplinary work. This chapter seeks to explain ways in which these subject matters can be used in concert to explain a growing predicament in American culture—gun violence among male youth. Guns have been a part of American culture and American folklore for centuries. While the presence of guns in folk music and tales predates the arrival of modern technology, what was once passed on by word of mouth has been replaced by more advanced forms of transmission. Guns are frequently depicted in film, television, music, print, and other forms of popular media such as the internet and video games. Representations of firearms can be seen in art, jewelry, clothing designs, and even tattoos. The way that guns are presently represented and discussed in American culture has created a strong passion for the firearm that has surpassed any perception of the various general functional uses for firearms that people have traditionally and currently recognize. Furthermore, many of the current representations of firearms that most American youth are exposed to today are also parts of extensive marketing schemes that are directed toward young people for the sole purpose of generating capital. Likewise, many of the negative repercussions of firearm usage are also felt by the same group—more specifically, the young Black male population who are more likely to carry guns for self-defense. Since many youths do fetishize guns, carrying them oftentimes catalyzes violence to levels of fatality more often than when there are no guns present. In part, due to the predominance of this phenomenon, America's fascination with guns can be interpreted through the lenses of folklore and fetishism.

NEGOTIATING IDENTITY WITH GUNS

Fetishism has been defined in a number of ways, but in its simplest form fetishism can be defined as the overvaluation of any object whether it be material or otherwise. According to E. L. McCallum, "The definition of fetishism has consistently boiled down to the use of an object to negotiate (usually binary) differences to achieve an immaterial end, whether it be economic gain, cultural prestige, or psychical satisfaction" (1999, xi). Based on this interpretation of fetishism there is much to be gained from it, at least from the perspective of the fetishist. The gun fetishist's fixation on guns is primarily a productive thing (for the fetishist at least) although outsider interpretations will almost certainly yield different perspectives. In fact, we know this to be the case when speaking in terms of guns and American male youth. Guns have been a fascination in American culture dating back to the seventeenth century (Squires 2000, 18–57). It is the history of this attraction to guns that we have to turn our attention to in order to better understand why and how guns have become fetish objects among male youth today.

In this chapter, first I will discuss ways that guns have always been an integral part of American culture. Secondly, I will consider the theoretical concept of fetishism as a useful tool for understanding ways in which guns work as powerful symbols. Third, I will analyze narratives of incarcerated youth who have been deeply influenced by America's gun culture and underground gun economy to determine how and to what extent they fetishize firearms. Finally, I will examine Black folklore for examples of legends involving gun violence and discuss ways that this imagery has influenced popular media and Black male identity.

Guns are fetishized not only for what they do, but also because of what they have come to represent. They have become a cultural symbol that embodies many of the characteristics and values that numerous Americans continue to believe are necessary to survive in a culture where agency and autonomy are valued over all other virtues. The ability for one to thrive and determine one's own fate through the use of firearms has always been an attraction for Americans and even immigrants seeking to come to America. An English colonist writes in 1774 that "there is not a man born in America that does not understand the use of firearms and that well . . . a gun, is almost the first thing they purchase and take to all the new settlements and in the cities you can scarcely find a lad of 12 years that does not go a Gunning" (DeConde 2001, 3).

GUNS AND AMERICAN CULTURE

Traditionally, in America the right to own a gun has been a right that has been intrinsically connected to what Alexander DeConde (2001) describes as "self-reliant patriotism" and is thus considered one of the most important components of the American constitution. Early English settlers seeking to reestablish themselves in North America depended on the firearm to eventually win the American Revolution. Centuries later, over six hundred thousand Americans died during the Civil War. What followed the Civil War may be described as the frontier movement in American history (1865–1890), where both white and Black settlers migrated westward to homestead lands that previously belonged to Native tribes.[1] Gun fighting was intrinsic as various groups struggled to carve their own existence into what seemed like free territory.

Battles have not always been of the physical sort. They have also been fought on philosophical fronts. In addition to defining and sustaining a sense of national identity, the gun has also been branded as a source of disagreement and divergence. The fight over how to interpret the Second Amendment is one of the most prevalent debates today. The most common question that has emerged in this fight is what should be done when guns fall into the hands of the wrong people? "The wrong people" is a comprehensive term that would most certainly always include children. At an alarming rate, guns are being used for purposes that fall outside of the confines of the law. According to DeConde,

> Available statistics tell us that in exercising this alleged right Americans have used guns, particularly in the twentieth century, "more often to assault, maim, and kill one another" than most other peoples in the world. In the 1990s, for instance, Americans killed more people with guns in a typical week than did western Europeans in a whole year. This record stands out because peoples in other technologically advanced countries have not had, and do not have, homicide rates connected to shooting as high as those of Americans. Nor have those countries allowed their citizens to possess firearms with a freedom comparable to that tolerated in the United States. (2001, 3)

"With freedom comes great responsibility" is an age-old saying that effectively characterizes the nature of the problem that DeConde describes.

Americans are currently faced with the predicament of deciding how to best regulate the sale and use of firearms so that they are not illegally

44   YOUNG GUNS: FOLKLORE AND THE FETISHIZATION OF GUNS

obtained or used with harmful intentions. While most would agree that making the country free of gun violence is an impossible task, they would also agree that many of the current statistics on gun violence illustrate a pressing need for law makers to do something to remedy the problem. Some of the most alarming statistics have emerged within the past two decades. According to Phillip J. Cook and Jens Ludwig, authors of *Gun Violence: The Real Cost,*

> In 1997, over 32,000 Americans died of gunshot wounds—more than died from AIDS or liver disease in that year, and in the same ball-park with motor vehicle crashes (42,000). Since 1965 more than *one million* people have been shot and killed, more than the number of Americans killed in all foreign wars combined during the twentieth century (617,000). Our firearms death rate is not the highest in the world—Columbia's, for example, is higher—but exceeds that of any other developed nation by a wide margin. (2000, 16)

These findings are comparable to the findings of DeConde. They both high-light the fact that gun violence is a much bigger problem in the United States than in any other western, developed, or technologically advanced nation.

Cook and Ludwig add another layer to the equation. They describe a new method of categorization that statisticians have developed to account for the overwhelming number of young people that are affected by gun violence in America in relation to other age groups:

> Gunshot fatalities impose a disproportionate public-health impact because so many of the victims are young. A measure that takes account of the fact is "years of potential life lost before the age of 65" (YPLL-65). Firearms injury was ranked number four in YPLL-65 during the early 1990s, behind only unintentional injury, cancer, and heart disease. Actually the Vital Statistics do not usually group gun deaths together; instead they are found with the homicides and sui-cides (both of which have guns as the agent in the majority of cases) and unintentional deaths. Homicide and suicide each rank among the top four causes of death for youths age 10–34. (2000, 16–17)

Additionally, statistics show Blacks and Latinos are disproportionately tar-geted by gun violence. Black people are at least eight times more likely to be shot to death across all fifty states. Likewise, Latinx people are killed by gun violence at a rate that is almost double the murder rate of whites (Mitchell and Bromfield 2019).

Alfred Blumstein, professor of urban systems and operations research at Carnegie Mellon University, discusses the phenomena of youth gun violence in "Youth, Guns, and Violent Crime" (2002). According to Blumstein, "The period from 1985 to 2000 saw some sharp swings in the rate of violence in the United States. Much of that swing is attributable to changes in violence committed by young people, primarily against other young people. Beginning in 1985, the rates of homicide and robbery committed by people under age 20 began to rise drastically, as did the use of handguns to commit those crimes" (40). The rapid increase that Blumstein discusses here is followed by a significant decrease in the rates of youth gun violence, but only after they peaked in the early 1990s. However, this decrease does not necessarily signal an approaching end to the growing crime epidemic; in fact, it may only signal a leveling off as lawmakers scrambled to devise and impose stricter gun-control laws for youth. Blumstein also explains that other forms of youth gun violence such as school shootings also began to surface during this same era. Our urban male youth may be committing gun crimes at increasingly alarming rates, but contrary to the belief of many experts, it is not chiefly due to a new breed of "superpredators" that suffer from nihilism in its most extreme forms. Blumstein recognizes various cultural elements that have also contributed to the rise of juvenile gun violence over the past two decades. Among these elements Blumstein lists "the rise of illegal drug markets, particularly for crack cocaine, the recruitment of youth into those markets, and an increase in gun carrying among young people" (39).

The increase in the number of juveniles that carry weapons is significant because the presence of guns, in most cases, serves as a catalyst that enables juveniles to transition quickly from regular fights with fists to committing sudden homicide. However, it is the prevalence of all these social variables together that contributes to a rise in youth gun violence. If current statistics regarding gun violence tell us anything about the society in which we live, they tell us that the fetishization of guns by juveniles can only be unproductive for young people and for American culture as a whole. However, this essentialist argument only includes the outsider perception. For one to see the problem holistically one must, at some point, place the perspective of the fetishist above all other common knowledge. One must be willing to consider ways in which the fetishism of guns can be viewed as a productive act that is in fact beneficial to the life of the fetishist. After all, if the fetishization of guns did not have something to offer the people that engage in it, one must assume that they would not do it.

FETISH THEORY: FROM FREUDIAN PSYCHOANALYSIS TO WILLIAM PIETZ AND E. L. MCCALLUM

The most universal notion of fetishism came about in the nineteenth century with the rise of psychoanalysis. Sigmund Freud brought forth the argument that the actual act of fetishism is indeed a replacement for the female phallus. According to Freud, the child in a prepubescent state is faced with the sudden realization that their maternal figure is not what they originally understood her to be—to the child's own consternation he discovers that his mother is without a penis (Freud 1928). This discovery leads the young child to believe that the woman has been castrated and therefore places the ownership of his own penis in jeopardy. The apparent shock of this discovery along with the fear of castration lies at the center of the Freudian psychoanalytic school of fetish theory. As Freud contends,

When now I announce that the fetish is a substitute for the penis, I shall certainly create disappointment; so I hasten to add that it is not a substitute for any chance penis, but for a particular and quite special penis that had been extremely important in early childhood but had later been lost. That is to say, it should normally have been given up, but the fetish is precisely designed to preserve it from extinction. To put it more plainly: the fetish is a substitute for the woman's (the mother's) penis that the little boy once believed in and—for reasons familiar to us—does not want to give up. (Freud 1928, 152–53)

When thinking along the lines of psychoanalysis, fetishism may be viewed as a productive act for the fetishist because the fetish replaces something that was once considered a source of security for the male child—the female phallus. One must presuppose in interpreting Freud's theory that these processes are taking place entirely on subconscious levels especially in applying them to individuals' lives beyond childhood.

Freud is often credited with popularizing fetish theory, but historians recognize that fetishism came about long before Freud existed as a way of negotiating cultural differences among various groups that encountered one another through trade routes. As E. L. McCallum points out to us, it is

William Pietz [who has] shown in his extensive discussion of fetishism's history [that] the term first came into use in the sixteenth century as Portuguese sailors and West African societies encountered one another and began to establish trade relations; in that context, technological and economic changes were transforming the boundaries that delineated national interests and identities. The term that emerged in this cross-cultural space has accrued significance in a rather astoundingly vast number of contexts: religious, aesthetic, cinematic, commercial, and sexual. (1999, xii)

As McCallum explains, traditionally it has always been important for us to consider a multitude of ways in which fetishism may be relevant to society. She asserts that it is the changing social dynamic that is to blame for fetishism's importance. This also sheds additional light on the significance of Pietz's historical analysis. Through fetishism, social roles that were previously thought of as fixed have come to be unstable and thus increasingly subject to interpretation. It is the kinetic nature of identities that, according to McCallum, requires us to continue to use fetishism as a lens that will allow us to take a much closer look at the nature of subject-object relations as well as ontological, epistemological, and cultural practices.

The terms in which we view subject-object relations must be critically analyzed if we are to understand the multitude of ways in which people relate to objects. Previously, people viewed subject-object relations in one way; that is subjects create objects and subjects also formulate the roles that these objects play in our lives. This notion is at the heart of western philosophy, but eastern philosophical thought calls for us to take into account the view that subjects relate to objects and also the notion that subjects sometimes believe that these objects possess the ability to relate back (McCallum 1999). It is the reciprocal nature of the subject's exchange with objects that has traditionally separated the "primitive" societies from those that were once considered "savage." This one distinction was used to shape the rules of engagement between seemingly incompatible cultures and also as a way to justify imperialist projects that lay ahead for wealthier nations.

Conceptualizing an epistemological view of fetishism requires us to reevaluate knowledge. Fetishism forces us to think critically about the things we believe to be true and the things we simply want to believe to be true. Thus desire, as an act of will, cannot be entirely alienated from knowledge. Additionally, an epistemology of fetishism forces us to unpack the loaded systems of signs that we have always relied on to interpret our own behavior and also the world around us. What has been traditionally regarded as signifier and signified may take on new and different meanings and new levels of importance in the process of interpretation.

In many cases, fetishism reassigns boundaries that serve as important social markers making it necessary for us to think critically about the multitude of elements that we depend on as identity markers. Elements such as age, race, ethnicity, sex, and gender become disengaged from notions that were previously thought of as fixed. The process of rethinking identity and how we view objects serves to elucidate entirely new systems of meaning. The role that desire plays in this thought process is a prominent one. Desire along with a belief in knowledge makes an epistemology of fetishism possible. Fetishism tells us that what we know to be true has the ability to falter. More specifically, what we recognize as true regarding objects, how we identify objects, and how we choose to relate to objects is in a constant state of flux. It is this state of iterability which allows the fetishists to retain a sense of agency. This is also one of the reasons why fetishism may be viewed as positive or productive for the fetishists. According to McCullum,

> A fetish object . . . could produce, through iteration, a subject with confidence and a stronger sense of self in the face of the threat of loss—of death, obsolescence, or waning prestige. But because the investment is in an object with its independent existence, the renewed fetish subject will never be confused with the object the way the man of genius is conflated with genius. The fetish relation holds the elements apart . . . with its meanings, remains distinct from the owner. This is similar to how, as a paraphilia, fetishism throws sexual difference into sharper relief against the norm of heterosexual subject-subject relations. (150)

THE YOUNG(GUNS) SPEAK: ANALYZING THE DATA

Discussion of why and how fetishism may be considered beneficial for the fetishist is best supported by specific examples of fetishism. For examples of male juveniles who fetishize guns it would be useful to turn our attention to a case study performed by Bernard E. Harcourt, professor of law at the University of Chicago and author of *Guns, Crime, and Punishment in America* (2003). Harcourt's case study was performed in the fall of 2000 at the Catalina Mountain School (CMS), located in the scenic Catalina Mountain foothills twelve miles north of Tucson, Arizona. The school is very secluded and surrounded by the hot and dry Sonoran Desert. Even though it is a correctional facility, the place is much better than what most people imagine when they think of incarceration. At CMS all the students are required to attend classes and abide by strict curfews. The school grounds are very neat, clean, and well kept. The students are even forced to wear uniforms: grey khakis and white shirts. There are also a number of armed security guards that patrol the school grounds around the clock. The facility is owned and operated by the Arizona Department of Juvenile Corrections. Harcourt's case study involves interviews with thirty of the over 150 young males between the ages of twelve and seventeen that call CMS home. The juveniles are being incarcerated mainly for the recidivism of charges that include "burglary, robbery, auto theft, drug possession and sale, firearm possession, criminal damage, running away, and curfew violations" (69). The young men have not been convicted of felony charges such as murder or armed robbery, for if they had been, they would have been tried as adults and sent to adult prisons to serve out their sentences. Everyone is released from CMS once they reach the age of eighteen (Harcourt).

Harcourt's main focus is what he calls "the semiotics of the gun" (2003, 70). He is concerned with the symbolic meanings of the gun and how these assigned meanings work to shape the lives of youth. Harcourt feels that understanding more about the way young people feel about guns can help us to better manage the problem of gun violence among youth. Furthermore, he hopes that research of this nature will be beneficial in the future for things such as restructuring laws and planning public policy. The endless possibilities of studies of this kind become even more apparent when one takes into account the fact that of the thirty students that were interviewed, 87 percent of them admitted to possessing a gun at some point in their lives, 77 percent of them admitted to carrying a gun on their actual persons, and 63 percent of them admitted to having an extensive background involving both gun possession and gun carrying. Surprisingly, the majority of these respondents were incarcerated for nongun related offenses (Harcourt). If the criminal justice system is not effectively detecting gun usage among youth, then studies such as Harcourt's may mediate between the court system and the young people that are impacted the most by gun violence.

Harcourt uses a method of systematic random sampling to choose his respondents.[2] He then conducts semistructured interviews of thirty detainees. The interview process begins with a set of free association prompts and then the students are shown three color pictures of handguns that come from the November–December issue of *American Handgunner*. The first photo is of an HS 2000 full-size 9mm service pistol from I. M. Metal of Croatia. Harcourt describes it as "a polymer semiautomatic, black plastic-looking pistol that resembles closely a Glock or SIG 9mm" (2003, 70).

Figure 1.1. HS 2000, 2020.   Figure 1.2. P-14 LDA, 2020.

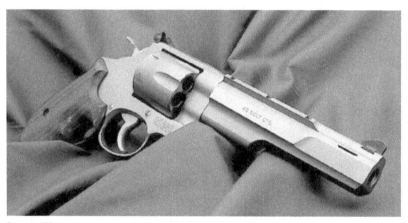

Figure 1.1. HS 2000, 2020.

The second photo is of a Para-Ordinance P-14 LDA. It is described as a "full-size .45 semiautomatic pistol with a five-inch barrel" (70).

The third photo is of a Smith and Wesson .45 Colt CTG revolver (Harcourt).

The free association prompts that are provided to students include: "What are you thinking of right now?" "What are the first experiences that these guns remind you of?" and "What do these guns make you think of?" (70). By posing free association prompts Harcourt is also able to collect a lot of information regarding their histories with guns including ways in which they used guns, how often they carried guns, their attitudes towards guns, the attitudes that their peers have towards them, how they obtained the weapons, and what the guns actually mean to them in terms of symbolism.

In analyzing Harcourt's qualitative data, it is clear that many of the students strongly identify in various ways with the images of guns that they are shown. The statements that many of the students make can easily be interpreted as evidence of fetishism. Harcourt never explicitly uses the term fetish, but his language and data clearly indicate that for the students, guns are much more than simply material objects. This is especially evident in Harcourt's closing remarks: "Guns are . . . deeply fascinating objects of desire to the male youths detained at the Catalina Mountain School. They hold a surprisingly powerful grip over these youths. They generate deep passion. They are seductively dangerous" (2003, 88). Harcourt stops short of applying the term fetish in his study; however, it is evident that fetish theory could help to better illuminate the roles that guns play in the lives of youth—more specifically the roles that they play in the formation of identity and subject-to-subject interactions.

In thinking critically about the language that the students use when speaking about guns it becomes evident that the students see guns as fetish objects. Aside from the traditional materialistic forms, the guns (in and of themselves) are also viewed as protectors (in a supernatural sense), feminized sexual objects, currency (in the form of exchange value), and death. Simultaneously, the students use the gun to negotiate various aspects of their own identities—aspects such as gender, sex, and group affiliation. In these ways the gun fetish may be viewed as being productive even if only for the fetishist.

Some of the respondents see the gun as both protector and protection. According to one respondent it is inevitable that one will be harmed or killed without one. One youth says, "Trouble come automatically when you don't have a gun" (2003, 71). He sees the gun as protection, but he also seems to ascribe some element of the supernatural to guns. In order to avoid harmful situations, one must be "strapped" at all times as if the very act of carrying the weapon is the protection. No further action is required on the part of the owner. It is as if the gun were actually alive. The gun is afforded agency for the purpose of defending the fetishist.[3] Harcourt explains that the respondents' notion of self-defense is twofold. On one hand, they believe that a gun will protect them from being physically injured. On the other hand, they feel the need to protect their image with it. They fear being harassed, humiliated, or intimidated by other youth (Harcourt). This is important because protection from physical injury may require a weapon, but emotional maltreatment would not. The respondents make no distinction between the two.

The guns also embody death for some respondents. They speak of Incidents in Ich guns have been fired accidently, injuring or killing someone in the process. One respondent says "They look nice, but they're dangerous . . . Like, they're, they look nice and everything. They can do powerful stuff, but like, they're dangerous" (73). Another youth responds to the photos by saying that "they're pretty deadly" (73). The language that the respondents use may also indicate that they find the weapons awe-inspiring—the constant juxtaposition of the visual aesthetic and the physical function of the weapon being indicative of trepidation. One may also interpret their language as the respondents ascribing tangible personality traits to the weapons. The adjectives "nice" and "dangerous" are generally applied only to people. Yet the respondents seem to personify the weapons—it is the gun itself that is either "nice" or "dangerous" and not the owner. In this sense the gun has been ascribed a personality of its own entirely—one that may be comparable to that of a Dr. Jekyll and Mr. Hyde. This may be an unconscious attempt on the part of the fetishist to disavow human involvement in the often-deadly outcomes that guns may have produced in their lives. Much like the young child that disavows the mother's sexual difference in Freud's psychoanalytic interpretation. This disavowal is a coping mechanism that simultaneously accepts and denies through the fetish (Steele 1996, 14; McCallum 1999, 24; Penglase 2011, 418).

Many of the youth who were interviewed also saw guns as feminine sexualized objects.[4] Harcourt explains that several of the responses that are interpreted by him as intense desire are also accompanied by certain physical signals as well. These signals include fixation on the photos, laughter, giggling, or even quiet moaning—all attributes that most would associate with intense lust. In effect, the statements portray desire and sexual gratification. If one were to replace the word "guns" with "girls," much of the intended rhetorical meaning would remain intact. Each of the following statements is made by separate respondents as they are being shown the photos:

"Guns are nice . . . They just, I don't know, I just, I just like guns a lot."

"I want to go shoot them . . . Yeah, I want to see how they handle."

"I would love to have one of these. . . . I always want, I always like, I always like guns."

"I'd say they look pretty tight."

"Those are some tight guns. I like the guns on there. I like them. I like the way they look."

"Those are some pretty tight guns."

"It's just tight right there. I like it. It's just tight like the way it looks. The way you can shoot. Those can shoot like ten rounds, huh? But they get jammed a lot. I had one."

"Nice guns."

"They look nice."

"That's a wicked looking gun . . . [*laughter*] I just haven't seen guns in a long time."

"I kinda like how they look. I just want to go shoot them."

"I love guns. Hell ya, I love guns. [I love] everything about a gun." (2003, 74)

Language such as this resembles what one might hear during an intimate conversation between lovers. The repetition and subtle nuances in some of their statements may indicate that they have become completely spellbound by the weapons that they are shown. The gun is spoken of in terms of the feminine sexualized body. The desire to physically "handle" or fire the weapon can be interpreted as sexual yearning. One may also draw the conclusion that there is a sense of satisfaction derived from the very thought of firing the weapon. The fact that some of the respondents go as far as to verbalize their "love" for guns may be indicative of belief (*on subconscious levels*) that a reciprocal relationship truly exists. Another statement made by a seventeen-year-old Mexican American gang member takes the feminine sexual association one step further by expressing that a certain level of commitment is involved in this subject-object relationship. He says:

I had me two baby 9s. I fell in love with those. They look beautiful to me. They were chrome, like perfect size, they had some power to them. I was like damn, I really don't use them because I don't want to get them burned. Somebody's body to it . . . I don't really use those. Those just like, I'm gonna keep those for a long time. . . . They're like tight. They're just all chrome. (86)

Again, the satisfaction that the respondent expresses in the weapons as well as the fact that he wants to keep the guns and protect the guns (seemingly forever) display characteristics that most would only attribute to the sacred institution of marriage. Perhaps in the mind of the fetishist finding the perfect gun is in fact like finding the perfect wife.[5] For gun fetishists all weapons are not simply one in the same. This meticulous nature of the fetishist seems to suggest that beauty lies solely within the eyes of its beholder. Yet this does not fully explain why the gun fetishist would find the gun to be so physically attractive or even why they would go so far as to impress female characteristics upon the weapon. Here Valerie Steele's discussion of a "dominance-failure" interpretation of fetishism is particularly useful. She writes,

> Dominance and rank-related aggression seem to be characteristic of human males, not only because men compete for access to women (and other resources), but because women who preferred to pair with high-status males would on the whole be more successful in raising and protecting children. Dominance and aggression as evolved sex-linked characteristics may also be related to the much greater prevalence of paraphilias among men. A "dominance-failure" interpretation of fetishism has received some empirical support: Male students who were told that women found them unattractive showed temporarily diminished interest in women and a greater response to objects such as shoes and underwear. (1996, 24)

Like shoes and underwear, the gun is something that the fetishist can dominate and also retain complete control over. When seen through the "dominance-failure" model the selective process of choosing the right gun, the sexual aggression that is associated with firing the weapon, and also the commitment to protecting the gun are all inherent social behaviors that have been disassociated from their original context and reified in the form of a subject-object relationship—the degree to which fixation on the gun replaces subject-subject interaction would have to be examined on an individual basis.

Some of the respondents looked at the photos of the guns and saw exchange value only. They did not see the guns for their intended functional purposes. They saw them as potential bartering leverage instead. Some recalled instances when they exchanged guns for drugs, money, or other material items. One of them says, "Sell those and party and buy things, you know . . . stereos, gold, help my family out, rent hotels, buy all kinds of beer, get all faded, live the fast life. Party hardy, all kinds of drugs, coke, cook all kinds of crack, sell it too, you know" (Harcourt 2003, 87). Another respondent also thought solely along the lines of commodification. He says, "This one [9mm pistol] I would keep. These two [.45-caliber pistols] I would sell. I would keep that one [9mm pistol] personally. Forty-fives always sell and that's what I did" (76). As Harcourt points out, for some of the respondents, guns may have been the first available and only means of participating in a market economy. In many ways the very exchange value of the guns may be interpreted as a fetish in and of itself. William Pietz helps to explain how fetish theory and Marxism can be used to elucidate relationships that may exist between the fetish and an increasingly consumer driven culture. In the following passage Pietz discusses the fetishistic nature of exchange value. He says,

> Exchange value is identified as the syntagmatic dimension wherein different commodity-signifiers circulate through exchange transactions that equate their economic value, rather the way words in a poetic text are substituted for each other through metaphorical equations of meaning. Such circulation itself produces novel value representations (meaning-effects) because the exchange values borne by commodities have a certain independence from their alleged use values (their "proper meanings"). (1993, 123)

This statement helps to explain the significance of the fetishists' ability to isolate the gun's practical use from its monetary value. The statement also helps one to see the subjective nature of exchange value. The fetishist must be able to negotiate between multiple levels of exchange value in order to be able to assign a certain exchange value to the guns that they wish to sell. They must be knowledgeable of preexisting market values, current street values, and also the value that they place on the weapon. For the fetishists, it may be a good thing that they see guns in the same way that most others only view currency. It may be one of their few methods of survival and also their only way to experience any measure of personal autonomy in a consumer driven culture.

For some, the sharing of guns is something that impacts intergroup relationships to a great extent. Having guns may mean the difference between having friends and not having any at all. Having a gun or even being willing to hold a weapon for someone else may mean that you are becoming a valued member of that group. As a physical gesture it may even be symbolic that a certain level of trust has been formed. One respondent describes a situation in which he frequently held guns for one person in particular. He says, "'It was given to me by an older friend of mine . . .' 'Hey if you need this, have this, in case anything happens' . . . 'So if you hang around with us, you just might need this, so take this. But be careful with it, don't play around with it'" (Harcourt 2003, 82). The group member is older than the respondent and he is also showing some degree of concern for the respondent's safety and well-being. Furthermore, the phrase "if you hang around with us" indicates that it was not just a physical transaction, but rather a welcoming into the group or a rite of passage. This special rite of passage may be significant to the respondent for a number of reasons. The group identification may provide him safety from rival gangs or from other opposing groups of youth. It may also provide him safety from the threat of incarceration, that is, only if they are able to seek shelter or go into hiding when needed.

Even after recognizing the transition as a rite of passage, one may still inquire as to why a youth would place themselves in such a dangerous predicament by accepting the weapon. From an outsider perspective, the transaction can be viewed as both a gift and a curse. Being caught by authorities with an unregistered weapon is no small offense, even as a juvenile. It could potentially cost one their freedom for decades, if not a lifetime. According to fetish theory, the origin of the problem does not lie in the functional use of the gun, but rather with the functional use of the *fetish* in the process of group identification or interpersonal affiliation. These are some of the more difficult aspects of fetishism to understand. Louise J. Kaplan, *Cultures of Fetishism* (2006), provides us with more insight into the nature of the problem:

> We crave to be the same as, if not better than, everyone in our immediate social order. We want and desire, sometimes more than any freedom offered to us, to be considered normal—which means to be just like everyone else. Even after we open our eyes and are able to see the symptoms of the fetishism strategy all around us, it is still immensely difficult to choose to be different. For those sorts of changes might make us seem weird. . . . The fears of being different and out-of-step with our neighbors are sometimes much greater than the desire to liberate ourselves from the shackles of the fetishism strategy.[6] (182)

For some young male gun fetishists, the threat of rejection from a group could be feared far more than the threat of imprisonment or the threat of any kind of physical harm. If what Kaplan writes is true, then it may be useful to reconsider the roles that we assign to all material objects in our culture and not just guns.

A material object such as a gun becomes cultural currency through the process of reiteration and repetition. Whether gun imagery is shared through oral traditions (such as ballads about badmen, folk tales about gun wielding heroes, or gun-toting legends), films, music, or even folk material culture, the guns' value as a cultural symbol will only continue to increase. While the medium does not dictate the message, it does determine who the messages will eventually reach. Today, millennials often turn to the internet, where they find gun imagery in films, on streaming services, and across various social media platforms. In many cases, guns are identity markers intended to express some aspect of a human being's character. Regardless of the message that they convey, the more people see guns, the more they will continue to think about guns; and from a Freudian perspective, the gun, as a powerful cultural symbol, will only continue to occupy the innermost recesses of people's consciousness. Furthermore, some scholars believe that using guns to negotiate aspects of one's own identity may have much more serious implications for teenagers and young Black males who may still be searching for a sense of self.

BADMEN AND SELF-IMAGE

Self-image is another reason why some male youth fetishize guns. Jeffrey Fagan and Deanna L. Wilkinson (1998) make critical correlations between the formation of self-image and gun violence among teens. They say, "Teenagers may situationally engage in violent behavior to form or maintain certain social identities within the broader social context of the neighborhood. Projecting the 'right image' may have consequences for personal safety, social acceptance, and self-esteem among individuals. Within the isolated social world where respect and valued social standing is limited, the threat of gun violence introduces new complexities for the development of social identity" (149). This information speaks to the importance for some male youth to be perceived as being tough by other male youth in and around their own neighborhoods through the use of guns.[7] Furthermore, once violent behavior is initiated, it becomes more and more flagrant through the act of repetition (149). One respondent who carried a gun explains that he did so only because he wanted to be more like the tough, gun-carrying figures that he encountered frequently on the streets and also on the screen. He says, "When I was younger, I used to kick with those fools and I was looking. 'There's a bad mother fucker right there. Look at that shit. Nobody fucks with that fool'. And in the movies, 'Man that's a bad mother fucker'. And I just wanted to be a bad mother fucker. . . . Like nobody, nobody crosses him" (Harcourt 2003, 72). Possessing a gun may provide youth with a shortcut to attaining the dangerous persona that this respondent describes, but for reasons why, culturally, so much implication is placed on being "bad" in the first place that one may find some answers in the field of folklore.

Frequently in films and other mediums the "bad mother fucker" carries guns and is given license to do as he pleases without the fear of retaliation from rival forces. This notion of the "bad mother fucker," in many ways, can be viewed as an embodiment of the "badman" motif that has been a part of African American folklore for centuries. As a motif it has survived and eventually migrated into many areas of popular culture. This phenomenon may be attributed to the important role that firearms play in the formulation of this archetypal character. The badman of African American folk tradition arose during slavery in response to a social, economic, and political system that did not afford African Americans equal protection and opportunities. The badman with his gun in hand was seen as a way of leveling the playing field—much like the respondent's desire to keep would-be rivals at bay. The badmen of old would sometimes do things such as rob from the rich and give to the poor, as seen in the case of a badman named Railroad Bill. There were many gunslingers who became a part of American oral tradition, but as Eric Mottram points out, African Americans had no use for "white killer myths" (1976, 81). Folklorist John Roberts explains further. "Although Black badmen were invariably conceptualized as individuals who, like Railroad Bill, were accused of breaking the law and became heroic because of their crimes, their acts of lawlessness were conceptualized within a tradition of folk heroic creation that African Americans recognized and accepted as normative expressions of their heroic ideals" (1989, 173). Some characteristics of the badman include supernatural powers (marked by the ability to fly or to shapeshift), the carrying of a large gun or pistol, and an uncanny shooting ability. There exist countless versions of the Railroad Bill legend that are told in the form of legends, ballads, and even folk songs. He remains important to the African American heroic tradition. However, he is not the sole badman figure. There are other important badmen as well and they include (but are not limited to) Devil Winston, John Hardy, Harry Duncan, and Stagolee.

Folklore that involves badmen is generally based on real people and events. The verisimilitude of the tales suggests that society has always been intrigued by the dangerous gun-toting types. For instance, Morris Slater, an Alabama turpentine worker, became legendary after killing a white police officer in 1893 after the officer confronted him in the hope of confiscating his gun. Reincarnated as a folk hero, Slater became the iconic figure that we now *only* recognize as Railroad Bill. The act of an African American male shooting and killing a white police officer in the nineteenth century was virtually unheard of. Such an action, no matter how justifiable, would nearly always result in the African American man being lynched by an angry white mob. The public perception of Slater's fearlessness and toughness in the face of a hostile and racist environment may be the single most important character trait that has allowed his legend to persist for so many centuries. The need for the public to celebrate Slater's crime can certainly be seen in the following lines from one version of the legend: "Railroad Bill was mighty sport/Shot

all the buttons off high Sheriff coat/Den holler, 'Right on desperado Bill'"
(Roberts 1989, 171). The sheriff was executed for attempting to confiscate the
very symbol of Railroad Bill's toughness—his gun. For him, as in the case
of most badmen, the firearm is the main source of their tough persona. It
is a defining characteristic of their identities. This is most certainly the case
in the folk legend of Stagolee. Like the legend of Railroad Bill, the legend
of Stagolee also survives in countless forms. It is also widely believed to be
based on real people and events. However, in this case, there is much more
evidence to substantiate such claims. Folklorist Cecil Brown explains that it
was an actual bloody bar room fight that occurred in 1895 on a Christmas
night in St. Louis between Lee Shelton and Billy Lyons that would eventually
be born into the folk legend that we now know as Stagolee.

> Soon they began to exchange blows by striking each other's hats.
> Shelton grabbed Lyon's derby and broke the form. Lyons said he
> wanted "six bits" from Shelton for damaging his derby. Then Lyons
> grabbed Shelton's Stetson. When Shelton demanded it back, Lyons
> said no. Shelton said he would blow Lyons' brains out if he didn't
> return it. Next Shelton pulled his .44 Smith & Wesson revolver from
> his coat and hit Lyons on the head with it. Still Lyons would not
> relinquish the hat. Shelton demanded the Stetson again, saying that
> if Lyons didn't give him his hat immediately he was going to kill him.
> Then Lyons reached into his pocket for the knife his friend Crump
> had given him and approached Shelton, saying, "You cock eyed son
> of a bitch, I'm going to *make* you kill me." . . . After shooting Lyons,
> Shelton walked over to the dying man, who was still holding on to the
> bar, and said, "N****r, I told you to give me my hat!" He snatched his
> hat from Lyons' hand, put it on his head, and walked out. (2003, 23)

In addition to numerous eyewitness accounts and other documents, the most
visible and socially relevant evidence comes in the form of the folk ballad.
The very first Stagolee ballad ever to be collected was sent to John Lomax
in 1910 by a Texas woman by the name of Ella Scott Fisher (Brown 2003,
9), and surprisingly enough, it retains many of the events' original details.

> 'Twas a Christmas Morning
> The Hour was about ten
> When Stagalee shot Billy Lyons
> And landed in the Jefferson pen.
> O lordy, po' Stagalee!

Although the ballad seems to add other elements such as a jailer and the appearance of Billy Lyon's grieving widow it stays true to much of the story's original content. "You've gone and shot my husband/With a forty-four gatlin' gun" (10). Fisher's version even describes the weapon accurately.

Despite the transformations of the badman becoming somewhat less apparent and even less traceable to the present as we transition from oral tradition to the most modern forms of visual media, the oral legends of Stagolee and other badmen reemerging in the forms of literature, hip-hop, blues, and even rock and roll still helps to substantiate the claim that the African American oral tradition has effectively helped to pattern what we currently regard as modern gun culture. This cultural influence includes the implementation of firearms and the implicit and explicit social approval of the badmen who used them. Taking the most historic evidence into account, Black folklore, the present-day fetishization of the guns by juvenile males may be interpreted as an extension of an earlier blueprint that was meant to instruct, establish behavioral models, and communicate values—in addition to being used as a method of negotiating difference.

Notes

1. Quintard Taylor discusses extensively the pivotal role that African Americans played in American westward expansion in *In Search of the Racial Frontier: African Americans in the American West, 1528–1990.*

2. Harcourt's respondents are referred to by number and they range from twelve to seventeen years of age. They also represent a variety of ethnic backgrounds including Mexican, Irish American, and African American, and come from various regions around the US.

3. In *Lost Bullets: Fetishes of Urban Violence in Rio de Janeiro*, R. Ben Penglase discusses the fact that *stray bullets* are seen as living as opposed to inanimate objects. According to Penglase, "They are alive, even if confused and misguided" (415). I juxtapose this view of bullets with the way that CMS respondents seem to compound their definitions of protection to encompass all notions of physical harm and emotional discomfort. The gun is afforded agency to prevent both.

4. Anne McClintock in *Imperial Leather: Race, Gender, and Sexuality in the Colonial Contest* discusses a process by which men project masculine power and agency onto physical landmarks represented in maps. This projection involves both conversion and disavowal. The city is thus manifested in the mind of the fetishist as something that is "more easily represented and made docile for male knowledge and power, for such representations could depend on the prior fact of the social subordination of women" (82). Analyzing these processes may help us to better understand how and why the male juveniles are able to ascribe feminine characteristics to material objects and the social dynamics that are involved.

5. Here the gun is feminized, but it can also be seen as a phallic symbol, as discussed in Carl P. Eby's *Hemingway's Fetishism: Psychoanalysis and the Mirror of Manhood*. Although Eby applies Freudian theory to literature, his discussion illustrates the complex and personal nature of the fetish.

6. Louise J. Kaplan's *Cultures of Fetishism* prefers the term *fetishism strategy* as opposed to *fetishism* because of the complex mental processes that it connotates.

7. Jeffrey A. Brown in *Dangerous Curves* discusses ways in which women in popular film use guns for much of the same purposes as the male youth—females depicted as heroines utilize the gun (as a phallic representation) to impose threat on other characters. He says, "The symbolically loaded image of women with guns . . . [is] an ingredient of gender performance, in other words, [it is used] as a semiotic device . . . in films like *Aliens* and *Terminator 2* to align the female leads with a clearly masculinized subject position" (130).

References

Bjerregaard, Beth, and Alan J. Lizotte. 1995. "Gun Ownership and Gang Membership." *Journal of Criminal Law and Criminology* 86, no. 1: 37–58.

Blumstein, Alfred. 2002. "Youth, Guns, and Violent Crime." *Future of Children* 12, no. 2: 38–53.

Brown, Cecil. 2003. *Stagolee Shot Billy*. Cambridge: Harvard University Press.

Brown, Jeffrey A. 2011. *Dangerous Curves: Action Heroines, Gender, Fetishism, and Popular Culture*. Jackson: University Press of Mississippi.

Cook, Philip J., and Jens Ludwig. 2000. *Gun Violence: The Real Cost*. Oxford: Oxford University Press.

DeConde, Alexander. 2001. *Gun Violence in America: The Struggle for Control*. Boston: Northeastern University Press.

Eby, Carl P. 1999. *Hemingway's Fetishism: Psychoanalysis and the Mirror of Manhood*. Albany: State University of New York.

Ellen, Roy. 1988. "Fetishism." *Man, New Series* 23, no. 2: 213–35.

Fagan, Jeffrey, and Deanna L. Wilkinson. 1998. "Guns, Youth Violence, and Social Identity in Inner Cities." *Crime and Justice* 24: 105–88.

Freud, Sigmund. 1928. "Fetishism." *The Standard Edition of the Complete Psychological Works of Sigmund Freud*, translated by James Strachey, 152–53. London: Hogarth Press.

Harcourt, Bernard E. 2003. "'Hell No, You Can't Jack That Fool. He Stays Strapped. He's Strapped All the Time': Talking about Guns at an All-Boy Correctional Facility in Tucson, Arizona." *Guns, Crime, and Punishment in America*. Ed. Bernard E. Harcourt. New York: New York University Press. 68–88.

Kaplan, Louise J. 2006. *Cultures of Fetishism*. New York: Palgrave Macmillan.

Lewis, John E. 2001. *The Mammoth Book of the West, The Making of the American West*. New York: Carroll and Graf Publishers.

McCallum, E. L. 1999. *Object Lessons: How to Do Things with Fetishism*. New York: State University of New York Press.

McClintock, Anne. 1996. *Imperial Leather: Race, Gender and Sexuality in the Colonial Contest*. New York: Routledge.

Mitchell, Yolunda T., and Tiffany L. Bromfield. 2019."Gun Violence and the Minority Experience." Ncfr.org/ncfr-report/winter-2018/gun-violence-and minority experience. Last modified January 10, 2019.

Mocan, Naci H., and Erdal Tekin. 2006. "Guns and Juvenile Crime." *Journal of Law and Economics* 49, no. 2: 507–31.

Mottram, Eric. 1976. "'The Persuasive Lips': Men and Guns in America, the West." *Journal of American Studies* 10, no. 1: 53–84.

Penglase, R. Ben. 2011. "Lost Bullets: Fetishes of Urban Violence in Rio de Janeiro, Brazil." *Anthropological Quarterly* 84, no. 2: 411–38.

Pietz, William. 1993. "Fetishism and Materialism: The Limits of Theory in Marx." *Fetishism as Cultural Discourse*. Ed. Emily Apter and William Pietz. Ithaca: Cornell University. 119–51.

Roberts, W. John. 1989. *From Trickster to Badman: The Black Folk Hero in Slavery and Freedom*. Philadelphia: University of Pennsylvania Press.

Steele, Valerie. 1996. *Fetish: Fashion, Sex, and Power*. Oxford: Oxford University Press.

Squires, Peter. 2000. *Gun Culture or Gun Control? Firearms, Violence, and Society*. London: Routledge.

Taylor, Quintard. 1998. *In Search of the Racial Frontier: African Americans in the American West, 1528–1990*. New York: W. W. Norton & Company.

Chapter 2

MOMS WHO CARRY

Femininity and Firearms in Vernacular Digital Photography

ANNAMARIE O'BRIEN MOREL

TRIGGERING THE LIBS: GUN GIRLS AS CONSERVATIVE ICONS

From sharpshooter Annie Oakley to countercultural figures like Kathleen Cleaver and Patty Hearst, armed women have been an ongoing source of public interest and outrage in the United States. More recently, controversies surrounding digitally circulated photos of conservative female gun-rights activists, including Sarah Palin, Tomi Lahren, Dana Loesch, and the Kent State Gun Girl, demonstrate both the contemporary alignment of firearms with conservatism and a steadfast cultural fascination with images of gun-toting women. In *Her Best Shot: Women and Guns in America*, Laura Browder discusses the shifting politics surrounding popular depictions of armed women by tracing both the portrayals of women with guns in advertisements and the news over the past century. The 1960s and 1970s mark a turning point in the depiction of women with guns in both sexualized and politicized contexts—exemplified in the rise of sexploitation films and action heroines concurrent with the coverage of radical leftist, Black nationalist, and feminist activists resembling female guerrillas in the news. However, armed women are increasingly associated with conservatism in the 1980s–1990s following the National Rifle Association's (NRA) explicit alignment with the Republican Party with their endorsement of Ronald Reagan in 1980, and prominent events involving right-wing extremists such as the violent stand-offs at Ruby Ridge and Waco in the early 1990s (Browder 2006, 189).

63

Accompanying "the gun industry's embrace of the female consumer" in the 1980s, the NRA began sponsoring women's gun ownership organizations, firearm training programs, and gun magazines (Browder 2006, 2–3). According to Browder, in the attempt to normalize firearms for middle-class suburban women without alienating their conservative-leaning base, the gun industry sought to present "gun ownership as a choice no more controversial than a woman's favorite shade of lipstick" (222). As a counter to women-led gun-control movements like the Million Mom March and Moms Demand Action, which positioned women as natural advocates for nonviolence, the gun industry began to center "armed womanhood" as "an avatar of strength and female achievement while remaining respectable and embodying family values" (212). At this time, conservative gun advocates began to incorporate women's rights rhetoric, positioning women as independent consumers and emphasizing their right to firearms as part of self-defense.

By presenting firearm ownership as a means of self-defense, and an extension of family values and motherhood, the gun industry recast the issue of gun control through the voices of conservative women. Following the alignment of gun ownership with right-wing politics, and the unabated public interest in images of women with guns, images of armed conservative women have played an increasingly prominent role in public discourse on guns and are a part of contemporary visual culture. Controversies surrounding photos of conservative women with firearms include an infamous photoshopped image of Palin wearing a bikini and holding a gun in 2008, glamorous photos of former NRA spokeswoman Dana Loesch, social media posts by conservative commentator Tomi Lahren, and the graduation photos of the "Kent State Gun Girl," Kaitlin Bennett.

The scandal around Kaitlin Bennett is particularly relevant to the rest of this chapter, which explores women's concealed-carry posts as part of the social media landscape. In May of 2018, Bennet's Kent State graduation photos became headline news after she tweeted images of herself carrying a firearm as commentary on debates over guns on campus. Wearing a short white sundress with long curly blonde hair draped over an AR-15 style rifle strapped across her back, Bennett catapulted herself into the public eye. The painted words on the top of her graduation cap made her message crystal clear: "COME AND TAKE IT." The photo went viral on Twitter when Bennett posted the photo with the caption, "Now that I graduated from @KentState, I can finally arm myself on campus. I should have been able to do so as a student—especially since 4 unarmed students were shot and killed by the government on this campus. #CampusCarryNow" (Bennett 2018a). Referencing the infamous 1970 National Guard shooting of thirteen protesters on Kent State University campus, Bennett embedded her otherwise typical graduation photos with political valence and historical significance. The contrast between the big black gun and the delicate, frilly white dress on her small frame—along with the overtly political message—drew the attention of both conservative and liberal commentators.

News coverage about the photo and the subsequent backlash online became an ongoing source of notoriety for Bennett as she fashioned herself into a conservative pundit by documenting her confrontations with liberal college students on camera (Rodriguez 2020; Eltagouri 2018). As her notoriety grew, Bennett began working as a reporter for conservative and conspiracy-oriented media establishments including Infowars. The camera continues to be one of her primary tools of expression. She continues to post posed gun photos with political messages in captions and frequently embedded in her selfies on graphic T-shirts with progun slogans. Much of the subsequent attention on Bennet, from both conservative and liberal commenters, focused on her femininity, with praises of her beauty on the one hand and denouncement of her styling and looks on the other. Critical memes and commentaries often allude to her body, hair, nails, and clothing, belying an underlying concern with her enactment of gender in a visual medium and her role as a female gun advocate.

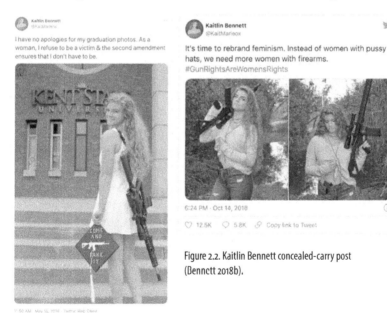

Figure 2.2. Kaitlin Bennett concealed-carry post (Bennett 2018b).

Figure 2.1. Kaitlin Bennett's graduation photo (Bennett 2018a).

The controversy surrounding the Kent State Gun Girl demonstrates the way in which photos of women posing with guns are politicized and circulated online, as well as the potentially far-reaching effects vernacular photos like snapshots and selfies can have on contemporary discourse. This sets the stage for the discussion of gun selfies posted on Instagram. In these selfies, women actively participate in shaping gun discourse using images of themselves to articulate political sentiments and advocate for firearms—refashioning the connection between firearms and femininity along the way. This chapter focuses on how women portray guns as part of everyday life in a gendered framework in a relatively common format—the concealed-carry photo.

An early example of a concealed-carry photo that I encountered was a selfie posted on Instagram with the caption, "It was a little tricky to find a good spot at the park where I can see the entrance/exit, play with the 2-year-old and still be in the shade, but I'm making it work" (callin_th_shotz 2018). The photo is a casual snapshot-style self-portrait taken on a summer day and is fairly typical for the user "callin_th_shotz," a self-described "American Momma" and ardent supporter of the Second Amendment. The photo is a selfie depicting a young woman sitting on a shady patch of blue playground turf with a half-eaten bag of chips beside her, lifting up the bottom of her floral shirt to reveal the gun tucked into a holster under the waist of her pink jean shorts. Slightly tilted and closely cropped, the woman's face is not featured in the photo. Her outfit and the reveal of the gun take center stage. The photo and caption together provide vivid documentation of an everyday moment in her life, offering an intimate glimpse of the firearm she carries beneath her light summer outfit and her navigation of the duties of motherhood.

Firearms discreetly worn in everyday scenarios and depicted in this manner are referred to as concealed-carry weapons and are explicitly categorized by Instagram users through hashtags such as #concealedcarry and #everydaycarry. Callin_th_shotz weaves several additional hashtags into her comments on the image, including #girlswhocarry, #concealedcarrywoman, #glockgirl, #concealcarrynation, #womenwhoshoot, and #momswhocarry, connecting her image with thousands of others with similar content on Instagram. As a subgenre of the gun selfie, the concealed-carry post generally features women armed beneath everyday attire, evoking before-and-after-style photos in a casual context, in stark contrast with the vast sea of erotically charged images of women with guns shared in other venues online and in popular culture. The concealed-carry selfie emphasizes the woman's innocuous presentation before revealing her hidden firearm, playing on the ability of the camera to both obscure and reveal underlying truth.

Figure 2.3. Search results for gender-neutral concealed-carry hashtag, #concealedcarrynation (Instagram 2020).

I collected photos shared publicly on Instagram by following several hashtags related to firearms and gender, focusing particularly on those relating to concealed carry (such as #concealedcarryfashion, #concealedcarrymama, #womenwhocarry, #carrylikeagirl, and #concealandreveal) and women's self-defense (including #shootlikeagirl, #momswhoshoot, #mamabear, and #refusetobeavictim). While observing photos posted through these hashtags, I noticed a few trends. First, before-and-after-style selfies depicting the transition between the outer appearance and the hidden weapon were extremely common. Second, the vast majority of selfies posted publicly with these hashtags seemed to explicitly link firearms and self-defense with family and motherhood. Third, posts frequently alluded to feminism through captions that linked guns to women's self-empowerment.

Browsing the hashtags that do not explicitly address gender (like #everydaycarry, #9mm, or #guns) demonstrates a range of snapshot photos of guns from a first-person perspective, as well as selfies and portrait-style photos of men and women with guns in hand or shooting. However, in my research I found that even in these gender-neutral categories, women appear more frequently in photos than men, despite representing a minority of gun owners (Parker et al. 2017). When men are depicted in gun photos, selfies are uncommon, and even concealed-carry photos are much less likely to depict significant portions of their body, with the image closely cropped on the weapon or holster.

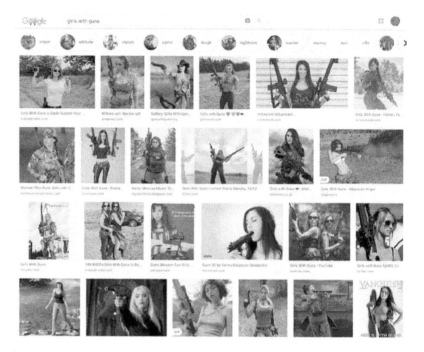

Figure 2.4. Google image search results demonstrating glamorous and objectified depictions of women with guns (Google 2020).

Depictions of women with guns that are not selfies shared under the general hashtags such as #firearms and #9mm are more likely to be overtly sexual than concealed-carry photos. Portrayals of women with guns in this manner, in revealing clothing with glamorous makeup and studio styling, correspond to an existing cultural fixation on images of young, attractive women carrying guns as "action babes" and "gun girls" (Brown 2011; Browder 2006). Photos shared with hashtags like #girlsandguns, #gunsandbuns, #gunbunnies and #gunbabes, often carry on these tropes, featuring highly stylized portrayals of glamorous women in provocative poses with guns. Provocative, glamour portraits of women with guns contrast sharply with concealed-carry selfies, pointing toward the role they inhabit in progun discourse. While concealed-carry photos certainly also depict women's bodies prominently alongside guns, they do not carry an air of fantasy but are firmly grounded in everyday settings through the norms of casual snapshot selfies. As women reveal their firearm beneath everyday clothing, they participate in progun discourse in an intimate way.

THE "SNAPSHOTS" AND GUN VISUAL CULTURE

Photos shared on Instagram constitute one facet of the interconnected networks that mediate vernacular gun discourse online. In "Gunnets: Why a Theory of Heterogeneous Volition Is Necessary in the Study of Digital Communication," Robert Glenn Howard describes the importance of vernacular discourse surrounding firearms in gun forum posts and the role they play within the broader digital ecosystem on sites like Facebook and Reddit, which "each have their own large volumes of vernacular discourse about guns" (Howard 2017, 124). However, the vernacular discourse represented by selfies is distinct from that of a text-heavy forum and are also distinct from other photos of guns shared online. While Facebook, Twitter, and Reddit have various groups and posts featuring guns, Instagram has a particularly vibrant scene for selfies.

There is relatively little scholarship on women and guns in American culture, despite recent studies that show that women's gun ownership has been rising over the past two decades (Deckman 2016, 218). According to a 2017 study by the Pew Research Center, 22 percent of women say they own a gun and an additional 18 percent of women report that they do not personally own a gun but live in a household with someone who does (Parker et al. 2017). The scholarship that does exist about women and guns in the United States tends to focus on historical figures and celebrity women with guns (e.g., Browder 2006), or on gun violence against women (e.g., Kelly 2004), rather than on women's everyday participation in image-making and discourse.

To explore concealed-carry selfies, I consider the historical and cultural contexts for portrayals of women with guns, performance of gender and visual qualities of the selfies, and the way in which they position guns in relation to motherhood and domesticity and self-empowerment. Visual texts are an essential part of contemporary gun culture, and gun selfies are an example of how guns have become a powerful vehicle for folkloric expression online. In this chapter, I contextualize gun-selfie photography through depictions of guns in popular culture, advertisements, and firearm advocacy in the United States, incorporating close readings of concealed-carry photos and the discourses that surround them. In this approach, I offer groundwork for future considerations of women's participation in vernacular gun discourse online and the political and expressive use of photography in social media.

The photos I examine of women with guns, created and shared online by individuals, are a form of vernacular photography (sometimes called snapshot, amateur, or domestic photography), with social functions existing alongside the expressive attributes. In his article, "Picturing Hunting," Jay Mechling points out that the relationship between vernacular photography and guns is embedded in the word "snapshot," which refers to casual, amateur photography. According to Mechling, "The word 'snapshot' actually originated in hunting to describe a shot taken in a hurry, with little time to aim" and began to be applied to photography as early as the 1860s (2004, 69).

Mechling argues that hunting photos, and vernacular photography at large, can be examined by folklorists as documents of folk performance or as a "coded image" considered in terms of "the visual conventions it creates and mimics" (2004, 55). Mechling lays out a clear way to approach photography from a folkloric perspective:

> We can examine a snapshot and parse out the text, texture, and contexts, just as we would any item of folklore, understanding that the "meanings" of a snapshot arise through all three of these elements— the manifest content of the image (the text), the visual aesthetic of the image (the texture, see Dundes 1964), and the concentric circles of contexts, from the most personal, esoteric context to the broadest social and cultural contexts, including the intertextuality between the image and other images or visual experiences. (60)

The term "vernacular" is useful to refer to the selfies shared in social media because it conveys the elements of informality and expressive qualities, as well as the relationship with broader institutions and commercial platforms. The term vernacular is used in both folklore and media studies to describe forms of popular and everyday expression online (Blank 2009, Kirshenblatt-Gimblett 1995, Howard 2008, Burgess 2009, Shifman 2013, Nakamura 2008). Selfies may be considered a form of vernacular photography, as they are a common and informal mode of communication within a society, shared on social media. Concealed-carry photos often blur the lines between commercial and personal photography, especially in the increasing saturation of aspirational "influencers" in social media who link to vendors. They are not produced by commercial retailers or affiliated with official institutions, but they use hashtags associated with brands to draw attention to themselves. Influencers are useful to brands because they have a sense of authenticity that professional commercial content does not, and the snapshot selfie is one way of creating that authenticity.

In "Vernacular Authority Speaks for the Glock: Heterogeneous Volition in an Institutional Proverb," Robert Glenn Howard identifies "gun porn" as an emic genre, describing it as "the practice of taking and sharing pictures of one's own guns." Unlike commercial photography that seeks to sell guns, gun porn is pornographic in the way that it celebrates the visual images of guns. Howard claims that amateur gun porn, unlike professional gun photography that is used to sell guns, "functions as a way to assert one's identity as a member of one sort of subgroup or the other in the larger recreational gun-user community" (Howard 2019, 84). As an emic genre of vernacular discourse, concealed-carry photos, like gun porn, are used to connect with others in their community; however, they are also meant for consumption by others outside of that particular audience.

Andrew Peck also addresses visual images shared online as part of vernacular discourse through memes in his discussion of photoshopped pictures of the pepper-spraying cop. Peck argues that "these user-based visual appropriations are valuable not only as forms of personal expression and civic engagement but as a complex example of how Web users continually negotiate themselves through vernacular discursive practices online" (2014, 1659). Gun photos similarly may function as a means of personal expression and civil engagement online. As women frame themselves in these images, everyday photography is used to articulate personal identity and beliefs.

SEX SELLS (GUNS)

As phallic objects par excellence, visual representations of guns in American popular culture and folklore have often been framed through masculinity and Freudian symbolism using psychoanalytic frameworks. The ongoing association of the gun with maleness and phallic imagery is addressed in Richard M. Dorson's treatment of cowboys in Westerns, Américo Paredes's discussion of the pistol as the ultimate symbol of machismo, and Simon Bronner's expansion on the phallic coding of guns in rituals and humor in "This is Why We Hunt" (Dorson 1963; Paredes 1971; Bronner 2004).

Sexualized images of women with guns contradict other stereotypical notions of femininity as soft, passive, and harmless, with the masculine coding of guns as hard, powerful and violent phallic objects. In *Dangerous Curves: Action Heroines, Gender, Fetishism, and Popular Culture*, Jeffrey Brown examines the portrayal of women with guns in action movies, arguing that the visual association of women with guns both fetishizes the female form, and eroticizes the gun. Brown writes, "Action cinema eroticizes the female form by visually associating women with guns. . . . The use of guns by beautiful women eroticizes violence, but it also cements the fetishistic representation of women and reinforces the underlying themes of castration

Figure 2.5. Search results for #momswhocarry (Instagram 2020).

anxiety at play in the genre" (2011, 101). Ultimately, he argues that "the combination of guns and strippers, who are clearly marked as sexual spectacles" eroticizes the gun and amplifies the femininity of the woman portrayed with it (130).

Despite the symbolic masculinity associated with the gun, women's bodies are frequently part of the visual culture surrounding guns in American culture, likely because of commercial appeals to a male audience. In *Her Best Shot: Women and Guns in America*, a detailed history of the representation of women with guns, Laura Browder discusses the emergence of sexualized images of guns with women in advertisements and movies. According to Browder, "From the late 1960s to the present day, women in firearms ads have tended to be scantily dressed models posing with ultramasculine weapons. Women's sexuality has been used to enhance the appeal of these guns" (2006, 10). The marketing of guns to men resulted in a paradoxical positioning of women with guns as a novelty or spectacle for visual consumption and an extensive archive of images depicting women with guns.

Portrayals of women as decorative props or objects of desire in visual media are addressed extensively in feminist media criticism, often through Laura Mulvey's conception of the male gaze wherein the "active/male" figure is contrasted with the "passive/female" and the "determining male gaze projects its phantasy on to the female figure which is styled accordingly" (1975, 6).

Mulvey's analysis of the connotation of "to-be-looked-at-ness" that styles the female figure for the male gaze extends to portrayals of women with guns in vernacular photography in the way women pose for photos. While there are elements of the male gaze that can be parsed in concealed-carry photos, namely in the prevalence of women sharing photos of themselves, and the particular focus on the body in the image, the performance of gender does not seem to be reliant on sexual objectification, but rather on the embodiment of femininity through allusions to family and domesticity.

AUTOBIOGRAPHY, REALISM AND THE BEFORE-AND-AFTER

Based on my observations of images collected from these accounts and hashtags, it is evident that women's concealed-carry selfies share distinctive stylistic characteristics. Not only do concealed-carry photos harness the cultural significance of guns as symbols of power and sexuality, but they also solidify the connection between firearms and conservative family values. Within the image and caption, the potent symbolism of the gun is juxtaposed with normative, family-oriented femininity, representing progun politics in a nuanced narrative framework. The remainder of this chapter highlights my findings in my examination of concealed-carry photos, and the importance of selfies as an expressive genre of photography that allows for the rearticulation of gender norms. Through visual and narrative elements that imply authenticity and intimacy, women's concealed-carry posts recast the armed woman as a figure standing for domestic safety and self-empowerment. Much of the power of concealed carry posts comes from the sense of intimacy, authenticity, and realism articulated through the digital photo as well as the accompanying text. Women's concealed carry selfies often include first-person captions that create a realistic representation of everyday life. Autobiographical anecdotes detailing relatable experiences or self-deprecating jokes are frequently paired with pragmatic advice about carrying concealed weapons. For example, one popular account opens a concealed carry post with a lightly self-deprecating reference to her "mummy tummy" before launching into an anecdote about the hassles of grocery shopping and potty-training children. User tacticoolmom writes, "How to conceal in a fitted tee. Squish that gun into your mummy tummy! I was able to go out grocery shopping by myself today. It was such a luxury. I haven't really been out of the house in a few days since we're in the middle of potty training" (2019). Another user, momswhocarry, posts a photo of herself wearing a loose T-shirt draped over her concealed weapon with a similarly

Figure 2.6. Concealed-carry post with "Nurture and Protect" T-shirt (Instagram 2019).

self-deprecatory tone, offering a positive spin on perceived shortcomings. She writes, "I know it's a fashion 'faux pas,' but for you other mommas who have better things to do than to iron your tshirts 😅 . . . Wrinkles honestly do aid in concealment! . . . no one will bat an eye at your wrinkles, and it makes it even easier to conceal a weapon on a thin frame when the outline of the gun is still somewhat visible (2019)."

These captions offer a window into strategies women use to incorporate guns into their daily lives, and hint at the value they place on firearms as a form of self-protection. Pragmatic advice for the management of a concealed-carry weapon is offered in the context of navigating the difficulties of everyday life. The first-person perspective creates a brief, informal personal narrative that frames the image, paralleling the sense of intimacy and authenticity that takes place in selfie photos.

A selfie is inherently autobiographical to some extent, reflecting the life of the one who produces it. As autobiographical narratives, selfies generate a sense of realism through self-representation, tied to the articulation of first-person perspective (Kirshenblatt-Gimblett 1989; Titon 1980). However, the selfie generates a sense of realism in ways that other forms of expression cannot. Selfies generally appear to communicate "real" information about a particular occurrence, and they are frequently used in everyday communication garnering them a sense of authenticity and informality. Glamour photos and staged "gun porn" photos, by contrast, are not necessarily concerned with the accurate transmission of one's own personal perspective as much as they are with the creation of a desirable representation of the subject. Through the use of realistic imagery, free of improbable, ornamental, nondiegetic elements, the photos assume a factual quality, regardless of how staged they may have been. The gun and holster, as well as the outfit that conceals them, are presented as part of the existing scene that the selfie captures. Because concealed-carry photos convey a sense of casual spontaneity, grounded in reality rather than artifice, they sometimes have qualities associated with amateur photography snapshots. In "Photography as Communication," David Nye suggests that because the subject matter is the most important aspect of photography meant for family and friends, the photos are often "out of focus, overexposed, badly cropped, poorly framed, or otherwise technically weak . . . made with confidence that the viewers will themselves supply the surrounding context" (1986, 33). The composition may be odd, centering the body in front of the camera at close range and cropping the subject in unusual ways, or have a blurry or over-exposed quality.

As a mode of representation in visual expression and literature, realism evokes a credible connection between the image and the existing world. According to art historian W. J. T. Mitchell, realism "is associated with the capacity of pictures to show the truth about things. It doesn't take power over the observer's eye so much as it stands in for it, offering a transparent window onto reality, an embodiment of a socially authorized and credible 'eyewitness' perspective" (1995, 325). In the context of concealed-carry selfies, photos are used to evoke a "transparent window into reality," revealing the firearm that is hidden beneath the surface. The image provides proof and turns attention to the embodied aspects of concealed carry.

In concealed-carry posts, the sense that the image accurately reflects what it depicts is facilitated through informal styling and poses that allow a glimpse of humble everyday domestic surroundings rather than scenic or luxurious locales. Instead of incorporating studio lights, decorative props, or artificial backgrounds, objects and lighting in the frame appear native to the scene. Backgrounds are minimal or nondescript domestic interiors, or occasionally everyday locations outside of the home like a local playground or grocery store.

Concealed-carry selfies are reliant on realism as a representational strategy as they depict the firearm's incorporation into daily life and the articles of clothing that facilitate concealment. While clothing ranges from formal wear to business to leisure attire, revealing, tight clothing is relatively uncommon. Instead, photos tend to feature casual or work-appropriate everyday attire, like jeans and T-shirt with a jacket or sweater layered on top, or button-down shirts with dressy pants or knee-length skirts. Regardless of the formality of the outfit, photos tend to depict a coordinated, neat, put-together look, with clean styled hair, clothing, and home interiors.

Alongside the central subject posing with her gun, photos may include objects associated with childcare, references to domestic chores, and personal hobbies or occupations. For instance, some of the selfies I encountered depict the subject with a coffee in hand, a Bible on the lap, or a steering wheel in front of the subject. While this may seem incidental, posing a selfie to reveal a gun in a hip or thigh holster while capturing contextual details or background is not always easy. However, these seemingly trivial details provide additional information about the "real life" moment—indicating she is not just carrying by herself in her room, but on her way to work, at church with her family, or grocery shopping.

The organization of space in the image creates a sense of intimacy in most selfies. Hand-held selfies, either taken with the front-facing camera or with the help of a mirror, appear more commonly than timed selfies because they are conducive to quick and spontaneous photos, and do not require extra accessories (like stands or remotes) and streamline the review process. Hand-held selfies also create an intimate first-person perspective. Front-facing selfies, taken with the phone held out at arm's length with the screen facing the body, typically create a slightly distorted perspective because of the wide angle of the lens and its fixed focal length. This exaggerates the size of the objects closest to the camera, in comparison with our natural vision, making them appear more prominent. Because selfies are typically limited to the arm's length (lengthened occasionally with a selfie stick), the background is also minimized, resulting in closely cropped images that draw the eye into closer proximity to the subject. Mirror selfies, taken by pointing the camera at a mirror to capture the image oneself, can capture a larger area of space than front-facing camera selfies, allowing for more context or capturing more of the subject in the image. Mirror selfies also fix the perspective of the camera, photographer, and subject in the visual space of the photograph. Both forms of selfies take advantage of the technological features of the mobile phone and camera interface.

However, unlike glamour selfies and pin-up style "gun girl" photos, concealed-carry selfies generally forego dramatic lighting and filters that drastically alter the hues and contrast in the image, preserving the photo's relationship with the subject according to audience expectations and creating a sense of realism (Rose 2001, 40). The sense of realism in a photograph is heightened when an image presents its subject using colors and perspectives that appear to match our natural visual perception of that subject. Filters are used sparingly in concealed-carry selfies, which both maintains the legibility of the objects that are portrayed and creates a sense of indexicality, or that the photo is truthfully representing the subject of the photo.

Another way of creating a sense of indexicality is through the presentation of concealed-carry selfies as before-and-after images. The before-and-after is a common format for women's concealed-carry posts in my observations (see figures 2.2, 2.6, and 2.7). Before-and-after posts consist of at least two photographs, showing the concealed-carry weapon as it looks when it is hidden beneath the clothes, alongside a nearly identical "reveal" photo that shows the gun beneath the clothing. This effect is often achieved through posts that contain multiple images, allowing the viewer to swipe back and forth between them, making the before-and-after an interactive experience. Other before-and-after posts are created by inserting both photos together into the same image to create a side-by-side juxtaposition, or with a short video clip in which the woman shows herself with the weapon concealed and reveals the weapon.

In before-and-after posts, the camera is used to show both the outward appearance and the "truth" in a visual manner. The before-and-after is a standard trope, particularly common in commercial uses of portrait photography to show the efficacy of beauty products, and weight-loss or fitness regimens, dating back to at least the mid-nineteenth century (see Rooks 2000, 43). In *Before-and-After Photography: Histories and Contexts*, Jordan Bear and Kate Albers describe the importance of this format and its underlying power, playing upon the contrasts of "the visible and the unseen, the certainties of proof and the imagined processes of transformation" (2017, 10). According to Bear and Albers, "If there is any universal feature of the before-and-after pair, it is their reliance on a viewer's imaginative investment in the temporal dimension offered in the visual exchange" (10). In the concealed-carry selfie, the before-and-after pair of images invites the viewer to imagine the relationship between the two images, while reinforcing the sense of objectivity conferred by the photograph as visual proof.

The visual format is sometimes referenced explicitly in the post through hashtags like #concealandreveal and #beforeandafter, and through commentary on the efficacy of the concealment. Some concealed-carry posts are linked to commercial content, acting as a testament for concealed-carry accessories with brands tagged in the post, reinforcing the before-and-after image's roots in advertising. While they draw on established visual vocabulary, concealed-carry photos are unique, conveying both the absence and presence of the firearm through the contrast of the images. The first image, in which the woman presents herself passively—a prime target for criminals or assailants, is positioned as a "lack" that the gun in the second image satisfies. The second image proves that she is actually armed, prepared to attack and defend herself and her family.

The before-and-after helps to sell a fantasy (literally in the case of quasi-advertisement posts by influencers): the promise of fulfillment, and a sense of safety attained through a concealed firearm. The reveal of the firearm, concealed beneath innocuous attire, corresponds with the sense of private and individual safety the gun represents. The realistic and autobiographical nature of the posts, as well as the informality of the selfie aesthetic build a sense of authenticity, illustrating the role of the gun in everyday domestic life. The accessibility and the familiarity of the before-and-after acts as a visual shorthand for concealment, a frame for articulating progun sentiments—and dramatizes her transformation from a vulnerable woman into a fierce defender.

PINK-WASHED GUNS AND SHAPEWEAR HOLSTERS

Feminine sensibilities and the role of the woman as a mother are reinforced in many ways in captions and in the focus on fashion and self-styling in the image. In my observations, many women display their values literally through garments with slogans on T-shirts. Some of the popular T-shirt slogans include: "Coffee, guns & messy buns," "Nurture & Protect," "Just an ordinary mom trying not to raise communists," "Keep Calm and Carry," "Liberty Loving Mama Bear, Hands Off My Cubs" and "Fierce as a Founding Mother" (primerandco 2020; liberty_belle_co 2020). Several designs incorporate a gun—the "My Mama Didn't Raise a Victim" T-shirt superimposes a rifle on the word victim, another replaces the letter L with a handgun in the word "FEMALE." These T-shirts reinforce the messages that surface in the images and captions, normalizing potentially divisive firearms with references to coffee and messy buns, as well as motherly love and protection.

Feminine identity is highlighted rather than downplayed in the focus on fashion and self-presentation, as well as motherhood. Rather than featuring unisex items like backpacks, jeans or hoodies, the concealed-carry posts feature accessories geared toward women. This includes pink guns, bedazzled holsters, and concealed-carry purses, in addition to highly feminized articles of clothing like concealed-carry leggings, corset and bra holsters, and garter-style thigh holsters. Captions and discussions often present the holster as a fashion accessory, with commentary on the outfit's success in camouflaging bumps and gun prints, or on the difficulties of dressing in a way that is feminine and flattering while carrying. The magic of the before-and-after photos that demonstrate the perfect preservation of the feminine silhouette as well as the consistent emphasis on the performance of traditional, domestic gender roles offset the potential masculinity associated with carrying a gun.

According to Jeffrey Brown, portrayals of women with guns often counteract the masculine associations of guns by objectifying the feminine body (2011, 130). While there are many images of "gun babes" on Instagram that demonstrate this form of objectification, concealed-carry selfies do not typically rely on the performance of an overtly sexualized version of femininity. However, the performance of revealing the body in concealed-carry posts does seem to evoke a subtle sensuality at times. Often revealing a slice of midriff, women pull up their shirts to show guns tucked into appendix holsters or draw up a skirt to reveal a thigh holster. The reveal of a flash of intimate skin or body parts that were previously concealed is associated with the "striptease"—and the connection between concealed carry and stripping is obliquely referenced in the playful use of the hashtag #concealandreveal (a hashtag also used by burlesque dancers). Simultaneously, the concealed carry seems to defy expectations of the striptease, with the reveal of the firearm representing a subversion. Rather than a striptease as a means of passive sex object, the display of the gun reveals them to be a potential threat.[1]

In *Good Guys with Guns: The Appeal and Consequences of Concealed Carry*, Angela Stroud describes the "pinkwashing" of guns, including the production of pink and bedazzled guns and firearm accessories geared toward women consumers. Pinkwashed gun culture, according to Stroud, highlights the assumed masculinity of guns in contemporary culture. "While pink accessories might be appealing to some women," Stroud explains, "these feminizing embellishments inadvertently reinscribe the notion that 'normal guns,' 'real guns' are for men and novelty guns are for women. Thus, paradoxically, pink gun grips are part of the discursive formation whereby guns are defined as masculine" (2015, 10). The pinkwashing of guns is evident in hashtags like #messybunsandguns, #elegantandarmed, #armedandbeautiful, #pistolsandpumps, #bulletsandbombshells, #heelsandhandguns, #stilletosandshotguns, and #ladyandtheglock. These hashtags play on the contrast between guns and women or feminine articles of clothing.

Concealed-carry posts incorporate cute details in the display of shapewear holsters, and provide fashion tips about maintaining a feminine look while carrying a firearm. Following Stroud's argument, the emphasis on feminine styling may be seen as a strategy for compensating for the inherently masculine nature of guns, ultimately reinscribing traditional gender

Figure 2.7. Before-and-after thigh holster concealed-carry post highlighting fashion and body (shelcheesy 2020).

norms. Thus, the styling of photos, like the narratives that address women as targets of violence, positions the gun as a masculine remedy for gender-based inequality, using its association with masculinity and power in juxtaposition with femininity.

When considering the intersection between women's bodies and gun discourse, the multitasking shapewear holsters, and the emphasis on visually portraying the body while carrying a firearm may take on additional significance. The insistence on maintaining a traditional feminine silhouette while carrying a gun preserves assumptions about sexual dimorphism, upholding progun discourses predicated on the physical differences between men and women, like "gun as the ultimate equalizer" (Deckman 2016, 221). Stroud, among others, describes this narrative emerging in her interviews with women who carry guns, but points out that for these women, "carrying a gun does nothing to fundamentally alter their view that they are inherently vulnerable to men" (2015, 69). Furthermore, she argues that "the idea that there is 'very little' that she could do to defend herself from a man because of average physical differences dramatically inflates the extent to which women are weak vis-à-vis men," citing several studies (70).

In general, posts that discuss motherhood and concealed-carry garments draw attention to the incongruity of stereotypes of passivity associated with femininity and the power figured by guns. In concealed-carry posts, the image visually attempts to resolve the conflict. Contemporary gender norms tend to reward women for their appearance, to the extent that some feminist scholars have argued beauty has superseded other values traditionally associated with femininity, such as caretaking and motherhood. In *Aesthetic Labour*, Ana Elias explains that in a postfeminist culture, the woman's body is valued "less for what it can do than for how it appears, which is figured both as the locus of womanhood and the key site of women's value—displacing earlier constructions of femininity which highlighted particular roles or characteristics (such as motherhood or caring)" (Elias, Gill, and Scharff 2017, 46). Concealed-carry posts show how women incorporate a maternal identity into their conceptions of femininity, grappling with expectations about their appearance and clothing framed in the context of motherhood. To wear flattering, feminine attire while carrying a baby, with a firearm at the ready is to be the ideal mother-protector.

MAMA GRIZZLY PROTECTING THE FAMILY WITH FIREARMS

Firearms and family are coupled in concealed-carry content, with guns portrayed in the context of domesticity and motherhood. While posts may invoke patriotism, incorporating American flags and references to Second Amendment rights, they tend to incorporate this into narratives that center the position of the woman in the home and her role within the nuclear family. Many women cite motherhood as a primary motivation for carrying a firearm in their posts, and many include children in the image, posing with a baby on her hip and a handgun tucked into pants. Discussions about the mechanics of concealed carry often extend to the challenges of caring for children while carrying a firearm, and the ability to wear traditionally feminine clothing.

The connection between motherhood and gun advocacy on Instagram is evident in the numerous hashtags like #concealcarrymama, #momswhocarry, #pistolpackinmama, #mamabear and #momswhoshoot. Many of the profiles that posted concealed-carry content also address their connection to family in their usernames, with names like tacticalmom and mamabear, and in their brief self-descriptions in their bios, with statements like: "Not Your Average Mom," or "Momma Bear guards this house. Wife to Riley," and "Dog mom, Wife, and human mom to be." For instance, one self-described "Wifey & Mama Bear," frequently posts photos of herself carrying a small child while revealing a concealed gun. One of these posts depicts her appendix belly band holster while carrying her child, and a caption highlighting the importance of protection and motherhood: "Never underestimate a Mama Bear 🐻 #whyicarry #dontmesswithmyfamily #protectthoseyoulove #childsafety #firearms #momswhocarry #mamabear" (bullets.n.bows 2019).

The "mama bear" trope is common in concealed-carry posts and relates to what Jennifer Carlson identified as "martial maternalism," in "Troubling the Subject of Violence: The Pacifist Presumption, Martial Materialism, and Armed Women in Contemporary Gun Culture." Drawing on earlier discourse about the "Mama Grizzly" archetype in conservative feminism and the romanticization of motherhood, Carlson argues that the mama grizzly represents an attempt to create an identity that "complements rather than critiques men's own prerogative to protect" (2016, 90). Expectations for women to arm themselves in order to defend the home, according to Carlson, are framed as an empowering choice through the mama grizzly trope, although "the longstanding expectation that women must sacrifice for their children is hardly feminist" (102–3).

The idealization of motherhood invoked here through the "mama grizzly" trope offers an alternative to some of the prescriptions of contemporary femininity—especially in the depiction of women with guns in popular culture. In these gun selfies, women are not depicting themselves as passive victims or glamorous gun models, but instead portray themselves in a relatively realistic manner as protectors of the home, caring mothers, and enterprising wives. This representation parallels the shift in portrayals of guns in advertisements in the late-twentieth century—from a tool for hunting or defense against wild animals to defenders of the suburban home. In this era, the gun was recast as a symbol of defense against the encroachment of the ills of civilization—namely urban crime (Browder 2006, 2).

Women's concealed-carry posts shaped around motherhood often invoke the image of the mama grizzly, while paradoxically citing traditional gender norms as women portray themselves armed as domestic caregivers in the private sphere and mention the inherent vulnerability of unarmed women in public. In nearly all concealed-carry posts shared by women the firearm is positioned as a tool that assures her safety when the police or her husband are not on hand.[2] The concealed weapon helps meet the needs of her children and family and enables her to navigate the public sphere alone.

#WHYICARRY

According to several studies, self-defense is an important reason women purchase guns, citing fear of crime, mass shootings, and fear of violent or sexual assault from strangers (Stroud 26; Carlson 2014; Browder 2006). While most concealed-carry posts reference protecting oneself from "bad guys," including criminals, mass-shooters and the government, many studies show that women are especially vulnerable to gun violence in the home, perpetrated by a friend or loved one (Carlson 2014; Sorenson and Schut 2018). Despite studies that demonstrate women's victimization by guns, progun discourse generally presents firearms as a means for protecting oneself against outside threats, and rarely mentions threats of domestic violence or suicide. Concealed-carry posts echo these sentiments through captions that often invoke images of violent attacks by strangers in brief narratives that explain their need for protection.

One clear example of how this discourse is expressed on Instagram is in the prevalence of "Why I Carry" narratives. These narratives, sometimes explicitly designated with the hashtag #whyicarry, are commonly appended to concealed-carry posts to articulate the need for firearms as protection against the threat of criminals and outsiders. According to Melissa Deckman's research, stories about defenseless women forced to defend themselves as they are caring for children were popularized in the early 2000s as politicians and gun lobbyists sought to combat gun-control legislation. Though she does not mention other forms of social media, Deckman demonstrates the repetition of similar stories in conservative women's blog posts, including one titled "Why I Carry" (2016, 224). The origin of the "Why I Carry" narrative is beyond the purview of this project; however, its continuation on Instagram with #whyicarry stories incorporated into concealed-carry posts demonstrates the way in which this narrative has been traditionalized and has been incorporated into online gun culture. In my observation of concealed-carry posts, "Why I Carry" statements cite news stories, crime statistics, and everyday encounters with the public, framing them within the same narrative framework.

Personal #whyicarry narratives posted by women often recount a potentially scary encounter with a stranger in a seemingly safe public location and highlight the vulnerability of women with children. For example, one typical before-and-after style concealed-carry post included a brief #whyicarry statement that cited the grocery store. The user captions, "Because even the grocery store can be scary lately. Every day, everywhere I can," followed by several hashtags including #personalprotection, #womensselfdefense, #womencarrytoo, and #refusetobeavictim (2persevere 2020).

Some "why I carry" posts incorporate copy-and-pasted text, as text-based memes passed around from person to person (colloquially known as "copypasta"). For example, a post by another woman with over twenty-six thousand followers begins with a personal statement about why she carries a firearm that is typical in its emphasis on motherhood and vulnerability to random violence. She writes, "With how crazy the world and the people in

Figure 2.8. Example of "why I carry" narrative, incorporating language of individual empowerment (freedom.concealed 2018).

it are, it is SO important to carry and carry safely. As a mother of two girls it is vital that I am able to protect them and myself if ever needed" (ellie_stines 2020). Below this introduction, she pasted the following text:

> I stand behind you in line at the store with a smile on my face . . . and a gun under my shirt and you are none the wiser, yet you are safer for having me next to you. I won't shoot you, it can't just go off. However, rest assured that if a lunatic walks into the grocery store and pulls out a rifle, I will draw my pistol and protect myself and my family and therefore protect you and your family . . . I won't die a helpless blubbering heap on the floor begging for my life or my child's life . . . I won't be that victim. I choose not to be, As for you, I don't ask you to carry a gun . . . But I would like to keep my right to choose to not be a helpless victim. (ellie_stines 2020)

This text has been circulating online with some minor variations since at least 2016 (Adiona 2016) and encapsulates various points that are commonly raised in "Why I Carry" narratives, and concealed-carry posts in general. This includes concern about safety in a public everyday space, choice and personal freedom, and the imagined role of the citizen-protector, described by Jennifer Carlson in *Citizen Protectors: The Everyday Politics of Guns in an Age of Decline* (2015). Similar narratives raising the specter of the helpless victim and the citizen protector were paralleled in early campaigns for women by the NRA, including in the "Refuse to Be a Victim" campaign discussed below.

"REFUSE TO BE A VICTIM" AND #GUNRIGHTSAREWOMENSRIGHTS

Advocates for gun control often cite the need to protect women from harm, while advocates for women's gun ownership often cite the need for guns for women's self-protection. Both of these stances on firearms rely on the image of the vulnerable woman alongside politically charged narratives of crime, victimhood, and the family. The rhetoric of these political campaigns, along with visual portrayals of women with firearms, plays an important role in the way that femininity is framed in relation to firearms.

In her analysis of conservative and Tea Party women, Melissa Deckman found that conservative women activists and media figures began using gendered rhetoric to argue for the importance of the Second Amendment in the 1980s and 1990s. According to Deckman, "Pro-gun women maintain that women should have access to any gun they may need as a way to protect themselves, viewing self-defense as an important feminist principle" (2016, 216). For instance, former NRA spokesperson Dana Loesch makes the argument in her 2014 book that gun control is the "ultimate war on women," framing guns as an equalizer for women (Deckman 2016, 225). Deckman also notes the invocation of feminist choice rhetoric in the promotion of concealed-carry legislation, which use gendered arguments about personal safety by contending that guns "advance feminist principles by empowering women to take control of their own lives" (232).

Concealed-carry posts that integrate identity and rhetoric surrounding women's empowerment into gun advocacy demonstrate underlying values of individual empowerment. In addition to the discussions of women defending their families as mothers, many reference gender as a motivation for protecting themselves with captions about women's self-determination and empowerment with firearms. Many also include hashtags alluding to women's empowerment or associated with feminist politics, including #strongwomen, #womensempowerment, #girlpower, #shootlikeagirl, #dontbeavictim, and #gunrightsarewomensrights. These hashtags draw on established language surrounding women's empowerment, while reinforcing established rhetoric of individualism, self-defense, and gender that have been baked into American culture. The empowerment suggested by these hashtags often relies on an individualist mentality, isolating the individual from systemic forces that foment violence, condoning personal vigilance in everyday situations and normalizing gun use.

Some hashtags like #gunrightsarewomensrights and #yourpocketsyourchoice explicitly appropriate feminist prochoice slogans, joining other hashtags like #keepcalmandcarry and #allgunsmatter by altering existing memetic phrases that circulate on social media. In a sense, these hashtags act as proverbial sayings with the grammar of the social media platform dictating parameters in content and form, producing a traditionalized form of mediated communication. In many of her posts, Kent State Gun Girl, Kaitlin Bennett, includes variations of these memetic phrases. For instance, she has used the hashtag #gunrightsarewomensrights as well as variations of the phrase "refuse to be a victim" in several of her gun posts—including the infamous campus carry photo (Bennett 2018a; Bennett 2018b).

It is important to note, however, that some particularly popular commercial hashtags used by laypeople, #dontbeavictim, #beyourownhero, and #refusetobeavictim, are each directly tied to the NRA's "Refuse to Be a Victim" (RTBAV) campaign. Launched in 1993, the RTBAV campaign offered self-defense training in the context of firearms sales and advocacy with the stated goal of empowering women to "choose to refuse to be a victim." The course is still offered today, with certification for instructors advertised through the NRA website, and thousands of courses offered by local firearms distributors, gun ranges and police departments (National Rifle Association of America 2020). The phrase "choose to refuse to be a victim" sparked significant feminist criticism for the way in which it plays on women's fears for commercial gain, and because it places the onus on women to defend themselves, implicitly blaming victims (Blair and Hyatt 1995, 117).

The message underlying the NRA slogan "Refuse to Be a Victim," that women need firearms as protection against random acts of violence and crime, is a crucial part of the contemporary gender politics surrounding guns in the United States. In her discussion of the history of firearms in advertising, Browder argues that the NRA helped to form a new model for the armed woman in the conservative home "based on a privatized notion of citizenship, a refutation of so-called victim politics" (2006, 229). A woman who is self-reliant in this context "will not entrust her safety to the hands of others and then whine when no protection is forthcoming. Rather, she will use a gun to accomplish what the state is no longer qualified to do" (229).

The "Refuse to Be a Victim" campaign represents a culmination of changes that started with conservative politics in the Reagan era, which positioned guns as a "defense against anonymous violence, a task that the government is clearly not up to. No longer touted for use in a friendly forest, firearms for women are meant to ward off urban menace" (Browder 2006, 11). For the first time, "good mothers and responsible single women needed to carry handguns to ensure their own safety and the safety of their families," which was embedded in the public through new images that emerge in advertisements

Figure 2.9. Screenshot of the NRA "Refuse to Be a Victim" campaign site (National Rifle Association of America 2020).

Figure 2.10. Positioning of guns as equalizers and language of empowerment in women's concealed-carry posts (tacticalgalnyc 2019).

and popular culture: "Housewives, lovingly tucking their children into bed, kept a revolver on the nightstand; ads featuring women without children played on fears of urban crime" (10). The shift toward guns as domestic protectors for women is evident in concealed-carry selfies, suggesting that the gun industry plays a critical role in establishing the role of firearms in vernacular social media.

The popularity of the hashtag #refusetobeavictim and the language of empowerment in these posts demonstrates two things: the extension of discourse about "selfie-empowerment" beyond "body-positive" contexts (Sastre 2014), and how corporate interests (like the NRA) are deeply intertwined with vernacular expression on social media. According to Howard in "Vernacular Authority Speaks for the Glock: Heterogeneous Volition in an Institutional Proverb," the incorporation of commercial language into proverbs gives corporate interests a sense of vernacular authority. When individuals employ proverbs that originate in or support the firearm industry, it represents a "hybrid vernacular-institutional-expressive practice" that reinforces the "already powerful institutions in the global military industrial complex" (2019, 21). The use of NRA slogans in women's concealed-carry posts demonstrates the interplay between individual vernacular practice and the interests of massive industries in ways that are difficult to untangle.

SELFIE EMPOWERMENT AND
POSTFEMINIST GUN ADVOCACY

While there are occasional comments about the difficulties of navigating the world as a woman with guns and the coding of guns as a man's thing, very few posts invoke revolutionary action (or even the disruption of social norms). Posts do not confront toxic masculinity, or power differences that may enable men to victimize women; this is accepted as part of the natural and unchangeable divisions based on biological gender (Stroud 2015, 70). By assuming violence to be part of men's nature and a natural part of society, responsibility is shifted away from perpetrators and society and displaced onto individual women. Posts emphatically advocate for individual protection of the family unit, turning attention away from collective solutions. The only way to achieve safety is through self-defense and empowerment, echoing the premise of the NRA's "Refuse to Be a Victim" campaign. In their reliance on individualist ideals, concealed-carry selfies help to construct a family-centric, but choice-based, femininity that aligns with gun advocacy.

The authenticity of the selfie, and the narratives of self-empowerment culminate in an image of the All-American woman who *chooses* to enact traditional femininity as a woman and mother and *chooses* to carry firearms to "refuse to be a victim." Individual choices, rather than political change or solidarity, are the focus of this form of empowerment. The underlying premise is that one must purchase a gun and take self-defense courses, championing personal vigilance along with consumerism and self-improvement over community engagement. It is the woman's individual decision to carry a gun and protect herself and her children, not the duty of the government or society to provide a world in which she feels safe.

By positioning the gun as a tool of self-empowerment and the selfie as the medium for the message, concealed-carry women become part of a broader postfeminist discourse about individual women's agency. Individual choice is a crucial aspect of postfeminist notions of femininity, dealing with "notions of choice, agency, autonomy and empowerment as part of a shift towards entrepreneurial modes of self-hood" (Elias, Gill, and Scharff 2017, 46). Choice, agency, and empowerment are common themes in concealed-carry photo captions, as they prop up the decision to be a mother and to carry firearms, as well as the desire to conform to gendered expectations regarding clothing and appearance. Criticisms of postfeminist discourse point out the way in which the focus on the individual minimizes the role of institutions and power structures on personal choices and behavior (Dobson 2015; Tasker and Negra 2007). The construction of self-empowerment through firearms similarly elides questions about the role of men as perpetrators of violence, the cultural norms that place women as passive victims, and the economic, racial and social strictures limiting women's choices.

Women's experiences with and attitudes toward guns are complex. As Jennifer Carlson notes in her ethnography of women's gun groups, "The visceral, lived experience of guns is contradictory and contested. A woman's gun can be a tool of embodied empowerment, but it can also be a vehicle of complicity with masculine protectionism. It might even be both, simultaneously" (2015, 25). In my observations of social media, women who participate in progun discourse directly engage with this complex discourse, arguing that women should learn to protect themselves and their family, articulating their attitudes toward firearms through selfies with narrative captions.

Together the image and text represent an autobiographical expression that articulates the experience of carrying a concealed weapon, and attitudes toward firearms, family and femininity. The force of concealed-carry photos comes partly from their sense of indexicality and the power of the digital photograph as a truth-teller. By portraying herself with a concealed weapon on the way to the grocery store with a toddler on her hip, a woman can convey a sense of strength and momentary security. The selfies are then positioned in progun discourse to encourage the use of firearms by other women. By articulating a deeply personal connection to the gun, wearing it close to the body, and framing it in terms of family and the home, concealed-carry selfies demonstrate a way in which vernacular photography becomes part of public discourse.

Progun posts by women reject some aspects of traditional femininity that emphasize passivity and victimhood and embrace the traditionally masculine role of protector. They do this by invoking the traditional language of family values with the progressive language of "girl power," balancing the performance of femininity and motherhood with gun ownership, and self-empowerment with conservative distrust of feminist politics. Overall, these posts create a visual narrative about women's self-defense, depicting the gun as part of the presentation of domestic femininity in a composed, happy home.

They also are actively producing a distinct visual culture around women's use of firearms. The individual, intimate, and domestic focus of these selfies illustrates the textually expressed beliefs about guns, violence, and the role of women in the home. Within concealed-carry posts, women with guns are cast as defenders of traditional values and the integrity of the nuclear family.

In their combination of women's empowerment and progun advocacy, the concealed-carry posts demonstrate one way in which women are politically engaged through selfies. Concealed-carry photos act as a form of literal self-fashioning using one of the most potent symbols of nationhood and masculinity, while maintaining a sense of femininity and intimacy. These photos present a clear and public position on gun ownership, while inviting the viewer to see the private measures taken by individuals and their subjective perspectives through the selfie format.

Notes

1. From a psychoanalytic perspective, the reveal of the gun and the sense of subversion that accompanies the concealed carry may suggest a phallic threat. The threat of the woman with the gun evokes phallic imagery in the context of the striptease and suggests that rather than a passive recipient she may be a violent aggressor.

2. While some posts mention support for the military or police, comments that indicate distrust in their efficacy against personal domestic threats are just as common.

References

2persevere. 2020. "Because Even the Grocery Store Can Be Scary Lately. Everyday, Everywhere I Can. #icarry." Instagram. March 25, 2020. https://www.instagram.com/p/B-K2K8HJBVQ/.

Adiona, Abeona. 2016. "Why the Viral 'If Evil Has a Gun . . .' Facebook Post Is So F**ked Up." 14 June 2016. http://www.chicagonow.com/courts-excellent-adventures/2016/06/why-the-viral-if-evil-has-a-gun-facebook-post-is-so-fked-up/.

Bear, Jordan, and Kate Palmer Albers, eds. 2017. *Before-and-After Photography: Histories and Contexts*. New York: Bloomsbury Academic.

Bennett, Kaitlin. 2018a. "I Have No Apologies for My Graduation Photos. As a Woman, I Refuse to Be a Victim." Twitter. May 15, 2018. https://twitter.com/kaitmarieox/status/996462786027950080.

Bennett, Kaitlin. 2018b. "It's Time to Rebrand Feminism. Instead of Women with Pussy Hats, We Need More Women with Firearms. #GunRightsAreWomensRights." Twitter. October 14, 2018. https://twitter.com/KaitMarieox/status/1051644881850925058.

Bennett, Kaitlin. 2018c. "Unlike Today's Feminists, I Feel Empowered by Putting My Protection into My Own Hands . . ." October 20, 2018. https://www.instagram.com/kait.meow/.

Blair, M. Elizabeth, and Eva M. Hyatt. 1995. "The Marketing of Guns to Women: Factors Influencing Gun-Related Attitudes and Gun Ownership by Women." *Journal of Public Policy & Marketing* 14, no. 1: 117–27.

Blank, Trevor, ed. 2009. *Folklore and The Internet: Vernacular Expression in a Digital World*. Logan, UT: Utah State University Press.

Bronner, Simon J. 2004. "'This Is Why We Hunt': Social-Psychological Meanings of the Traditions and Rituals of Deer Camp." *Western Folklore* 63 no. 1/2: 11–50.

Browder, Laura. 2006. *Her Best Shot: Women and Guns in America*. Chapel Hill: University of North Carolina Press.

Brown, Jeffrey A. 2011. *Dangerous Curves: Action Heroines, Gender, Fetishism, and Popular Culture*. University Press of Mississippi.

bullets.n.bows. 2019. "Never Underestimate a Mama Bear 🐻 🔫 " Instagram. November 22, 2019. https://www.instagram.com/p/B5Lxg8GA5PD/.

Burgess, Jean. 2009. *YouTube: Online Video and Participatory Culture*. Malden, MA: Polity.

callin_th_shotz. 2018. "It Was a Little Tricky to Find a Good Spot at the Park Where I Can See the Entrance/Exit, Play with the 2 Year Old and Still Be in the Shade." Photo. Instagram. 24 July 2018. https://www.instagram.com/p/BlnuV-FHhMp/.

Carlson, Jennifer. 2014. "From Gun Politics to Self-Defense Politics: A Feminist Critique of the Great Gun Debate." *Violence Against Women* 20 no. 3: 369–77.

Carlson, Jennifer. 2015a. "Carrying Guns, Contesting Gender." *Contexts* 14 no. 1: 20–25.

Carlson, Jennifer. 2015b. *Citizen-Protectors: The Everyday Politics of Guns in an Age of Decline*. Oxford University Press.

Carlson, Jennifer. 2016. "Troubling the Subject of Violence: The Pacifist Presumption, Martial Maternalism, and Armed Women in Contemporary Gun Culture." In *Perverse Politics? Feminism, Anti-Imperialism, Multiplicity*, edited by Ann Shola Orloff, Raka Ray, and Evren Savci. Bingley, UK: Emerald Publishing Limited.

Deckman, Melissa. 2016. *Tea Party Women: Mama Grizzlies, Grassroots Leaders, and the Changing Face of the American Right*. NYU Press.

Dobson, Amy Shields. 2015. *Postfeminist Digital Cultures: Femininity, Social Media, and Self-Representation*. New York: Palgrave-Macmillan.

Dorson, Richard M. 1963. "Current Folklore Theories." *Current Anthropology* 4, no. 1: 93–112.

Elias, Ana Sofia, Rosalind Gill, and Christina Scharff. 2017. *Aesthetic Labour: Rethinking Beauty Politics in Neoliberalism*. London: Palgrave Macmillan.

ellie_stines. 2020. "With How Crazy the World and the People in It Are, It Is SO Important to Carry and Carry Safely." Instagram. August 15, 2020. https://www.instagram.com/p/CD7VxC9HK9o/.

Eltagouri, Marwa. 2018. "The Story behind the Viral Photo of a Kent State Graduate Posing with Her Cap—and a Rifle." *Washington Post*, May 17, 2018. https://www.washingtonpost.com/news/grade-point/wp/2018/05/16/the-story-behind-the-viral-photo-of-a-kent-state-graduate-posing-with-her-cap-and-a-rifle/.

freedom.concealed. 2018. "#whyicarry I Am a Young Woman Who Spends Most of Her Time on a College Campus, and I Refuse to Be a Victim." Instagram. March 24, 2018. https://www.instagram.com/p/Bgt7ngeBZ9N/?hl=en.

Gleisser, Faye, and Delia Solomons. 2018. "Introduction: Armed/Unarmed: Guns in American Visual and Material Culture." *Journal of Visual Culture* 17 no. 3: 263–71.

Howard, Robert Glenn. 2008. "Electronic Hybridity: The Persistent Processes of the Vernacular Web." *Journal of American Folklore* 121, no. 480: 192–218.

Howard, Robert Glenn. 2017. "GunNets: Why a Theory of Heterogeneous Volition Is Necessary in the Study of Digital Communication." *Cultural Analysis* 16, no. 1: 18.

Howard, Robert Glenn. 2019. "Vernacular Authority Speaks for the Glock: Heterogeneous Volition in an Institutional Proverb." In *Folkloristics in the Digital Age*, edited by Pekka Hakamies and Anne Heimo. Helsinki: Academia Scientiarum Fennica.

Kelly, Caitlin. 2004. *Blown Away: American Women and Guns*. New York: Gallery Books.

Kirshenblatt-Gimblett, Barbara. 1989. "Authoring Lives." *Journal of Folklore Research; Bloomington, Ind.* 26, no. 2: 123–49.

Kirshenblatt-Gimblett, Barbara. 1996. "The Electronic Vernacular," in *Connected: Engagements with Media*, ed. George E. Marcus. University of Chicago Press.

liberty_belle_co. 2020. "Patriotic Apparel." Instagram. November 17, 2020. https://www.instagram.com/liberty_belle_co/.

Mechling, Jay. 2004. "Picturing Hunting." *Western Folklore* 63 no. 1/2: 51–78.

Mitchell, W. J. T. 1995. *Picture Theory: Essays on Verbal and Visual Representation*. Chicago: University of Chicago Press.

momswhocarry. 2019. "I Know Its a Fashion 'Faux Pas,' but for You Other Mommas Who Have Better Things to Do Than to Iron Your Tshirts . . . .'" Instagram. 21 August 2019. https://www.instagram.com/p/B1bcDaxBIVo/.

Mulvey, Laura. 1975. "Visual Pleasure and Narrative Cinema." *Screen* 16, no. 3: 6–18.

Nakamura, Lisa. 2008. *Digitizing Race: Visual Cultures of the Internet*. Minneapolis: University of Minnesota Press.

Nye, David E. 1986. "Photography as Communication." *Journal of American Culture* 9, no. 3: 29–37.

Paredes, Américo. 1971. "The United States, Mexico, and 'Machismo.'" *Journal of the Folklore Institute* 8 no. 1: 17–37.

Parker, Kim, Juliana Horowitz, Ruth Igielnik, and Anna Brown. 2017. "America's Complex Relationship with Guns: An In-Depth Look at the Attitudes and Experiences of U.S. Adults." Pew Research Center. https://www.pewsocialtrends.org/2017/06/22/americas-complex-relationship-with-guns/.

Peck, Andrew M. 2014. "A Laugh Riot: Photoshopping as Vernacular Discursive Practice." *International Journal of Communication* 8 (January): 1638–62.

primerandco. 2020. "Primer & Co 2A Clothing." Instagram. November 17, 2020. https://www.instagram.com/primerandco/.

"Refuse to Be a Victim®." 2020. National Rifle Association of America. https://rtbav.nra.org/seminar-topics/.

Rodriguez, Adrianna. 2020. "Kent State 'Gun Girl' Who Walked Campus with AR Confronted by Protesters at Ohio University." *USA Today*, 18 February 2020.

Rooks, Noliwe M. 2000. *Hair Raising: Beauty, Culture, and African American Women*. New Brunswick, NJ: Rutgers University Press.

Rose, Gillian. 2001. *Visual Methodologies: An Introduction to the Interpretation of Visual Materials*. Thousand Oaks, CA: Sage.

Sastre, Alexandra. 2014. "Towards a Radical Body Positive." *Feminist Media Studies* 14, no. 6: 929–43.

Shelcheesy. 2020. "Now More than Ever It's Important to Take Your Protection into Your Own Hands . . ." Instagram. June 4, 2020. https://www.instagram.com/p/CBBCsSFJqoX/?hl=en.

Shifman, Limor. 2013. *Memes in Digital Culture*. Cambridge, MA: MIT Press.

Sorenson, Susan B., and Rebecca A. Schut. 2018. "Nonfatal Gun Use in Intimate Partner Violence: A Systematic Review of the Literature." *Trauma, Violence, & Abuse* 19, no. 4: 431–42.

Stroud, Angela. 2015. *Good Guys with Guns: The Appeal and Consequences of Concealed Carry*. University of North Carolina Press.

tacticoolmom. 2019. "How to Conceal in a Fitted Tee. Squish That Gun into Your Mummy Tummy!" Instagram. July 22, 2019. https://www.instagram.com/p/BoPXphXg1wv/.

tactigalnyc. 2019. "Ladies, Use What's Perceived as Our 'Weaknesses' . . ." Instagram. October 3, 2019. https://www.instagram.com/p/B8pBjbhJA_d/.

Tasker, Yvonne, and Diane Negra, eds. 2007. *Interrogating Postfeminism: Gender and the Politics of Popular Culture*. Durham, NC: Duke University Press.

Titon, Jeff Todd. 1980. "The Life Story." *Journal of American Folklore* 93, no. 369: 276–92.

Chapter 3

BETWEEN THE FOREST AND THE FREEZER

Visual Culture and Hunting Weapons in the Upper Midwest

TIM FRANDY

It was after one of the far-too-many tragic school shootings in the spring of 2018 when a Facebook friend shared a meme comparing the much-maligned AR-15 (used in some of the most horrific mass shootings in American history, including at Sandy Hook, San Bernadino, the Pulse, Las Vegas, Sutherland Springs, Stoneman Douglas, Buffalo, and Uvalde) with a Ruger Mini 14. Like all memes, multiple versions of this meme comparing these two rifles exist, with minor variations in the images used, or in the text.

While this version mentions one rifle being "scary," other versions critique performative legislation to ban assault rifles as security theater or reflect longstanding fears about people coming to "take your guns." Although it's worth noting certain features of the pictured AR-15 (like magazine size, weight, and buffer tube) are not present on the Ruger, the meme makes a legitimate point about the disconnect between a firearm's technical capacity and the way people perceive its outward appearance. All the versions of this meme that I've seen suggest a rifle's appearance should not ultimately matter in a firearm's regulation. However, the meanings that are created through people's interactions with and through guns extend far beyond their technical capacity, into complex networks of expressive identity. Although these memes seek to minimize it, the visual culture of guns matters a great deal in the way meaning and values are communicated through firearms.

Having grown up in a hunting family, in Wisconsin's Northwoods—home to vast and diverse communities of hunters—I have long been versed in how different hunters express themselves and their values through variations in their expressive patterns of hunting. There is a world of difference between the trophy hunters who drop thousands of dollars on a single hunt and Anishinaabe hunters who offer asemaa (tobacco) to the spirits in exchange

This is a Ruger Mini 14:
Semi automatic
Uses .223 ammunition
Has readily available 30 round magazines
Looks like a non-scary hunting rifle so it's a-ok.

This is an AR 15:
Semi automatic but for some reason is commonly called
an assault rifle
Uses .223 ammunition
Has readily available 30 round magazines
Looks like a scary military weapon so OMG ban it.

Scary guns

Figure 3.1. One version of the meme comparing the technical capacity of two rifles.

for a deer; between people who "hunt" by enjoying drink and merriment at deer camp and those who silently stalk a single deer for an entire day through a snow-covered forest; between those who want to fill their freezer and those who prefer antlers to meat. We could see these differences in their hunting attire, whether a cobbled together mix of blood-stained hand-me-down wools and flannels passed through generations, or fully matched wardrobes of the latest scent concealing synthetics. We could smell the differences between blaze orange coats smelling of raked-up oak leaves, of bar and cigarettes, or of purchased deer scents. We could hear the differences in the woods: a single shot, perhaps followed by another; the whoops of drivers pushing deer; or a barrage of semiautomatic shots increasing in frequency as the frustrated hunter misses again and again. We knew how to read each other. These expressive minutiae were as communicative as a human voice.

My family was perhaps somewhat different from many hunting families in the United States. Or, at least, I felt it to be a little different when I heard others talk about the ways they hunted. We weren't interested in blood sport, nor in hunting to ritualize some kind of conquest of nature (Harrison 1992, 69). We didn't hunt to perform masculinities or to escape women. And we certainly didn't hunt "for fun" or "for sport," "to bond," or "to make memories" (cf. Bronner 2004). Even the traditions of hunter-conservationists—which we most commonly used as "available narratives" (Somers 1994) to explain our practices—were not perfect fits to describe our tradition. The notion of "fair chase" seemed reasonable (Posewitz 1994), but our hunting was not ultimately about the pursuit of and competition with animals that we depended on to feed our family. Such notions were as foreign to us as the idea of "competing against" the blueberries we found in pine barrens deep in the national forest, or "the chase of" the tomatoes we grew in our gardens.

Rather, our own practices taught us about balance and humility, about knowledge and respect, about how we live in relation to animals, plants, water, and earth, and about our interdependence with other species in broader cycles of life and death. As an adult, I learned that many of these attitudes had deep roots in the animist ecological worldview of my mixed Finnish and Sámi ancestry. In both traditions, subsistence hunting, fishing, and gathering in the arctic and subarctic were crucial for survival. They were—and still are—deep parts of the ways we perceive the world and humankind's place within it, and the ways we communicate and construct our own identity. From ritual offerings and prayers to animals, to the verb used to hunt (Finnish: *pyytää*; North Sámi: *bivdit*) which means "to ask or request," hunting was traditionally an act of humility and ecological relationality, not one of androcentric dominance. It is within this larger context that this auto-ethnography and investigation of my own family folklore takes shape.

NARRATING GUNS AT HOME IN THE LAKE SUPERIOR REGION

The Lake Superior region represents a loosely defined cultural, environmental, and economic region that spans through Michigan, Wisconsin, Minnesota, and Ontario. The region is densely forested with broad tracts of public land, dominated by pine, fir, birch, poplar, and maple, on the southern tracts of the northern coniferous forest biome. Tens of thousands of freshwater lakes and rivers exist in the region, creating rich fisheries that have supported subsistence and tourism over generations. Because of the long winters and generally poor soil quality—due to glaciation during the last Ice Age, approximately ten thousand years ago—farming is not terribly profitable in the region. For all these reasons, the region's Indigenous peoples and early settlers alike traditionally relied on a mix of hunting, fishing, gardening, and gathering edible foods—like berries, maple syrup, and wild rice—to eat (Gage 1982). These practices and the values associated with them have endured for generations, and within many families, wild food procurement is still important in—and sometimes central to—everyday life.

This system of informal economy has long existed alongside other economic waves, beginning as early as the fur trade era between approximately

1650 and 1850. Subsequent waves of mining for copper and iron, logging, shipping, and tourism have been important drivers of the region's economy, with each wave changing the region's cultural landscape (Martin 1986). Many of the earlier waves of settlers relied on subsistence practices to at least supplement their food sources, but newer residents who relocated into the region after 1970 were much more likely to be from cities or large towns, to be more detached from their own means of food production, and to consider hunting and fishing more as a recreational activity than as an important informal economic activity. Though subsistence practices are still common in the region—and even a common reason for children to miss school—they are not quite as prevalent as they formerly were.

Like many in the Northwoods, I grew up around guns: 30-30, .30-06, .270, .243, .22, and 8mm rifles; 12, 16, and 20 gauge shotguns, and an antique 10 gauge that hung above our fireplace; BB guns and pellet guns for the kids; even some old small-caliber pistols that muskie fishermen used to wear on their belts (up until it was banned in the mid-1960s, they'd reel the giant pike up to the boat and shoot them in the water). We didn't have a lot of firearms, but we had what we needed to hunt, a few seldom-used heirlooms, and a few things we picked up cheap along the way. Like many families, we had these firearms stored in a couple glass-door gun cases displaying them decoratively in the heart of our home. A simple lock was on the front of the case, with key stashed away nearby. Ammunition was stored elsewhere, as was only sensible with children in the house. We generally used them only to hunt, but every few years, we might shoot clay pigeons or shoot an unused rifle. Many years, we didn't even target shoot, and would use only as many shells as deer and grouse we'd harvest. In general, we appreciated guns as tools but didn't have tremendous interest in firearms beyond their use in hunting. There was only so much technical capacity we needed from a rifle, since we seldom could see past one hundred yards in the pine forests we hunted in. In fact, we respected the artistry of the old-timers, like my grandfather, who could use an open sight 30-30 to hit the thin side of a quarter at fifty yards.

Guns were a normalized aspect of everyday life for the greater community when I grew up in the 1980s. Students often brought rifles and shotguns to my high school so they could hunt on the way home from school. Because we were a rural school district serving a geographical area larger than the state of Rhode Island, many students had to drive—or snowmobile during the winter—up to an hour to get home through a state forest. Hunting an hour or two before dark on the way home was considered a productive and healthy activity that supported families economically. Many of these policies were already changing in the 1990s, when I began high school, when the

98   BETWEEN THE FOREST AND THE FREEZER: HUNTING WEAPONS

school clarified its firearms policies, prohibiting the legion of gun-rack filled trucks that formerly filled parking lots. With firearms displayed on home-made racks in the back window of the cab, these racks made for convenient storage and access for a variety of legal (or illegal) road hunting activities. By the time I began high school, guns were allowed at the school but not in the school; and in the parking lot, the guns needed to be kept in a locked vehicle and concealed from sight.

Northwoods gun culture has changed greatly over the past half century or so. To get a sense of some of these changes, in September of 2018, I asked my father and mother, Tom Frandy and Patty (Olson) Frandy, to share some of the stories that I had heard growing up and in my early adulthood about firearms. My father, Tom Frandy, is a retired high school teacher who taught at Lakeland Union High School, in Minocqua, Wisconsin—the same school he attended in the late 1950s and early 1960s. He grew up in Vilas County, with family members working as teachers, biologists for the Department of Natural Resources, fishing guides, loggers, and in the tourism industry. My mother, Patty, grew up on a dairy farm in Burnett County in northwestern Wisconsin and worked as an educator and as an administrative assistant for a church. They met in college, in the small city of Superior, Wisconsin, and were married in 1967. Most of the stories documented hereafter I'd heard before, but few were things I'd heard often enough to remember verbatim, allowing for a relaxed and relatively natural context for story swapping amongst the three of us.

Formerly, hunting and firearms were so normalized in rural northern communities that firearms appeared regularly in places where now they would cause great concern. Patty explains about visiting her daughter (my sister) and son-in-law in Alaska:

> This one time I was flying up to Alaska to visit Chrissy and Jay. I guess this would have been in the late 1990s . . . before 9/11. It was fall, and I was flying out of Rhinelander [a Northwoods town of 7600 people with a very small airport]. I was about halfway through the flight and I noticed that the flight was completely full of men with guns. They were holding them on their laps. They were in the carry-on bins. There were guns everywhere. Of course, they were all flying up to go hunting since it was the fall. I didn't even think anything of it. But you certainly couldn't do that now.

The presence of hunting weapons in public spaces—and not just private ones—was relatively common in hunting communities for the simple reason that firearms need transportation between home and hunting grounds. Patty recalls picking up a 30-30 rifle being fitted with a new sight from a gun store in the small town of Woodruff, Wisconsin. To even get to the parking lot, she had to cross the largest downtown intersection (which admittedly is quite small): "As I'm leaving the store with an uncased gun, there is a police guy coming in right when I'm leaving! I realized maybe I shouldn't be walking around downtown with a gun. But what choice did I have? Nothing happened, of course."

One of the most prominent shifts that Patty and Tom note is the differences that now exist in terms of minors having access to firearms. Tom explains,

When I was 14 [ca. 1958], I wanted to buy a pistol for my older brother Jack for a Christmas present. I had a note from my parents. And I talked to the school bus driver and had him drop me off at the hardware store in the next town down the road. I bought the pistol there, and then had my folks pick me up and drive me home when they were done with work.

Patty had her own similar experience with her tomboy cousin Kay, who herself grew up to be a well-known hunter and farmer in her small rural hometown:

This happened when I was at Pansy school. It was a one-room schoolhouse, you know. My Aunt Elsie was the teacher, and I was the only student in my grade. Well, Elsie had to do everything in that school: teach, cook, clean, everything. So one day, she must have been busy, and she asked if my cousin Kay and I would go take the trash to the dump for her. This is right in the middle of the school day. I'm about 9, and Kay is 13. She gives Kay the keys to her car, and we load the trash into her trunk. So we go off driving towards the dump. Kay's driving, since she's older. We go to the dump, which is just a big hole in the ground where we throw things in, and she asks me: "Hey, do you want to shoot some cans?" "Sure." So she pulls a gun out of the back of the trunk. We threw out the trash and then spent the next half hour taking turns shooting at cans. Eventually, she says, "Well, I suppose we should get back to school now," and we drive back. I don't think any part of this story could happen today!

These ex post facto narratives emerge from the ether of distant memories into existence through a process of remembrance and recollection. Hardly worth narrativizing during their own time (at least in the same way), these everyday happenings and their value as narratives emerge only because of the changed cultural context surrounding guns. Ironically, the final story was the one I heard most when I was young, perhaps less because of the guns than the unsupervised use of a teacher's car at such a young age. With time it accrued greater meanings associated with firearms and even the use of dumps to dispose of trash. Meanings in these narratives ripen over time as they mature and are harvested to understand (or at least contemplate the nature of) cultural shift.

In particular, many of these stories emerge only after the tightening of gun policies in rural schools in the 1980s and 1990s, and as the metaphorical meanings behind guns transforms from a symbol of food production to one of violence and self-protection. In the late 1960s, for instance, Patty explains of one student who brought a firearm to her classroom:

> During my first year of teaching, I was having my students give speeches. One of the students asked if he could demonstrate how to clean a gun as a speech. "Why not?" I thought. Seems like a good idea. The thought never even crossed my mind that this could be a problem. Although the principal did come and check with me. He saw this student walking through the hallway with a gun, and when asked about it, the boy said that it was for my class. Which it was. The principal seemed a little nervous about the whole thing.

Tom recalls a similar episode about a student selling him a rifle before guns were considered taboo at schools. Of note is that his principal concern at the time was the student having parental permission to sell an item of value.

> I don't remember exactly when it was, sometime in the 80s. A student approached me after class one day and asked, "Mr. Frandy, would you like to buy a gun? I'm selling my .22." "How much?" "$75." Which seemed reasonable. So I made him bring in a note from his parents, saying he had permission to sell the gun. I wanted to make sure that he wasn't trying to sell something he didn't have permission to sell, or even if he stole a gun from the parents. . . . I didn't want anything to do with that. So the next day, he comes walking into the school, right through the halls with an uncased rifle. He comes to my classroom, I give him cash, and I leave with it. I still have that [rifle].

Though these events occurred in the 1980s, this story likely emerged as a self-contained narrative only after firearm rules were tightened at the school in the early 1990s. For our family, the story wasn't told to nostalgically pine for a simpler past, nor to offer up some simplistic solution to a complex social problem. These stories offer no solutions. Rather, they serve as tools of what Ray Cashman terms "critical nostalgia," or "informed evaluation of the present through contrast with the past" (2006, 137–38). Such stories are told in both contemplation and humor, laughing perhaps at our own naiveté, while also bringing forth serious and existential questions about the shifting symbolic meanings of guns.

Although guns, power, and violence are difficult to fully decouple, numerous people raised in hunting communities downplay their innate linkage. For instance, during a panel on gunlore during the 2018 meeting of the American Folklore Society, discussant Tok Thompson recalled his own upbringing in Alaska, likening guns to chainsaws (note Thompson's concluding essay, where he revisits this discussion). Both are loud and powerful tools most commonly used by men, expensive, fairly dangerous, and associated with procurement (of food and heat). Thompson explained neither was associated with interpersonal violence, aside from in distant references to American popular culture, although both have tremendous capacity to do great damage to living things through their misuse. Even within a single community, however, guns carry divergent, overlapping, and intersecting meanings. In her essay "Hunting for Meaning: How Characterization Reveals Standards for Behavior in Family Folklore," Mary Ellen Greenwood explores her own family traditions (her father and uncle, Steve and Doug) with that of a neighboring camp (called the Clantons). The Clantons—classified by Greenwood as undesirable Montana Freemen types in her narrative typology—brandish sidearms, shoot unnecessarily at trash, and generally disturb and unsettle Steve and Doug. Greenwood explains, "Unlike the Clantons, who equate guns with power, Steve and Doug see guns as representative of memory" (2004, 92). Some of these contrasts, between people and the values and meanings that they impose on guns, play out in the visual discourses of firearms that exist within the Upper Midwest and beyond.

VISUAL CULTURE AND FIREARMS

Many older hunting rifles and shotguns, like the ones that fill my extended family's gun cases, are commonly ornamented with decorative motifs. Ornate gun-stock carving and metal engraving traditions were formerly common throughout the region. These traditions are at least partially reflective of the region's Germanic heritage, in which hunting was generally practiced as a recreational activity of the upper middle class. Hunting served as a performance

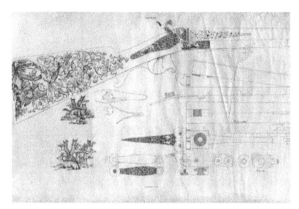

Figure 3.2. One of Ernst's pattern sheets found in Schlegelmilch's collections. Image courtesy of the Chippewa Valley Museum.

Figure 3.3. Ernst's pattern sheet in Schlegelmilch's collection depicting dogs and game. Image courtesy of the Chippewa Valley Museum.

of leisure and the wealth and sophistication it entailed. Firearms are expensive—today as in years past—and are symbolically heavy prestige items. As such, they and their ephemera (e.g., powder flasks) were even at early dates frequently adorned with design elements or motifs that emphasize the nature of the relationship a person has with their weapon. There was a particular emphasis on nature or hunting scenes embossed or engraved onto these tools.

Nineteenth-century gunsmiths, like Herman A. Schlegelmilch (1830–1903), incorporated such elaborate designs into their work. Born in Suhl, Thuringia (then part of Prussia, but today in Germany), a city known for its weaponry and gun manufacturing since the Middle Ages, Schlegelmilch learned the trade of gunsmithing from his uncle beginning at age fourteen. A journeyman gunsmith by the age of seventeen, Schlegelmilch eventually left for the United States in 1853. After stints in New York, New York; Bethlehem, Pennsylvania; Chicago, Illinois; Beaver Dam, Wisconsin; and Cedar Rapids, Iowa, Schlegelmilch and family (wife Augusta and daughter Dora) moved to Eau Claire, Wisconsin, in 1860. Schlegelmilch worked in Eau Claire to

Figure 3.4. Bill Frandy (left) with his ornamented hunting rifle.

establish *schützenverein* or gentleman's marksman clubs, where members shot, in addition to rifles, "bows, crossbows, air guns, or black powder muskets" (Pederson 2016, 8). According to Pederson, such clubs had origin in military traditions, although by the nineteenth century they had become more like country clubs, and they were often populated by politically influential or aspirational individuals. Schlegelmilch manufactured the entirety of firearms himself, from barrel to stock, using pattern books to finish his products with elaborate adornments that include wildlife, foliage, persons, and more. Schlegelmilch owned a collection of patterns designed by Gustav Ernst (1809–1899) of Zella-Mehlis (just five kilometers north of Suhl)—a town known for its master engravers (Vanek 2016). Such ornamentation—both expensive and impractical for a tool—helped distinguish the gentleman and sportsman from other gun users.

This ornate, high-style tradition is still common today in the work of some carvers who sell their services, including individual artists in the American West like Joe Cummings or resident Lance Larson, who both run online businesses. Larson learned the outdoors from his father in western Montana, where he worked as a fly-fishing guide, before taking up woodwork and moving to Arizona. Cummings grew up hunting and fishing in Utah's Wasatch Mountains and worked as a taxidermist for many years. Both Cummings and Larson depict a number of hunting-themed outdoor scenes in their

Figure 3.5. Bill Frandy's plastic inlay design recalls Western motifs while personalizing the 30-30 deer rifle.

Figure 3.6. The unusual "signing" of a gun stock may have been useful in deterring theft by tourists during the resort era of the early twentieth century.

Figure 3.7. Ornamental embossing on the hammer of a 10 gauge shotgun.

gun-stock carving, with game animals (elk, bear, deer, birds), animals used in hunting (horses, dogs) and foliage (most commonly oak leaves). Cummings and others sell instructional books or videos that teach individuals to carve their own firearms—seemingly appropriate within the discourse of self-reliance that runs through many contemporary hunting cultures. The visual motifs in these traditions are less about power than about a perceived balance and intimacy between humans, animals, and the forest. The ornate motifs suggest the elegance and beauty of the hunt, with the firearm positioned metaphorically as a link between these perceived separate realms.

Within my family's own Nordic contexts, where peasant-hunting traditions were the norm, while such elaborate ornamentation would be seen as beautiful, it perhaps would also be regarded as unnecessarily ostentatious.

My Finnish grandfather, Bill Frandy, modified his factory-produced 30-30 deer hunting rifle from the 1910s using subtle inlay design. The diamond motifs are little more than plastic inlay, held in place with adhesive and a nail.

They are noticeable only on the visible sides of the gun for a right-handed shooter. On the reverse of the stock is an engraved signature that appears to have formerly been painted white.

Such adornments reflect a close relationship between hunters and their tools, while suggesting the rifle's status as a valued, personalized item. Similarly, the distinctive features (particularly the signature) also bear a practical element too: they help prevent against theft and resale—an unfortunate but real concern with expensive, highly portable wares.

Although such highly ornamented firearms (in the style of Ernst, Cummings, or Larson) have always been somewhat exceptional, as firearms shifted during the 1800s to factory-production, main manufacturers preserved some of these ornamentation traditions, which are still abundant in contemporary firearm design.

These ornaments include geometrical motifs as grips, inlay on grips, and engraved metals with Western or floral designs. Seemingly every small surface was adorned with these decorative elements—including hammers, screw heads, and trigger guards. One key feature of these designs is their subtlety. The hidden motifs and subtle textures found within this embossed decorative style are elements gun owners may subconsciously recognize and respond to but do not really notice without more careful study of a particular firearm.

GUN CABINETS AND DISPLAY

Unlike the contemporary gun vaults and safes that are so commonly sold in sporting goods stores today, in the Lake Superior region guns were traditionally stored in glass gun cases—generally with some sort of simple locking mechanism. Adornment on cases, their placement in the home, and the assemblage of paraphernalia within the case call attention to how guns are understood within the context of a family space. In the home I grew up in, the main gun case was located in our living room, behind a television. Suitable for about half a dozen shotguns or rifles, it was filled with all sorts of hunting gear, including knives, compasses, and a drawer beneath it overstuffed with hunting regulations and maps. On each side, however, it is flanked by two matching cupboards packed full of china, dishes, and glassware. Flanking the cabinetry hangs a print of wildlife art, framed and mounted with decorative ruffed grouse feathers. A separate gun case can be found in a basement bedroom, which also houses a few World War II bayonets found by family veterans, some old awards from my brother's and my time in high school and college, and two drawers filled with unused hand-warmers from more than

Figure 3.8. John Frandy's homemade gun case.

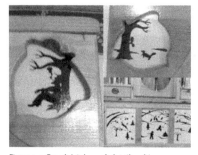

Figure 3.9. Frandy's ink-work detail on his gun case.

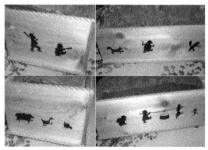

Figure 3.10. A mosaic of images John Frandy designed on a footstool, and later recreated elsewhere in his home library.

twenty years ago, and—somewhat to my embarrassment in writing this—a collection of old Pez dispensers.

My brother, John Frandy, a professor of physics at Waukesha County Community College, designed his own multifunction gun case with nature motifs of ink on wood that recall his own perception of hunting iconography.

A pipe-smoking hunter sits asleep in a tree stand waiting for deer. Oak motifs suggest his location near a food source for deer, and his efforts to de-scent himself. Deer run about and hide from hunters.

A fox chases a squirrel up a tree—evoking the hunt within broader cycles of nature. The food cycle is a common motif in John's work. A nearby footstool he made in 2010 has four inked sets of characters, one on each face of the footstool. A wolf, a bear, and a fox chase a sheep, a duck, and a chicken.

The predators are chased by two male hunters. Women and children chase the men with a pot, as if to prepare a meal from the game. The woman in the rear bears a slightly torn bag of grains, which leaves a trail of grain behind her as she walks. The chicken and duck follow the grain trail, and the chicken can be seen pecking up the grain. So too do we march in our endless progression, returning to the woods to harvest that which harvests us.

Even more interesting are the other items on the shelves of the gun case. The shelves house tea pots, felted creations, heirloom dishes, and books including early outdoor sportsmen's writing, collections of Swedish folktales, and the *Kalevala* (a compilation of Finnish and Karelian folk song, sometimes called the Finnish national epic)—reflecting a self-awareness of our family's hunting traditions and their situation within a variety of folk practices. John also remarked that it seemed appropriate for the gun case to be near the dining room table, as something of a reminder to help his children understand that food comes from somewhere other than the store.

Although this gun case, like my father Tom's, centers traditional masculinities (it's worth noting, however, that women who hunt in the region often have similar displays), both are situated within a familial context. With the tools of hunting (rifles and shotguns) centered in the cabinetry, it is situated entirely in relation to the tools we eat with (dishes, tea pots, heirloom china) that surround it. Underrepresented in the study of foodways, hunting and fishing practices remain—within many families who harvest for subsistence—central within the operations of the family's informal economy. This narrative emerges with the display of these two central gun cases in these two homes. The third case, in the basement bedroom, perhaps best marks transition from adolescence to adulthood: filled with air rifles, and .22s, with a few family heirlooms, commencement-related memorabilia, and even a child's youthful possessions left behind when departing for adulthood.

Recently, however, John explained that he had moved his gun cabinet to a more private and interior location of the house:

I had a friend who came over for dinner a while ago, and you know, I had the gun cabinet in our dining room area. He commented, "You know, it's been a long time since I've seen that." And it's true. I haven't seen a gun cabinet meant to display guns for a long time. And I even felt uncomfortable having my guns in such a public area of my house. Not because I felt it was wrong, but I just didn't want others to get the wrong sort of idea about us. So after I finished the library last summer [in a renovated garage space], I moved the gun cabinet back there.

With the move in 2018, the gun cabinet was moved to a peripheral room, and left half-lost amidst built-in bookshelves. Since the kitchen and dining areas were no longer nearby, the tea pot and decorative plates ultimately ended up separated from the rifles and shotguns. With kitchen remaining intact, the firearms were grouped with a room dedicated to books and the imagination—a move that seemingly resituates the hunt in even closer relation to the collections of folktales that formerly flanked it. The logics of placement and display are flexible and fluid, and as they evolve out of values, they at once shape them for people who encounter them.

I too have found it difficult to store my tools of hunting. Living for most of my adult life in university towns, it seemed strange to have hunting gear out, accessible, and visible. Away from my childhood home, it just didn't make sense to have these kinds of tools out on display in a place I did not use them, like hanging a set of wrenches in the living room. For years, I left my hunting rifle with my parents, where I hunted. And when I finally took possession of it, I squirrelled it away in closets or other hidden locations—periodically forgetting even that I was the owner of a firearm. I also learned it was easier to hide this part of myself, since I found it to be rather misunderstood by other university students and workers who came from backgrounds more suburban and more affluent than my own. It took me many years of graduate school before I admitted publicly exactly how little money I had, and that I routinely traveled back home to hunt and fish for the majority of meat I ate—both because I had to and because I chose to.

Although I no longer hide this side of myself, I still don't have great interest in displaying firearms in a case due to the way this visual discourse will be interpreted by others—at least so long as I live in a university town. The net effect of these shifts, however, is perhaps problematic. With guns increasingly associated with power-wielding and the performance of toxic masculinities, many people choose to disassociate and distance themselves entirely from these emergent cultural discourses. Yet such a response is perhaps of questionable wisdom. By going into hiding, it does few favors to sustain these kinds of hunting cultures that I would like to sustain—that which I personally would consider to be a healthy relationship between people, the foods we eat, and the tools we use to harvest them.

Although the meme I shared to open this essay suggests otherwise, the visual discourses of firearms matter a great deal. They communicate clearly and effectively a tremendous amount of information about a gun owner and his or her motivations for owning and displaying weapons. We can understand how firearms figure into a family unit by the centrality of the location in which they are displayed. We can unpack the visual discourses of firearm ornamentation to glean their perceived use in elegantly connecting hunter to nature. We can understand how gender intersects with guns by looking at what surrounds displays of guns. We can look at the ephemera in the assemblages of gun cases to understand how firearms are seen in relation to other objects of material culture. We can recognize that the rise in mass shootings and high-profile gun violence has impacted how people display and store their firearms. And finally, we can recognize that important cultural and discursive—if not technical—differences exist between the AR-15 pictured in the meme that opens this essay, the extravagant stylings of wealthy recreational hunters whose rifles serve as prestige items, and hunting weapons minimalistically adorned with natural motifs in glass cases in the heart of a home.

References

Bronner, Simon. 2004. "'This Is Why We Hunt': Social-Psychological Meanings of the Traditions and Rituals of Deer Camp." *Western Folklore* 63, no. 1/2: 11–50.

Cashman, Ray. 2006. "Critical Nostalgia and Material Culture in Northern Ireland." *Journal of American Folklore* 119 (472): 137–60.

Gage, Cully. 1982. "Wild Food." In *Heads and Tales: A Third Northwoods Reader*. AuTrain, Michigan: Avery Color Studios: 65–72.

Greenwood, Mary E. 2004. "Hunting for Meaning: How Characterization Reveals Standards for Behavior in Family Folklore." *Western Folklore* 63: 79–100.

Harrison, Robert Pogue. 1992. *Forests: The Shadow of Civilization*. Chicago: University of Chicago Press.

Martin, John Barthlow. 1986. *Call It North Country: The Story of Upper Michigan*. Detroit: Wayne State University Press.

Pederson, Chris. 2016. "The Eau Claire Schuetzenverein." *Currents* 42, no. 2. Chippewa Valley Museum Newsletter.

Posewitz, Jim. 1994. *Beyond Fair Chase: The Ethic and Tradition of Hunting*. Helena: Falcon.

Smoot, Frank. 2006. "Tale of the Gunmaker." *Currents* 32, no. 4. Chippewa Valley Museum Newsletter: 3–4.

Somers, Margaret R. 1994. "The Narrative Constitution of Identity: A Relational and Network Approach." *Theory and Society* 23: 605–49.

Vanek, John. 2016. "From the Forests of Thuringia: New Details from Germany about the Schlegelmilch Family and the Pattern Book of a Renowned Engraver." *Currents* 42, no. 2. Chippewa Valley Museum Newsletter: 11–15.

Chapter 4

4CHAN, FIREARMS, AND FOLKLORE

NOAH D. ELIASON (WITH ERIC A. ELIASON)

Firearms: they are tools of oppression, tools of liberation, tools for defending your rights, tools for animal population control, or even tools for armed robbery. They capture the imagination and evoke delight and fear. Various folk groups interested in firearms have traditionally gathered at gun stores, workshops,[1] family gatherings, hunting camps, and gun ranges to participate in shared customary practices and share stories, jokes, folk beliefs, customization techniques, and other lore about guns. They still do. But now—as is common with many other types of avocational folk groups—"gun guys" and "gun girls" often get online to gather and share.[2] As both a gun and internet culture enthusiast myself (and hence a native ethnographer), I eventually discovered the weapons board on the infamous website 4chan.[3] There I discovered a wide variety of folk culture, a few selections of which I share, and attempt to analyze, in this chapter. Some preliminary explanations are in order, since the lore of online folk groups can not only be notoriously baffling to outsiders and full of inside references that build on each other over time, but also highly shaped by the specific policies and software parameters of the forums that host online community interactions.

4CHAN AND THE "WEAPONS BOARD" OR "/K/"

4chan is an anonymous image board website. Each "board" on the website has its own topic of discussion and set of rules, but all the boards largely function the same. A discussion thread can be created at any time by anyone. And once a thread is created, anyone can reply to it. However, there can only be a finite number of threads on a given board. This means when a new thread is created, the thread at the bottom of the catalog is archived and can no longer be replied to. Which threads are the top and which threads are at the bottom

Figure 4.1. A patch design that has become an iconic symbol of the 4chan weapons board. Often, actual patches are made following this design and sewn onto range wear.

is determined by bump system. This means that every time somebody replies to a thread, the thread is bumped up on the list. So, threads that are inactive or have reached their reply and image limits are the ones dying whenever a new thread is created.

Rather than focusing on one genre of expressive culture across multiple groups, this chapter follows a folklife approach that focuses instead on one folk group and looks at a number of interconnected genres produced by the group. In this instance, one that gathers virtually entirely online.[4] Each 4chan thread is like a point in the lifecycle of this folk group. And even though thread titles and topics are completely up to the whims of the individuals making them, traditions and conventions have emerged, and you will see thread topics recur or "resurrect" if you use the website long enough. Often, as is the case with folklore, these recurrences will show both continuity with past manifestations and creative new features and variations.

/K/ATURDAY

For example, if you visit the weapons board on Saturday, you might see a cat photo posting thread in the catalogue. This follows one of the oldest, most widespread, and most familiar internet traditions, which actually began on 4chan in the mid-2000s. In these threads, users post pictures of their

Figure 4.2.

Figure 4.3.

cats on Saturday or "Caturday" ("Caturday"). The following images from the weapons board might have, and probably have been, cross-posted any number of places.

However, in addition to swimming in this larger stream of online culture, the 4chan weapons board has its own oikotype of the "Caturday" tradition (Dundes 1999, 137–40).[5] In the folktext of weapons-board posters, "Caturday" is often rendered "/k/aturday." Then"/k/" being shorthand for the weapons board since /k/ is how the weapons board is identified following 4chan's naming conventions. It appends the 4chan website URL in order to direct you to the webpage for the weapons board. "/k/aturday" posts might seem the same as any "Caturday" post, except that in addition to cats as a genre-defining element, usually something firearms-related such as a pistol, ammo, or ammo boxes are also included. The cats are often jokingly referred to a "battle buddies." Sometimes, posters will include a boundary-maintaining comment insisting that other posters adhere to their own perception of what is a necessary "/k/aturday" oikotype genre-defining motif, as in the "post guns or fuck off" comment seen below in post #44175366.

These threads' contents are /k/ folk-group-specific variants of the larger tradition on the internet of posting funny or cute pictures of cats. Such pictures, and many other internet pictures, can be considered a type of folk art. Even though sharing art is not necessarily the objective of these threads, photography is still the type of art, and it is clear that with many of these pictures at least some effort was taken to make them more aesthetically appealing.

"FAMILY" PHOTOS AND "GUN PORN"

Another example of a recurring thread where folk art features emerge is "family" photo threads. In these threads, users post pictures of all their guns together within the frame, as if the guns were sitting for a family portrait. As with the "/k/aturday" threads, pictures appear that display obvious effort and thought put into making them visually appealing—at least according to the aesthetic preferences of the /k/ community. One of these preferences is "the more and larger variety of guns, the better!" Even if little thought was put into making the image nicer looking, getting all your guns to fit in the frame efficiently still requires a certain level of skill and creativity.

Many firearm aficionados, on seeing the images below, might not first think of family portraits at all. They might instead go to the other end of the photography wholesomeness spectrum and think instead of the common gun-culture folk-speech term "click here to enter text.gun porn."[6] On one level, the term is tongue-in-cheek, but the metaphor has legs. In both "gun porn" and porn of pornography's traditional subject matter, the photos depict something lots of guys like to look at and might like to hold on to. When done according to the aesthetic conventions of their respective professional traditions, both kinds of porn pay special attention to lighting, shadow, lush colors, enticing detail, and evocative environments. Furthermore, as high-quality photographic equipment has gotten cheaper and YouTube videos proliferate on how to use it properly, the "male gaze" has shifted significantly away from professionally produced magazines like *Guns & Ammo*, *Recoil*, or the annual *Shooter's Bible* on store racks, and toward high-quality amateur "gun porn" online.

However, straight-up "gun porn" is not a prevalent term or feature on /k/. Nevertheless, in a roundabout way /k/ might be the originating source of much of the gun porn found elsewhere online, such as more popular mainstream social media like Reddit. 4chan users tend to be contrarian, anti-pop culture, and hence anti-gun porn, or any other kind of "-porn," which /k/ users find too straightforward and insufficiently ironic or edgy. Post a picture *from* Reddit on /k/ and get mocked off the thread. This vibe encourages users to upload original pictures of their guns rather than repost vanilla gun porn. As a result, and if true to /k/ users' perceptions, /k/ is likely a frequent origin of images that, perhaps in modified form, come to be called gun porn elsewhere. The attitude might be described as, "Gun porn is stupid; but we invented it!" Which is a kind of absurdism that the /k/ community understands and appreciates as one of its defining features.

The post #44428204 below incorporates vintage editions of *Shooter's Bible* as a backdrop in its nicely laid out design and may be a knowing wink showing that the poster is in on the joke that "family portraits" could be seen as a /k/ folktext variant for the larger gun culture's term "gun porn." If so, this is unlikely due to any /k/ community squeamishness about the word "porn" (since 4chan is in no way squeamish about that sort of thing), but rather another example of the internet culture's tendency to play with, subvert, and surprise when it comes to issues on which people often tend to have strong political feelings, like pornography and guns. Since being squeamish about the word "porn" is not what anyone would expect a 4chan discussion board to be, this might be exactly why some /k/ posters present this way by calling gun porn "family portraits."

On the other hand, since no one on /k/ seems to remember a discussion thread emerging about the irony inherent in the naming disparity between "gun porn" and "gun family portraits" despite the similarity of their content, this might not be going on at all. It might be that, sometimes, 4chan really is just wholesome—guns really are family to /k/ posters, just as cats, dogs, and other pets are "family" according to other boards' photo-sharing caption conventions. These two possible ways of interpreting gun "family" photos' relationship to gun porn (it's a joke or it means nothing) on /k/ are not mutually exclusive. Some posters may be thinking one thing; others another. Some are cognizant of both possibilities; some of neither.

While sometimes gun porn–like threads appear on the board, a distinction needs to be made between them and gun family photos. Family photo threads are more personal and intimate for the users on the board because they are taking unprofessional pictures of their own guns and sharing them with a community they care about. The folk art emerges as a result of the

Figure 4.4.

Figure 4.5.

tradition in the community rather than the goal being to create art in the first place. According to the most common understandings of the term, something would only be considered gun porn if the primary intention behind posting an image is for its visual appeal. While artistry and visual appeal can be part of the reason for taking a picture for a family photo thread, it is almost never the primary reason. Discussions in the family photo threads I have read over the years indicate photos get posted in these threads because /k/ommandos (/k/ users) have enough desire to feel like a part of the community that it outweighs their fear of the feds that are crawling all over the board. An image posted in a family photo thread doesn't become gun porn until somebody downloads it and posts it somewhere else as gun porn.

ND CONFESSION THREADS

Another example of a /k/ variant of a broader genre is the "confession thread." In these threads, users come forward and "confess their sins" so that they might be forgiven. This is often done with mock-serious use of the terms and tones of an evangelical camp meeting or revival. But being accurate with denominationally specific accoutrements is not really a /k/ priority. This can be seen in the fact that, despite the Protestant rhetorical flourishes, confession threads typically begin with the same genre-identifying device or visual opening formula—the cartoony drawing of a Catholic priest shown below. The sins being confessed usually include people not shooting their guns for a long time; or people not cleaning their guns for a long time; or, in more extreme cases, people will confess their personal ND stories.

ND stands for negligent discharge. A negligent discharge is when a gun is fired even though it wasn't the operator's intent to fire the weapon. The term has been consciously adopted by responsible gun owners and the military as a replacement for the previously used term "accidental discharge." The idea behind this terminological shift in shooter folk speech is that there is no such thing as an "accidental" firing. Guns don't just "go off." In fact, jokingly expressing the belief that they do is a way to mock one of the most infuriating phenomena to firearms enthusiasts—strident gun-banners (or "grabbers" in the /k/ lingo). "Grabbers" are imagined as those whose eagerness to take away other people's personal property and civil rights outstrips their willingness to disabuse themselves of the danger-exaggerating fundamental misconceptions about how guns work that probably lead to their misguided "stepper" stance to begin with.[7]

In reality, negligent discharges only happen as a result of someone violating one of the four firearm safety rules:

1) Treat every gun as if it is loaded, even if you think it is not.
2) Always be aware of where your muzzle is pointing and never point a gun at anything you don't want to see destroyed.
3) Keep your finger off the trigger until you have decided and are ready to shoot.
4) Be sure of your target and what is behind it.

These rules themselves are a kind of folklore. They are very well-known in gun communities. Variants of these four rules may differ a little in exact wording but their main points are identical. They are often ritually recited at the range before shooting, and veteran shooters often quiz amateurs on their four-rules catechism before shooting.

Figure 4.6.

Figure 4.7.

The image sequence below is a series of screen stills taken from a video originally posted on the videogaming livestream service Twitch. This video, and this streamer, were quickly booted off Twitch, but someone managed to collect the video before it disappeared. It has since circulated widely on the gun-related internet platforms including /k/, where it has been mercilessly mocked for breaking rule number one and, actually, all the four rules and then some.[8] As a result, an innocent can of G-Fuel was taken from this world.

NDs are regarded as a serious sin, and the quickest way to get yourself banned from a shooting range. But like with most any anonymous message board, you cannot expect serious matters to be taken very seriously all the time. So, I was not too surprised to find the story below in the confessions thread. The poster describes eight different times they NDed.

Most /k/ readers would immediately recognize this post as similar to a folktale or joke, in that most tellers and hearers understand the genre to be entirely

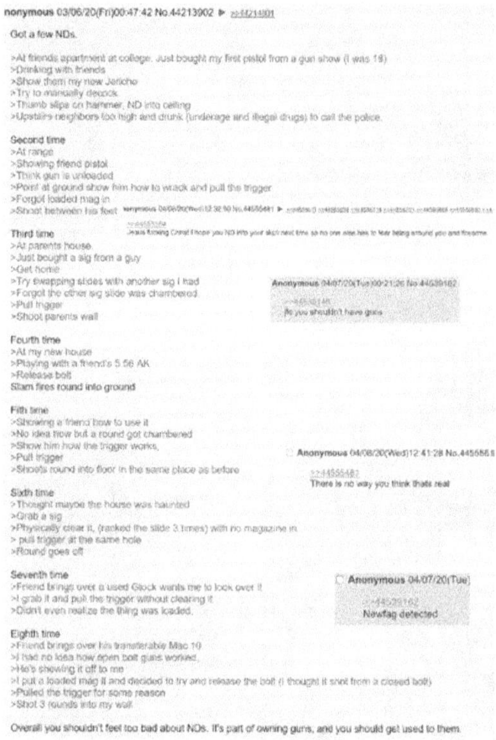

Figure 4.8.

fictional. But since folktales are usually third-person narratives and this tale is presented as a personal experience narrative (PEN), perhaps it could be called a PEF—personal experience folktale (like a tall tale where the sharer knows the story is bogus but attempts to fool the recipient). This particular PEF is also an example of copypasta. Copypasta is the native genre term in internet culture for a copied chunk of already written text that gets dumped onto a thread, often as if it were composed to fit that discussion. Responses to copypasta posts vary. Readers might be annoyed that any not-truly-organic-to-the-discussion text is getting dumped into an ongoing thread. Or they might take delight that a creative and apt deployment of a quite long and elaborate cut-and-paste reposting can seem to actually fit appropriately into an ongoing discussion for which it was not originally written.

This particular ND copypasta likely functions as a release valve for those taking firearm safety as seriously as they should. It also serves another function within the community as a kind of folk-group initiation tall tale/prank that exposes new users. New users who may have never seen this copypasta before might read the last line and be understandably upset. NDs are not

NOAH D. ELIASON (WITH ERIC A. ELIASON) 119

Figure 4.9.

something to be taken this lightly when handling firearms, and anybody who thinks that NDs are just part of owning guns is frankly dangerous. This attitude can be seen in the /k/ screen captures below.

When new users express such concerns, they out themselves as, if not new, then at least gullible, users. This prompts other users in the thread to begin calling them out with posts like the ones below. The first of the responses below seems to assume the horrified responders in posts No. 4455481 and 44539162 are themselves making a disingenuous attempt to get someone to bite by believing that they didn't get the joke. The old trick of, "I'm *so* not a noob that I can turn the tables by getting you to think I am one and thereby show *you* to be the noob!" The poster of post No. 445556111 is way ahead of this, showing they are not falling for it. However, it is still unclear from this exchange just how many levels of "I know that you know, that I know, that you know, that I know what I am doing," is going on.

Ambiguity surrounding responders' actual intentions and beliefs also shows up dramatically in the last example of /k/ folklore considered

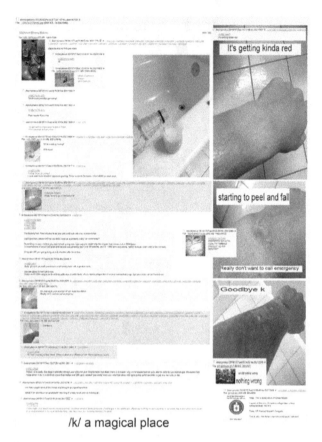

/k/ a magical place

Figure 4.10.

here—one of the most enduring urban legends on /k/ and other gun-related internet forums. Jan Brunvand (1981) identified grisly body-rending mayhem as one of the most common motifs in urban legends. Brunvand suggests that common urban legend themes reveal to us what our deepest concerns are. Urban legend-like morbidity shows up on /k/ as well.

On 19 September 2017, some /k/ommando (4chan weapons board poster) reported intentionally mixing two common chemicals together to produce chlorine gas, in their bathroom, because they wanted to test their gas mask. They made a post about it, and it quickly gained attention. What could go wrong? Well, as it turns out, when you try to commit a war crime against yourself, a lot can go wrong. It all starts to go downhill when the original poster (OP) uploads a picture of their arm turning red and says it hurts and they might have to go to the hospital. Then one of the users in the thread calls OP a fool and says chlorine gas will also burn your skin and soak into your surroundings. Then the one poster does a little napkin math and concludes that if OP only made four ounces of gas, that comes out to a 29,962 parts per million concentration. As little as 400 parts per million is generally fatal over 30 minutes and at 1,000 parts per million and above, death ensues within only a few minutes. OP continues to post pictures of their arm and describes their worsening condition in their last post. Their arm was in really bad shape. They say, "Goodbye /k/," and they are never heard from again. Some thread followers assume OP had died.

Fortunately, this magical moment was captured by an integrator who compiled it into a series of screenshots that highlights the important posts in the OP thread.

Spreading far beyond its original posing, this online urban legend has been shared in many other threads since that fateful day in the fall of 2017. (This is why my story recounting above was in present tense, to highlight that posting this narrative has occurred, is still occurring, and will likely occur again several times.) However, some have speculated that the whole thing was just an elaborate prank pulled off by a talented makeup artist. When passed on with this general assumption by reposters and responders, it might be called a folktale that functions as a kind of release-valve dark humor making light of the seriously dangerous things about which /k/ommandos usually tend to be very careful.

Taken together, "/k/aturday," gun family photos, ND PENs (or PEFs), and the "I died of my own homemade poison gas" urban legend all demonstrate common features of folklore—variation, oikotypes, narrative structures, and a creative dynamic between repeating familiar patterns, tweaking them, and introducing new ones. And they do so despite the traditional genres these items represent having migrated from oral face-to-face transmission to an anonymous online social media discussion board. Trevor Blank is indeed onto something arguing for a broad landscape of "digital folklore," ready for analysis, that a few years ago many folklorists might have found oxymoronic. However, /k/, its constituent genres, and the specific items of lore it fosters are not *simply* an example of folklore jumping from one vector medium to another—like Grimm's fairytales did transitioning from being mostly oral, to being mostly written, to being mostly Disney princess movies. It is this; but it is also more than just this.

/k/ shares a particular feature with many spaces in the complex world of internet culture, especially anonymous ones. Participants in online folkloric creation, consumption, and collaborative interaction with other members of their folk group can never be 100 percent sure just how serious anyone else is and what their actual meanings and intentions are. This is, of course, true in traditional face-to-face lore as well, but the problems (or opportunities for creative playfulness) caused by such opportunities multiply in online environments. Perhaps posters themselves don't always know how they feel and have ambiguous motivations for their ambiguous meanings. But in /k/'s particular corner of the internet, the zeitgeist often seems to be *not* to try to resolve these ambiguities, but to amplify them, making it a "magical place" indeed.

This ambiguous spirit might seem, to those unenculturated in the ways of /k/ and 4chan, to verge toward, or even plunge headlong into, the kind of trolling for which internet culture has often been criticized. Participant insiders seem rather to delight in the cheeky, gun-related traditions that enmesh people together on this forum. They see any ostensible hostility as the kind of welcome ribbing that would only occur among friends who felt comfortable with each other.

/k/ allows for the collaborative expression of a shared identity and set of sensibilities through the presentation and playfully creative manipulation of sets of shared signifiers that solidify their folk group insider credentials as firearms aficionados savvy to internet culture. This identity—at least for the time they are logged onto /k/—comes to the forefront as the primary of (likely) many self-identifications a poster/lurker may have of themselves. /k/ participants may also have many other political, ethnic, regional, etc. identities, but the customs of /k/ do not bring these up as much. Any /k/ participant may well also participate in multiple identities related to folk group affiliation. And there are any number 4chan boards, or other internet forums, ready to accommodate and provide a play-place to articulate these identities. This tendency of internet forums to take on a single unique character, by adopting a single topic-focused identity—while constituent participants may well have many and various other identities in other spheres of their lives—and the tendency of people to selectively and repeatedly-affiliate through the countless oikotypes of shared interest-focused forums, are displayed in any and every face-to-face, as well as online-emergent, folk group. *That* we gather around shared interests seems to be a universal human trait, even if the interests themselves are virtually endless and far from universally shared.

Notes

1. Unlike the term "workshop" perhaps more familiar to academics, I use "workshop" here in its traditional sense of a place with tools where people actually create and modify material things.

2. Folklorists have traditionally focused their research interests on expressive culture shared face-to-face in small groups. However, for over a decade now, Trevor Blank (2009, 2012, 2014) and contributors to his books have been carving out space in the discipline for those who have noticed many features of folklore active in digital culture as well. Robert Glenn Howard (2017, 116–33, 121) has looked specifically at the migration of gun culture online and how traditional face-to-face genres such as "folktales and ballads" have been eclipsed in digital space by new forms of expression and symbolic webs of signification.

3. 4chan's infamy stems in large part from its unregulated and freewheeling commitment to free speech compared to other social media sites such as Facebook, Instagram, Twitter, and Reddit—which more aggressively police expressions some may find offensive. Many creative and beautiful things happen on 4chan. But those less familiar with the expansive forum may only recognize the name 4chan from the frightful expressions of racism and misogyny reported on by the media. These only show up in some corners of a vast collection of ongoing, ever-evolving chats on thousands of subjects. Some such postings seem to reflect genuine belief. Some likely appear only because trolls know they will get a reaction. The more outrage elicited, the more enjoyable this is for the troll. Which buttons get pushed may tell more about the targets' sensitivities than the trolls' actual convictions. Some language may be intended as "edgy" or "ironic" posing, actually intended to mock misogynists and racists or even show solidarity with marginalized people, not always in ways that are appreciated, surely. (Read the word "fag" in the posts featured in this chapter with this in mind.) Chat-board banter throughout internet culture has long been characterized by a tendency to be deeply imbedded in complex matrices of inside jokes, ambiguous numbers of multiple layers of framing, and playful and purposeful obfuscations and misdirections. This makes deciphering actual intentions difficult. These features of the internet cultural landscape make it easy for a casual observer, lazy reporter, or grandstanding activist to paint the whole of 4chan with a broad brush as hateful, when it is also where many innocuous and mainstream memes (such as last decade's ubiquitous LOL cats) first emerged before migrating to other social media. In my own experience on the /k/ board, occasionally, some Nazi will pop up to post something racist. They typically quickly get invited to take that crap to some other board, or maybe even to "8chan," where such dreck is migrating as even 4chan begins to impose restraints to moderate its content.

4. On folklife see Don Yoder's ([1976] 2000) *American Folklife* and Don Yoder and Henry Glassie's (2000) *Discovering American Folklife*.

5. An "oikotype" is variant of any instance of folklore that displays characteristics specific to, and reflects distinctive features of, a locality, region, time period, or folk group such as ethnicity, religion, or avocational subculture. With just a few changes in the details of a narrative's text, such as the setting or a motif or two, a complex item of folklore that occurs with broad similarities across many distinctive cultures can be made to seem almost organically specific to a particular folk group in which the oikotype circulates. "Cat

pictures" are a widespread traditional form of expression with slight to significant variations across many internet subcultures. Only the "guns" part of "cat pictures with guns" is really distinctive to gun-related online forums like /k/. The term "oikotype" was coined by Swedish folklorist C. W. von Sydow ([1948] 1965, 219–42).

6. Along with phenomena like "food porn," "car porn," "real estate porn," and "closet organization porn," gun porn is a particularly well-developed kind of "non-porn porn." (See Howard's "Vernacular Authority Speaks for the Glock: Heterogeneous Volition in an Institutional Proverb.") What all these "porns" have in common, despite emerging from and appealing to different folk groups, is a kind of photography that provides glamourous and vivid instant visual pleasure without the work of actually having to make, buy, maintain, or develop a relationship with the depicted subject matter. The other thing these "porns" all have in common, is that they absolutely eschew depicting people in sexually provocative ways. Reddit even has an r/humanporn subreddit where redditors post amazing pictures of handsome people, in lavish traditional clothing, from a dazzling variety of ethnicities and global locations. But the one thing you will never see on r/humanporn is anything remotely like sexualized naked people (Nguyen and Williams 2019). While "GWG" (girls with guns) images have indeed long been a subgenre of pinup photography that occasionally shows up on /k/, this goes beyond the scope of this chapter.

7. "Stepper" is an online gun culture term for anyone who would infringe on the right to defend one's own life by banning, taking away, or otherwise restricting access to firearms—particularly agents of the state. It references the "don't tread on me" motto of the patriots' Revolutionary War–era Gadsden Flag in its updated internet variant of "no step on snek." This variant wording uses simplified grammar and goofy slang terms with childish spellings for animals like "doggo" or "pupper" for dog, "snek" for snake, and "hooman" for human. LOL cat captions like the famous, "I can haz cheezburger?" have made this "DoggoLingo" an internet meme staple. Employing it serves as a signal to indicate that the animal is speaking, which fits particularly well with the Gadsden flag, whose motto seems like a quote from the snake in both its historical and internet-culture versions ("The Weird Underside of DoggoLingo").

8. The streamer's "I swear to god I emptied the mag" is groanworthy on a number of levels. He obviously was not diligent enough in removing all the rounds from his weapon or his ND would not have happened. Guns don't magically generate bullets after you have taken them all out. And even shooters with the most rudimentary understanding of how semiautomatic pistols work (and their safe use protocols) know that even if you remove the magazine (don't say "clip," which is a shibboleth that will instantly identify you as ignorant of firearms folk speech), a single round will still be in the chamber if the weapon was cycled and ready to fire. So, removing ammo from a semiauto is always a two-step process. One does not simply remove the mag or ammo from the mag, one also then cycles the slide to eject any round that is chambered and ready to fire. And then one *still* keeps one's finger off the trigger, still (as always) treating it as if it were loaded. Of course, this gun clearing procedure won't work at all if the magazine is left in the firearm while cycling the slide, as happens in this sequence of images. His cycling removed a round for sure, but the magazine just fed another into the chamber. Then he fired it off with his atrocious trigger discipline. Perhaps he would have noticed his multiple mistakes were he not violating yet another cardinal gun safety taboo—namely, never handle firearms while drunk (Luke C. 2020).

References

Blank, Trevor J. 2009. *Folklore and the Internet: Vernacular Expression in a Digital World.* Logan: Utah State University Press.

Blank, Trevor J. 2012. *Folk Culture in a Digital Age: The Emergent Dynamics of Human Interaction,* Logan: Utah State University Press.

Blank, Trevor J. 2014. *Toward a Conceptual Study of Folklore and the Internet.* Logan: Utah State University Press.

Brunvand, Jan Harold. 1981. *The Vanishing Hitchhiker: American Urban Legends and Their Meanings.* New York: Norton.

C., Luke. 2020. "A Twitch Stramer's Negligent Discharge: This Is Why Guns and Alcohol Don't Mix." *The Firearm Blog.* 10 March 2020. https://www.thefirearmblog.com/blog/2020/03/10/negligent-discharge-twitch/.

Dundes, Alan, ed. 1999. "Geography and Folk-Tale Oicotypes: Carl Wilhelm von Sydow." In *International Folkloristics: Classic Contributions by the Founders of Folklore,* 137–40. Lanham, MD: Rowman & Littlefield.

Howard, Robert Glenn. 2017. "GunNets: Why a Theory of Heterogeneous Volition Is Necessary in the Study of Digital Communication." *Cultural Analysis* 16.1: 116–33.

Howard, Robert Glenn. 2019. "Vernacular Authority Speaks for the Glock: Heterogeneous Volition in an Institutional Proverb." In *Folkloristics in the Digital Age,* edited by Pekka Hakamies and Anne Heimo, 73–91. Turku, Finland: Folklore Fellows' Communications.

Know Your Meme. "Caturday." Last modified 2019. https://knowyourmeme.com/memes/caturday.

Nguyen, C. Thi, and Bekka Williams. 2019. "Why We Call Things 'Porn.'" *New York Times,* 26 July 2019. https://www.nytimes.com/2019/07/26/opinion/sunday/porn.html.

von Sydow, Carl Wilhelm. (1948) 1965. "Folktale Studies and Philology: Some Points of View." In *The Study of Folklore,* edited by Alan Dundes, 219–42. Englewood Cliffs, NJ: Prentice Hall.

"The Weird Underside of DoggoLing." *Internet Archive Wayback Machine.* https://web.archive.org/web/20190402163135/https://blog.oxforddictionaries.com/2017/08/01/doggolingo/. Accessed August 3, 2020.

Yoder, Don, and Henry Glassie. 2000. *Discovering American Folklife: Essays on Folk Culture and the Pennsylvania Dutch.* Mechanicsburg, PA: Stackpole Books.

Yoder, Don. (1976) 2014. *American Folklife.* Austin: University of Texas Press.

Chapter 5

PERCUSSIONED FLINTLOCKS

A Nineteenth-Century Folk Art

NATHAN E. BENDER

In the history of firearms, the nineteenth century is known for major leaps in technological advances, literally starting with black powder flintlock muzzle-loading guns, and ending with smokeless powder-cartridge breechloading repeating arms. This chapter begins with a brief review of black powder ignition systems, used for private trade as well as military arsenals. The change in design of firearms ignition from flintlock to percussion created opportunities for folk artistry.

The first of these advances was Rev. Alexander Forsyth's 1807 patent in Britain (no. 3032) for the use of a percussion ignition lock, in which a hot spark to fire a gun was created by smashing a small amount of a detonating compound, as opposed to a flintlock's sharp flint flake slicing minute slivers of white-hot steel from a hardened frizzen. Forsyth's patent success inspired a wide variety of improved percussion systems by other inventors (Gooding 1973, 283–97; Held and Held 1970, 170–78; Whisker 2008, 5–9). The most successful of these proved to be small, soft metal percussion caps with a detonating compound on their inside, which were fitted to coned metal nipples that screwed into gun barrels. After Forsyth's patent expired in 1821, the 1814–1817 percussion cap designs unsuccessfully patented by the English-born artist and inventor Joshua Shaw of Philadelphia (Whisker 2008, 5–9) quickly gained in popularity and became manufactured on both sides of the Atlantic.

Nearly all early percussion-ignition systems were based on flintlock designs that were modified or altered as needed (figure 5.1). As a result, once percussion-lock arms came into general use in the 1830s, many owners of flintlock firearms had their guns converted to a percussion ignition system rather than purchasing an entirely new firearm. The art of percussioning a flintlock was within the means of anyone skilled in metalworking. While

126

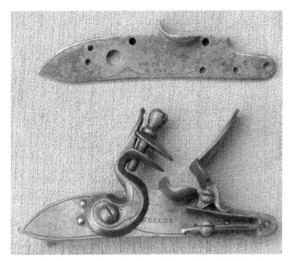

Figure 5.1. Flintlock from a Robert Wheeler trade gun, beneath a Wheeler & Son lock plate that has been stripped of its hammer, frizzen, and frizzen spring. William Basco collection, photograph by author.

local blacksmiths and gunsmiths probably did much of this work, it could also be done by private individuals with access to basic metalworking tools. Such private conversions are normally unmarked and unattributable. The arms further discussed in this chapter reflect original flintlock guns, later converted to percussion-cap ignition in North America in the nineteenth and early twentieth centuries.

Percussioning a flintlock gun involved changes to the barrel to accept a percussion nipple with a threaded seat, and a change in the flintlock cock to a striking hammer. Nipple seats were added to barrels by either drilling and tapping threads directly into a barrel, by welding on a reinforcing bolster to a barrel, or by screwing or welding on a side drum bolster (Sharpe 1995, 21). Breech bolsters became subject to patent designs and so could be quite sophisticated by being cast as a separate piece that screwed directly into the back of a barrel. These were often used on newly made guns and arsenal converted military muskets. Unpatented was the "American system" of screwing a drum bolster, a hollow iron or steel cylinder with male threads, into the enlarged and threaded touchhole of a barrel. Drilling and tapping a hole in the top of the drum created a place to seat the percussion nipple. These "powder drums" were usually left to be screwed in and out as needed. The inventor of this system is unknown, but it quickly became widespread (Madaus 1981, 75), being simpler and cheaper than welded-on or patent breech bolsters.

Figure 5.2. Tryon percussion lock and flintlock, with similar size lock plates. Percussioning by changing out an entire lock could be done when similar size lock plates were available. William Basco collection, photograph by author.

Figure 5.3. Use of original flint cock to hold a percussion striker. Nipple is set into the side drum of this English chief's grade trade gun by Galton. William Basco collection gun B21, photograph by author.

Percussion hammers were needed to strike a sharp blow to the detonating caps. One way to do this was to simply pull out the entire old flintlock and replace it with a percussion lock having a lockplate that could be fit into the mortice left in the wooden stock (figure 5.2). However, an existing flintlock could generally be altered to percussion. This can be achieved by unscrewing and removing the steel frizzen and the outside frizzen spring. The priming pan and supportive arm for the frizzen might be either unscrewed or cut and filed off to get them out of the way. Empty screw holes were then often filled to maintain an even lockplate surface. This left the old flint cock as the main feature on the outside of the lockplate.

This is where much of the art of the craftsman came into play. Some flint cocks were retained, being used to hold small metal strikers instead of pieces of flint (figures 5.3 and 5.4). A few flint cocks were apparently reforged or welded on to create a different hammer shape, though this seems to have been uncommon, and perhaps more trouble than it was worth. The most popular practice was to completely replace the flint cock with a specially designed percussion hammer, still using the same tumbler attachment and internal parts of the flintlock lock plate. Different sized barrels and locks required different sized hammers, with muskets using larger hammers than ordinary rifles or pistols. Hammers could be adjusted (i.e., bent to shape) to precisely hit the percussion nipple and cap to obtain solid functional performance (figure 5.5). There were also a wide range of sizes of nipples and caps, suitable for large muskets down to very small pocket pistols (Roberts 1952, 84–86).

Figure 5.4. Flint hammer holding a metal wedge, aligned with the percussion nipple on this rifle from southern Appalachia. Note that the converted flintlock is itself a replacement lock. Robert Tetro collection, photograph courtesy Robert Tetro.

Figure 5.5. Exaggerated "S" curve in hammer shaft, possibly to better align hammer nose with percussion nipple, on a restocked Ketland fowler with a Hudson's Bay Company marked gun barrel. Mark Bender collection, photograph by author.

Percussion hammers served as a platform for creative folk artistry. They show many C scrolls and S curves in their designs, coming out of a rococo ornamental craft tradition in Europe and America (Heckscher and Bowman 1992, 9–13). This tradition lends itself to very elegantly shaped hammer profiles, fitting well with rococo-based ornamentation of other gun furniture, such as trigger guards and sideplates. The back of percussion hammer shafts is flat to permit them to freely rotate just above the surface of the lockplate. It is the outward facing surfaces, head and spur, and overall profiles of the hammers most subject to stylistic creativity and tradition. Early hammer designs often have wide, rounded bases and wide shafts, as were many of the flintlock cock designs. By the mid-nineteenth century, however, many hammer designs for rifles and pistols came to feature very slim bases and shafts. Blank gun cock forms could be rough-cut out of iron or steel stock, stamped-out, or even purchased as finished hammers in different sizes (Greener 1884, 286–87; Johnston 1871, 35). Blanks were filed to shape, according to the desires of the craftsman.

A few early styles are particularly worthy of note because of their artistry. During a recent study of English trade guns sold and gifted to Native Americans (Bender 2018), several converted Northwest gun and Chief's grade gun flintlocks from the War of 1812 were observed to have similar styles of handcrafted percussion hammers (figures 5.6–5.9). This was interesting, as such trade guns were widely distributed in both Canada and the United States. The features these percussion hammers have in common are rather short hammer noses, a notable "U" shaped spur on the back, with wide bases and flat shafts (cf. Gale 2010, 165, 168; Gale, Ness, and Mikelson 2016, 97). These seem to fit the style of "dog's head" hammers used on American long rifle and

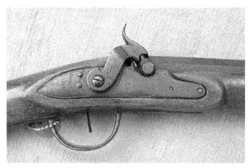

Figure 5.6. English trade gun flintlock by Barnett, dated 1812 with Hudson's Bay Company sitting fox view mark. The dog's head–style hammer has chisel cut and file decorations, fit to a powder drum and nipple in the American style. William Basco collection, photograph by author.

Figure 5.7. American trade gun from Springfield Armory, with flintlock dated 1808. The handmade dog's head style hammer shows vertical floral engraving. William Basco collection, gun A102, photograph by author.

fowler conversions and in converting military muskets from flint to percussion, such as at the nineteenth-century Fayetteville Arsenal, North Carolina (Madaus 1981, 74–77; Murphy and Madaus 1996, 192–97, 216). The trade gun examples, however, seem more stylistically pronounced, perhaps because of being formed by individual blacksmiths available to Native peoples from the 1830s through 1840s and later. Several of the trade gun specimens observed have engraved or chiseled designs on the shafts. Northwest percussion trade guns for Native Americans, not needing any conversion, became available as early as 1846 by the Tryon company of Philadelphia (Russell 1957, 126), even though flintlocks continued as a standard trade item well into the 1860s (Gooding 2003, 88–89). The Eley Brothers percussion caps from England were used for Hudson's Bay Company percussion trade guns (Roberts 1952, 84–85).

Figure 5.8. English chief's grade trade gun by Lowndes, having a handmade dog's head hammer with fancy decorative work. William Basco collection, B20, photograph by author.

Figure 5.9. American fowler, possibly attributable to Silas Allen c. 1820-1830, with an English Ketland lock having a crude handmade dog's head percussion hammer. Mark Bender collection, photograph by author.

In Bedford County, Pennsylvania, gunmakers had a recognizable long rifle style, distinct from those of Lancaster County. The Bedford County school developed a distinctive percussion hammer design, having a long spur artfully curved from the back of the shaft, and often a long, extended nose, its face drilled relatively deep to cover the exploding metal percussion cap. Illustrated in figure 5.10 is a converted Ketland flintlock imported from England, but with a Bedford County–style percussion gun cock, having a long octagonal nose. This lock was acquired by the author from muzzleloading firearms historian and trader Tom Pike, of Lisbon (previously New Lisbon), Ohio. It is worth noting that gunsmith John White had shops in New Lisbon and New Philadelphia, Tuscarawas County, Ohio, making Bedford County–style long firearms (Hanson 1960, 30; Whisker 1990, 134). This Ketland lock

Figure 5.10. English flintlock by Ketland & Co., with a Bedford County, Philadelphia, style percussion hammer. The distinctive long nose and high spur was a regional specialty, with this nose being octagonal. Author's collection.

Figure 5.11. English flintlock on a Robert Wheeler & Son chief's grade trade gun, with a commercial replacement percussion hammer having a crudely chiseled floral design. William Basco collection gun B31, photograph by author.

percussion conversion cannot be definitively attributed to John White, as Columbiana County lies across the Pennsylvania western border, and other nineteenth-century Ohio gunsmiths trained in the Bedford style are also known, such as Joseph Mills in Coshocton County, Ohio (Whisker 1988).

By and large, however, the overall trend of the nineteenth century for civilian rifle and pistol percussion arms was to use the gun cock styles coming out of Pennsylvania and England. These became somewhat standardized with slim shafts, the spur and nose at nearly right angles to one another, though still incorporating rococo-style curves (figure 5.11). Such percussion hammers became commonly used, including on plains rifles of the western frontier (cf. Gale 2010, 105, 119; Gale, Ness, and Mikelson 2016, 9, 109). John Chapman's 1848 book *Improved American Rifle* discusses only percussion arms and does not even mention the by-then obsolete flintlock ignition system. Jacob and Samuel Hawken of St. Louis made the famous Mountain Rifle with a percussion bolster (Bender 2006, 165–67), this nineteenth-century company also retrofitting other guns for pioneers heading west on the overland trails (Hansen 1960, 43). Some of these converted guns may have received the Hawken stamp on their barrels, making the Hawken brothers one of the few private gunsmithing firms doing percussion alterations that are now potentially identifiable.

Many military arsenal conversions of flintlock to percussion muskets occurred in the 1840s, though by the mid-1850s with the adoption of barrel rifling, additional breech reinforcements and modifications were needed (Madaus 1981, 77–78; Gooding 2003, 87). The American Civil War of the 1860s proved a tremendous incentive for the percussion conversion of additional flintlocks, especially for arms intended for and often used by Confederate forces (Murphy and Madaus 1996, 21–34, 71–97, 187–97, 454, 487–92, and 537–42). During and after the war, great progress was made in breech-loading firearms. Sturdy metal cartridges quickly proved much faster to load and reload during field use compared to using loose powder and lead balls, or even rolled paper cartridges with conical bullets as used in military muzzleloading caplock muskets (Roberts 1952, 93–97). Early breechloading gun designs often used outside hammers even with metal cartridges, though these guns eventually became antiquated. Center positioned hammers became expected with newer gun designs from Colt Patent Firearms, Winchester Repeating Firearms, and other industrial firearm manufacturers mass-producing affordable, high-quality firearms. Once modern smokeless powder replaced the older black powder in breechloading cartridges, traditional muzzleloading arms quickly fell out of fashion. Percussion conversions of older flintlock arms became much less frequent in the twentieth century as it was simply no longer worth the effort compared to the advantages to be gained with obtaining a new breechloading smokeless powder gun.

Reconversions from percussion back to flintlock started to be seen in the mid-twentieth century as gun collectors desired to return guns to their original condition. These modern reconversions are mostly done for the collector's market, as few of these guns are ever actually put back into regular use. The processes of reconstructing a flintlock are considerably more involved and difficult, as the end goal is to try to make a gun look like it "originally" did when first manufactured (McCrory 1989, 41–54). Some of these reconversions are expertly and beautifully done. But by doing so, there is inevitably some loss of vintage nineteenth-century examples of folk percussion conversion.

References

Bender, Nathan E. 2006. "A Hawken Rifle and Bowie Knife of John 'Liver-Eating' Johnson," *Arms & Armour: Journal of the Royal Armouries* 3, no. 2 (October): 159–70.

Bender, Nathan E. 2018. *The Art of the English Trade Gun in North America*. Jefferson, NC: McFarland & Company.

Chapman, John Ratcliffe. (1848) 1941. *Improved American Rifle*. With supplement by Ned Roberts. Manchester, NH: Clarke Press.

Gale, Ryan R. 2010. *For Trade and Treaty: Firearms of the American Indians, 1600–1920*. Elk River, MN: Track of the Wolf.

Gale, Ryan R., Larry Ness, and Gary Mikelson. 2016. *Rifles of the American Indians*. Elk River, MN: Track of the Wolf.

Gooding, S. James. 1973."The Development of Percussion Primers." In *Arms and Armor Annual*, edited by Robert Held, 1: 283–97. Northfield, IL: Digest Books.

Greener, W. W. 1884. *The Gun and Its Development; with Notes on Shooting*, 2nd ed. London: Cassell & Co.

Hanson, Charles E., Jr. 1960. *The Plains Rifle*. Highland Park, NJ: Gun Room Press.

Heckscher, Morrison H., and Leslie Green Bowman.1992. *American Rococo, 1750–1775: Elegance in Ornament*. New York: The Metropolitan Museum of Art and Los Angeles County Museum of Art, distributed by Harry N. Abrams.

Johnston, J. H. 1871. *"Wholesale Priced Catalogue of Guns, Rifles, Revolvers, Ammunition, and Sporting Goods."* Pittsburgh, PA: Great Western Gun Works.

Madaus, H. Michael. 1981. *The Warner's Collector's Guide to American Longarms*. New York: Main Street Press.

McCrory, R. H. 1989. *Lock, Stock & Barrel: Antique Gun Repair*. Union City, TN: Pioneer Press.

Murphy, John M., and Howard Michael Madaus. 1996. *Confederate Rifles and Muskets: Infantry Small Arms Manufactured in the Southern Confederacy 1861–1865*. Newport Beach, CA: Graphic Publishers.

Roberts, Ned H. 1952. *The Muzzle-Loading Caplock Rifle*. Harrisburg, PA: Stackpole Press.

Russell, Carl P. 1957. *Guns on the Early Frontier: A History of Firearms from Colonial Times Through the Years of the Western Fur Trade*. Lincoln: University of Nebraska Press.

Sharpe, Philip B. 1995. *The Rifle in America*. With an introduction by Julian S. Hatcher. Republished for the National Rifle Association, Fairfax, VA: Odysseus Editions, with editor's note by Jim Casada. First published in 1938.

Whisker, James Biser. 1988. *Ohio Long Rifles Vol. I*. Bedford, PA: Old Bedford Village Press.

Whisker, James Biser. 1990. *Ohio Long Rifles Vol. II*. Bedford, PA: Old Bedford Village Press.

Whisker, James Biser. 2008. "Joshua Shaw and the Percussion Cap." *Newsletter: Association of Ohio Long Rifle Collectors* 31, no. 2 (October): 5–9.

Chapter 6

NERF PUNK

The Firearm Folklife of "Alternative History" Cosplay

LONDON BRICKLEY

The time is 10:00 p.m., Sunday, September 2, 2018, in the downtown heart of Atlanta, Georgia. The Sheraton Hotel's ballroom opens its doors to a dimly lit interior. The sconces on the walls emit a pale golden light; the overhead chandeliers cranked down to the barest ember glow. Costumed attendees in a flurry of corsets, bustle skirts, and vests amble in, each added body slowly swallowing up the garish geometric patterns of the carpet. With all the stockings and gears, scrap metals and monoculars, the gathering feels a little bit like some kind of misfit prom. An assembly of characters from the works of H. G. Wells, Jules Verne, and Ray Bradbury come to life—a sentience breathed into clockwork toys, rusted robots, and airship captains. Adding to the ambience, the scratchy sonic melody of an orchestral band seeps through the speakers, embracing everything in its orbit with a cabaret sound of brass and strings. From off in the corner, on a makeshift platform stage, the evening's emcee lifts his mic, welcoming all who enter to this year's annual assembly of "The Mechanical Masquerade."

As my eyes adjust to the dim light, the ballroom begins to grow brighter. The electric bulbs are too pale to be fire, but the air still feels orange. Maybe it's all the costumes, which heavily favor sepia tones embellished with metallic accents of copper and bronze, that innately conjure up the errant vibe of candlelight. From overhead, the rapid tempo of the Lindy Hop slows into something morose, and patches of the dance floor follow suit, transitioning their movements into a Viennese waltz. Set outside the dancing horde, a man dressed in a deep-sea diving suit, made of thick, heavy-looking brass and an excess of rusted rubber tubing, shuffles over to embrace a pixie catcher. His movements are hindered by the weight of his gear, and yet he is careful to avoid the antique wicker birdcages hanging off the fey huntress's body, in

Figure 6.1. An Alternate West: *"Lady Luck"* by Anthony Sumrak.

Figure 6.2. Maverick Nerf Mod by old junkyard boutique.

which the woman's wee fairy captives are held. (Handmade and delicately glued to the bars, these "captured fairies" are small, beautiful figurines comprising taffeta wings on wire skeletons, which flicker with the heartbeats of tiny lights). Across the way an Edwardian "space pirate" talks to a Victorian gentleman about the schematics for a helium airship. When the dinosaur shuffles in—the inflatable T-Rex costume ruffling in the air-conditioned breeze—the gentleman bows and offers it his top hat. The hat slides off the smooth inflated head. But it's the grand idea of it, followed by the experimental attempt, that counts.

It is then, in this heightened ostensible fever dream of expressive performance and creativity, when I first really take notice of the prized "handgun" at the man's side. As the gentleman scoops to pick his hat back up from the floor, his sidearm gleams from where it rests in its holster—a custom overhaul of a Nerf "Maverick" model that gives his English turn-of-the-century ensemble a bit of an Old West flair. The gun, once a plastic children's toy, now looks more like art. Repainted with copper tones over an emerald-green base, glued-on gears, and an embedded functioning time piece, the aesthetic of the gun had been meticulously cultivated, reworked into something impeccably fitting to the ethos of the night at hand. The attention to detail in rebuilding the weapon made sense in context. It was, after all, an entirely essential accessory. For, as the gentleman himself soon took the time to explain to me, no self-respecting man of upper crust society would be caught out around town without his pistol: one never knew when they would be called to a duel.

And yet the inclusion of weaponized accessories among the evening's guests was not limited to the aspiring aristocracy. There were many flavors of dress in the room: courtly, apocalyptic, fey, military, industrial, proletariat, etc., and the gentleman was not the only one packing. In fact, even (or perhaps especially) during the high social event of the ball—tucked among the layered skirts and stacked belts of a significant majority of the event's attendees on that fine and humid evening—was an entire cache of handmade sidearms, each unique to the bearer. The pixie catcher, although she preferred to catch fairies with the aid of her giant butterfly net, still had her backup "stun gun" clipped to her side. The green glowing gel in the weapon's exposed core had, after all, been perfectly tailored to stun a pixie's central nervous system on impact. So too would the brass-laden diver (as he assured me upon my inquiry on the subject) never think of dipping three— let alone twenty thousand—leagues under the sea without his pressurized harpoon, a curious hybrid contraption that looked like a cross between an airsoft rifle, an oxygen tank, and a barnacle-encrusted trident. And *how*, the space pirate challenged, was he supposed to defend attacks against his zeppelin if not for the oversized bazooka strapped to his back? Like the others, this weapon too was another handmade custom job, which, made from a soldered-together string of tin cans and supporting a mess of antennas and rods, had been designed to attract and harness the lightning that was always flashing above his ship in the sky, transforming the bright electrical current into nature's ammunition.

As the night carries on, more bodies filter in and with them come the guns—rebuilt, reworked, and remixed: shotguns, spearguns, muskets, pistols, revolvers, even blunderbusses. And yet even though each costumed accessory is immediately recognizable as a "gun," there isn't a single one that looks like it quite belongs to any known reality. But then again, by design, nothing in the room that night is supposed to. Old world, futuristic, archaic, and otherworldly, this is the world of alternative history (AH) cosplay. A vibrant community whose folk expressions thrive off paradox, AH cosplay exists

138   THE FIREARM FOLKLIFE OF "ALTERNATIVE HISTORY" COSPLAY

somehow both within and outside of time—a sentiment that then extends to all the materials, participants, stories, performances, and even the guns that help build and maintain it. And as singular as this moment felt, this was only one portion of a larger, and rather unexpected and unorthodox, participant form of expressive gun culture. One that at least that weekend, like the mechanical ball itself, was nestled within a much larger event known as Dragon Con.

Held every year, when the late summer sun glows too hot over the streets of Atlanta, Dragon Con compels thousands of people—fans, gamers, cosplayers, and general "nerd" and "geek" culture enthusiasts—to gather together over the long Labor Day weekend. For many, Dragon Con, a five-day extravaganza "multi-genre event," is the social event of the season, attracting over eighty thousand attendees in 2019 (a number that has been steadily on the rise each passing year). During the 360 days leading up to the event, many attendees pass the time designing their wares, and every year more and more people come dressed to the geek chic nines. Latex-clad superheroes mingle with robot unicorns. Steampunk airship captains catch up with alien militia. The most devoted come in full character. Others simply accessorize. It's a sight to behold. For five days, downtown Atlanta becomes a wonderland of color and creativity.

Alongside the costumes, the characters, and the performances, this visual feast of subcultures and their material expressions is also—if one is looking for it—a grand showcase of handmade weaponry, including guns in a wild array of wonderous fashions and functions. Although not an official requirement, for many Dragon Con participants of the cosplaying persuasion, an outfit just isn't complete without a sidearm. And what those sidearms are, exactly—what these guns are made of, how they are made, and why they are carried—is where things get really interesting for those with a joint interest in folklife and firearms. Because these guns aren't ordinary, everyday weapons. Be it a Matchlock made from melted down trumpet barrels with piano key triggers, Gatling-type guns that shimmer and spark with Tesla coil cores, or clockwork-controlled rifles that spit out dayglow ammunition, cosplay weaponry collectively presents a rich material parade of a very particular form of material folk art. One that despite the seemingly endless possibilities of its form and execution nevertheless emerges and further operates within the rich preset boundaries of a communally understood folk tradition.

Handcrafted and tailor made, the cosplay gun is built for show—a visual spectacle emblematic of strange and fantastic worlds often set in an "alternative" time and place. Often (although not always) stripped of their ballistic functions, the question of what such a collection of fantastic but ballistically nonfunctioning objects, culled from scrap materials to evoke alternative realities, might have to do with guns in real life is a curious one. The answer, however—from the AH cosplay's gun manufacture to its employment within community spaces—is that these weapons of abstract reality have a lot more in common with actual historical and present firearms than a surface glance might suggest. And this is because the cosplay gun doesn't merely show, but also tells. A participant-based form of both individual and communal expression, the cosplay gun is both an object and a text. And like many texts, they are meant to be read. Each gun has a very real story to tell.

This chapter looks more closely at this material-semiotic phenomenon—at the simultaneous physical, figurative, and narrative nature of the alternative history cosplay firearm, as well as the ritualistic performances and reflections of real-world weapons embedded within alternative gunplay practices. The first section, therefore, looks more specifically at the AH gun as a material object and veritable folk art of the AH community through an introduction to the "makers" (folk artists), the physical processes, and the materials that go into the AH gun's construction. The second section of this chapter then turns to the AH gun's more abstract narrativity—the stories that the AH guns tell—in order to consider the ways in which the AH gun may not be so alternative to reality after all. Far from an insular expression of surface aesthetics and "toys," the various vernacular gunlore expressions shared among AH cosplayers serve as a transformative means by which this vibrant, fantastical world of folk art and performance uniquely expresses the complicated multitude of symbols that the gun has historically carried for its bearers throughout space and time.

BRAVE NEW WORLDS: ESTABLISHING THE BORDERS OF "ALTERNATIVE HISTORY" COSPLAY

Although the focus of this chapter is on the folk art, ritual practices, and symbolic revelations of the alternative-history firearm, as produced and carried by AH cosplayers, there are a few terms to cover before we can really begin. First and foremost, for those entirely unfamiliar with the cosplayer's landscape, "cosplay" itself is a hybrid collapse, or portmanteau, of "costume play," further defined as a performance art in which participants called *cosplayers* wear self-assembled costumes and accessories to represent a specific character or persona (either a replication of a preestablished figure in popular culture, one of their own creation, or even some sort of hybrid in between). Cosplayers are everywhere, finding adaptable habitats at anime, gaming, cosplay-specific, and other multi-media conventions, community-organized symposiums, performance events, online forums, social media platforms, and more intimate local gatherings. And just like the diversity of cosplay's physical outputs, the performances of cosplay can come in many forms. One of the more traditional and widespread (and therefore generally the most familiar form of cosplay known to outsiders) is the recreation or adaptation of already established, known characters from popular media (be they characters from books, TV, films, comics, anime, etc.).

Cosplayers who cosplay characters that are already known from popular media and other established sources engage with their craft in a very particular manner (see Cherry 2016; Hills 2014; Lamerichs 2019; Winge 2006). When you cosplay a character that isn't "yours," the backstory—and the weapon accessories that go with them—are already preestablished by the understood canon from which that specific character derives. Cosplaying a *known* character is about *replication*. It is about using the materials and tools available to create the most authentic replication of the original. This in and of itself is an intricate and artful process that takes great skill and dedication. There is a whole culture around cosplay replication (a category that includes not only media-based recreations but historical cosplay as well, such as Civil War reenactments). Replication cosplay is a practice worthy of study in its own right; this, however, is not that study. And that is because this chapter looks at a separate subset of cosplay that is a very different breed than the replicators and the adapters—one that wields a very different kind of gun. This form of cosplay comes in the form of "alternative history" (AH) cosplayers, something much different in practice and execution than those trying to replicate and emulate popular or historically known personas. And that difference starts, like the AH gun itself, with a story.

The baseline of all AH cosplay creation is the story. The AH firearm, in its final physical form, serves as a concrete material accessory scrapped together from all sorts of assembled pieces. Before those pieces can be properly assembled, however, there is quite a bit of backstory that goes into an AH gun's construction by its maker. And the very first step in such a process is determining the history to which an AH gun belongs. This brings us to a second important emic community term or expression to know before really delving into AH gunlore folk customs and their materials: "Alt (or alternative) history."

The cosplay gun is a real, physical object that exists in the known and present world, but those same guns also manifest out of and exist within the specific world build of the cosplay, which is almost always a realm different—be it slightly or vastly different—from our own. AH cosplayers call these brave new worlds "alternative histories"—a term that is marked by the seemingly simple idea that something or some part of a given historical place, moment, or time period has been altered from a more standard, "canonical" understanding of said time. In order to construct such hypothetical worlds, AH players operate under the premise of a deceptively simple thought experiment that ponders what would happen to the world if X occurred instead of Z, in which Z is what actually occurred in recorded or canonical historical memory, and in which X could be anything. Some of the premises found in AH thought experiments are broad and encompassing, positing scenarios that would have inevitably caused a ricochet of effects throughout history, incurring widespread global ramifications and drastically changing the landscape of the present or the future. (For example, *What if steam had remained the dominant form of power in England instead of electricity?* Or, conversely, *What if laser technology had been discovered, perfected, and institutionalized in a precolonized Indonesia?*) Other time-constructions are more isolated, carving out a space for occult or esoteric branches of time to explore in secret. (For example, *What if there had been a clandestine French voyage to the moon in 1816 that had discovered an alien subspecies who gave them magic atom-altering crystals, which were then only available and used in the weapons of the highly selective few people who knew about them?*)

Whatever the premise, each and every one of the AH thought experiments has some history-altering effect on the way the participant imagines the future and present. The options are limited only to the participants' imaginations, but commonalities among many or most AH projections are certain focuses on technology, science, and time—notably how obtaining certain technologies or a failure to develop certain sciences impacts society on every level, including culture, politics, fashion, custom, language, daily ritual, warfare, economics, etc. And what those world-building alterations are dictates the character or the persona that the AH cosplayer will subsequently construct. This includes what the persona's weapon will look like, and how it will function within the alternate space. As such, participants create their guns in kind, building their AH firearms from the ground up using a range of found materials and customs of construction shared by and learned from other participants in the community. In this way, AH participation often begins as a thought experiment, but through the process of manifesting the thought through the physical construction of a fully realized persona complete with all the material trappings, which is then further performed and shared among a group of self-identified participants, AH cosplay is also an art, a lifestyle, a culture, and a community—one in which "the gun" plays a surprisingly substantial role in the symbology of their performance.

In many ways, the construction and performances of alternative histories happen every day. AH participants are everywhere. Anyone can participate in envisioning new worlds and performing alternate realities, as evidenced by the diversity of the AH community, which ranges in age from small children accompanying their parents to an AH convention gathering in Ohio while enthusiastically dressed as space pirates, to senior engineers that tinker about on an AH model laser gun in their garage in Taiwan, uploading the process to share with others on the community forums online. Loosely gathered, AH participants are a self-identified, self-motivated subset of people, globally scattered in their general daily lives, who find and engage with others via the most convenient community connections available to them. Online, digital, and virtual spaces are always available for those who wish to discuss character ideas, seek costuming help, download design schematics, share their creations, or access DIY (do it yourself) tutorials. Meanwhile, scheduled physical gatherings of AH events occur throughout the year, appearing in the forms of more localized in-person casual meetups to formally organized popular conventions.

It is within these diverse spaces of intersection that the AH community comes alive, taking the opportunity to perform their cosplay of alternative realities ranging from simply accessorizing to completely embodying a fully fledged persona. Like many performance-based activities, at the heart of cosplay is the act of being seen. For many cosplayers, the opportunity to show or display the character—or even simply their weapons—that they have created is an important step in fully actualizing the process. As such, there is a rich visual archive of AH materials readily available to anyone who goes seeking them, each documented, shared, and spread freely by those who share in the embrace of the AH aesthetic. As Nicolle Lamerichs (2018, 202) observes from her own extensive research with cosplay communities, "Cosplaying at a fan convention is partly institutionalized through and motivated by specific events," further noting that "the most common of [such events] are fashion shows, photography sessions, and cosplay acts." However, even though the in-person visibility may seem like the primary display of a cosplay act, it is important to acknowledge the interwoven nature of both cosplay's virtual and physical spaces in the cosplay process. As Lamerichs observes,

Online forums and communities are devoted to providing mutual help with difficulties [in costume design]; . . . tutorials made by fellow fans in these forums lead to a culture in which fans help one another as peers. The community is crucial to the development of costuming skills. . . . The costume is a cultural product that can be admired at a convention, and spectators thus also play a role in guaranteeing authenticity [see also Winge 2006, 69]. Fans may evaluate the costume, appreciate the character being portrayed, or take photographs that again remediate the object and player. (Lamerichs 2018, 202)

Activities and actions in virtual spaces inform the materials that ultimately manifest in the more physical performances at conventions and other in-person gatherings (at which point the physical space of the cosplay may then recirculate back into virtual space as photographs and videos are posted online). Lamerichs's observations of the larger cosplay community remain in place within AH subsets, for which cosplay acts similarly strengthen the sense of community bonding and performance. For AH cosplay, the "institutional-ization" or the *validation* of the "reality" of their alternative space often comes down to the virtual collaboration along with the physical acts and instances of visibly existing (be it within the in-person convention space or in digital uploads) among the others who are both of and not of their own timelines. Performances, plays, comedy sketches, dramatic readings, "alternative his-tory museums," fashion shows and, most importantly, the AH tea parties and masquerade balls are essential venues to facilitate the act of being seen. It is among these different venues of visibility that the practices and performances of the AH gun can be similarly found, cultivated, seen, and "read" as both a physically material object and a narratively symbolic form of folk art.

"TIME TO MEET YOUR MAKER": METHODS, MATERIALS, AND OTHER BUILDING RITUALS OF ALT WEAPONRY CONSTRUCTION

The practice and participation in AH performance has no central organi-zational schematic. And yet, one of the largest and longest-running places for an AH enthusiast to be and be seen is Atlanta's yearly Dragon Con, which among its horde of more than eighty thousand fantasy- and gaming-convention devotees hosts its fair share of AH cosplayers. Like many city centers, Atlanta has a lot of hotels. Unlike certain other city centers, however, Atlanta's hotel spread is quite compact, built one on top of the other as the gridlocked streets grew. The Con continues to spread to more and more buildings every few years, but as of 2020, the event is principally housed in Atlanta's seven major rentable structures in the Peachtree Center area, with guest spillover into other nearby hotels, motels, or whatever spare couch one can find. The event is huge. Rooms in all the official hotels sell out quickly, with the holy trinity of the walkway-connected Marriott, Hilton, and Hyatt Regency serving as the central hub of all the action, the lobbies of which are great places to catch any and all schools of cosplayers on casual display if you can maneuver enough to weave your way through the crowded color burst of body paint and latex. In order to facilitate the great droves of people, the event has since divided itself into color-coded "tracks," with classes, conferences, speakers, and events that fit a certain genre of "geek culture" coded together for easier access. It is among this bright array of mingled lines that the "alternative history track" has slowly begun to grow.

As close as the hotels are to one another, there is one that stands a bit further south. Although it is only a handful of blocks away from the major hub of the event, the Sheraton has a bit of a reputation as often housing the tracks that have the fewest attendees. While several hundreds of people will line up to stuff themselves into one of the Marriott's ballrooms for a popular media panel, many of the tracks allocated to the Sheraton more often find themselves with a bit more leg room per panel—the gathering of people that filter through the doors of the upstairs meeting rooms is in the comparable several *dozens*. In August of 2018, I was one of those people who walked through one of the Sheraton's second-story doors. Full disclosure: I myself have always had an affection for cosplay communities. As a lifelong *Dungeons and Dragons* player who also dabbles with "LARPing" (live action role playing), I feel that cosplayers are my kind of people in a peripheral sort of way. I was aware of the practice—the artistry and dedication of general cosplay customs—even if I myself could never muster up the required levels of active motivation and skill to participate. But it was in one of these Sheraton rooms designated to the alternative history track that I first really came to understand the depths of creativity, production, community, and *lore* that goes into AH cosplay weapons. I had walked into the room because of a sign. Unlike many of the signs at the Con, most of which were professionally printed with that vibrant, glossy sheen, the sign in question was a simple scrap piece of computer paper, which, taped up to the side of the door and hastily scrawled over with hand-edited scribbles, read, "The Alternative History Museum." Intrigued, I entered.

In 2018, the concept of an alternative history museum was relatively new in the Dragon Con program, set up as a place for the creative "makers" (those in the scene who make, construct, build, or assemble costumes or accessories)[1] within the AH community to show off some of their wares. It was a pretty simple set up. Tables with white cloths had been pushed around the outskirts of the room to line the perimeter. On each table was a collection of fantastic objects built, made, and cultivated by AH participants. Alongside

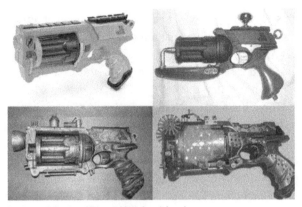

Figure 6.3. Selection of "Maverick" Nerf model mods.

their objects, many of the makers—dressed fully in their own AH persona ensembles—were there to explain their creations. And as it turned out, many of the wonders on display were weapons: pistols, lasers, "blasters," rifles, shotguns, firearms, muskets, bazookas, revolvers, or in a single word—*guns*. But not just guns—*alternative history guns*.

Looking upon an AH gun is (almost always) a rather fantastic experience. No two handmade guns are the same. But the singular quality doesn't stop there. There is a slight uncanny quality to an AH gun, particularly as, despite the gun's construction as an assemblage of odd objects, it still looks like a gun. There is often something familiar about the shape, enough so to hint at its firearm function: the spinal protrusion of a barrel; a familiarity in the frame; some container of an odd ammunition, be it a swollen cylinder of plasma or the sinuous shock of something electric, each tracing its way to a trigger to insinuate the action. The aesthetic is always just enough to make anyone who has seen a gun in their own historical timeline recognize the weapon for what it is. And yet, the AH gun is like nothing known to our own history's arsenal.

A mixture of metals—golds, coppers, and bronzes—tangled with knobs, wire, and lights, an AH gun displays its history proudly and openly through the aesthetic assembly of its materials. And those materials might be anything: hair curlers, flashlights, LED strips, wire, old clocks, trumpets, a violin bow, lace, a lamp, etc. Essentially, if it can be glued, sewn, or welded, it can be used in the making of a gun. As a result, every AH gun has a different composition and with it a different tale to tell. And yet, there are certain shared histories that produce commonalities among the base builds. It is, for example, incredibly common for many DIY makers to start with a Nerf gun at the base (with the Nerf "Maverick" model being one of the more popular to modify on account of its ubiquity as well as its "multi-historical" versatility).

There are several reasons why Nerf guns are so popular among makers: Nerf guns are easily accessible, including from secondhand retail options such as local thrift shops and garage sales; they are cheap; light of weight; easy to break (and reassemble); easy to paint; and easy to glue. As such, the most common practice among AH gun makers is to start with a Nerf foundation. Once obtained, the Nerf gun is usually washed thoroughly with dish soap to remove any semblance of grease and then matte painted black as a solid foundational primer. After that, the gun can be augmented at will, gluing any found objects that might add to the desired aesthetic and then painted again. In slightly more advanced builds, it is also fairly common to deconstruct and recombine multiple, different Nerf models, sawing the Nerf guns in half and hybridizing the pieces in a Frankenstein-like reconstruction of harvested limbs. Other select makers who possess the skill to do so might build entirely from the ground up, soldering metals and other found materials into creations entirely of their own designs.

Whichever path a maker selects, how-to guides are readily available in a variety of online spaces for any who want to get their hands actively engaged with the process (currently, the most popular of which are YouTube, Pinterest, and Tumblr). As each guide and gun makes clear, the raw creativity that pulsates through the scene is quite astounding, if not an essential element to the construction process. Makers who have been creating, building, and, well, *making* AH weaponry for a while have a tendency to collect objects wherever they find them, recognizing on sight that an old barometer or a broken trombone would be a great item to have on-hand in their personal cache of supplies. As one maker explained to me, "At some point, you just stop seeing stuff for what it is, and start to look at it for what it *can* be."

The possibilities with a build seem endless, and yet, despite the wide array of materials used in the assembly, there is a certain consistency among AH gun builds that makes them immediately recognizable for what they are. There is a certain unity present, something that tethers them all together despite the freeform nature of the build. This is because, like most great forms of science fiction, an AH object operates within the parameters of its own preset and consistent logical structure. It is not that there are *no* rules, just that the rules are not written in any manual. They are embedded in plain sight and implicitly understood by AH participants. The rules are located in the story of the gun, whatever that story might be. As such, although there are no *official* rules in a gun build, in that any and all materials are fair game, there is still an embedded understanding of logic-bound limitations—a certain understanding among participants that the AH gun must in some way be a *transformed*, reworked to fit into an alternative, but still a readable, object.

The final product must make sense as an object belonging to the oral AH it both derives from and represents. The gun should both be a *byproduct* of its story and it must *tell* that story. And that, I learned that day, while browsing through the hand-selected objects for display at the inaugural Alternative History Museum, was possibly the most paramount piece of their material folk art: all AH guns have a story.

The story of the AH cosplay gun is based on many variables, and like the multiplicity of its materials, is individually enriched through the details, but the major common base points among AH gunlore include special attention to these things: the narrative of the AH from which the gun derives; the narrative of the person/persona who bears the gun; and any further considerations on the effects such a derivation of time, technology, person, and place would have had on the subsequent manufacture of the gun on a material, social, and cultural level. The precise process of a gun's story construction is not exclusively bound to a specific number of steps in an exact order. A cosplayer may, for example, start with an already-made AH gun and work their way backwards, building a character and then a world around the already physical and present object. However, in the spirit of AH play, many first begin, before a gun is even physically built, with that AH thought experiment of reconstructed time, followed by constructing a character who might occupy that world. When and if such a completed character construction includes bearing AH arms (as many AH cosplayer characters do), the logical extension of the process then dictates that the gun should "fit" within the recreated reality. In short, either the object first produces the text, or the text first produces the object. But at the end of the process, both text and object should be inseparable.

This is a much more elaborate notion to think about than one might expect. Once again, in order to build a gun, you must start with the base. Not the base of the Nerf model but the grander philosophy of the object in question. As one AH cosplayer enthusiastically explained to me over an oolong tea, which he sipped from his own copper goblet at a table in the Marriot lobby's Starbucks, "Guns don't simply manifest out of nothing." Guns are material objects, products of their place and time in history—whatever that history might be. He continued,

When constructing a weapon you must think of the character and think of the era. What was the era like? What materials were available, what pigmentation of colors, and what objects? What were the functions of those objects? Would a craftsmen want to display or show the interior workings of the gun—the mechanics, or the ornate parts? (If

148   THE FIREARM FOLKLIFE OF "ALTERNATIVE HISTORY" COSPLAY

during a version of the Industrial Revolution, where man became fascinated with intricate machines, yes; if it's the apocalypse, where aesthetics are not a priority, probably not) What technology dominates the era? What powers a weapon and what kind of ammunition does it use? What region is your character from? What cultures and customs come with it? Is your character patriotic? Wanting to show off a make and model that distinctly represents manufacture from your own country? Or do you have an obsession with importing machines from foreign soil? What are the politics of the time, and how might that effect the open carry of weapons? Are people quick to display and draw their side arm, or must it be concealed? Do you want to intimidate with your weapon—carry a big gun that all can see? Or is the preference for something light and functional? Are others envious of your wealth? Do you wish to display class and social standing via the gun, or is your character desperate, scrapping together any parts they can to make a weapon? (Michael Gould, personal interview, Dragon Con 2018)

Essentially, even the smallest change in the course of history trickles down to affect the fundamental designs and uses of weapons, which are further modified individually to the character within the world. After all, the contextual trapping of "history" drives and forms the aesthetics, the people, and the guns that are produced from within its borders.

This makes sense. Material objects throughout time have always been heavily shaped by what materials are available, in fashion, legally (or illegally) accessible, and in demand. This is not only true of manufactured weapons in alternative histories but in the real world as well. What is also interesting, however, is that although the list of considerations goes on in terms of how the material reality of a gun's surroundings would shape the gun as a material object (including what kind of ammunition such a gun would use), the question of how a gun build would, even hypothetically, ballistically shoot that ammunition is not of any particular concern to most AH participants. AH guns (with very few exceptions) do not shoot in real life, nor are they built to. Although, curiously enough, AH guns don't need to physically be able to shoot ammunition to be talked about as if they do. In fact, it is a rather consistent and common folk custom that when talking about an AH gun, the participant, be it in or out of their cosplay persona, will talk about an AH gun as if it were "real" in every functioning capacity.

This was the second thing I learned very quickly at the museum that day. When describing their guns, even out of character, makers had a tendency to talk about their firearms in an active, present sort of way—"this one shoots electrical currents" or "this one is used in aviation combat"—in a shared semantic understanding that the presumed and suspended reality of the AH space is simply taken for granted by all participants. This emic language custom was something I myself was not privy to during my first AH gun conversation, which took place between me and a maker named Rocky Sawyer.

The gun lay on the white-clothed table, a sturdy twist of bronze that emanated a spectral pale blue from its core. "Can you tell me about this one?" I asked.

"That's the *Mctavish Blaster*," he informed me. "It shoots sonic lasers." The answer was so succinct, so simple, delivered in a crisp present tense full of easy conviction. I knew some guys in college who had built a fully functioning *Dr. Who* inspired robot Dalek for their engineering master's thesis. The Dalek had functioning lasers. It didn't seem beyond the realm of possibility.

"Does it really work?" I asked.

Something about the way I posited the question, perhaps a little too earnestly, had Sawyer hesitating. He eyed me skeptically, like I had perhaps gone a bit mad, mixed in with a dash of sympathy for the poor naïve amateur. "Umm. No," he clarified, before he patiently explained that the gun was made out of a melted down trumpet and LED light strips.

I offered only the most half-hearted of attempts to cover up my naïve blunder, because put like that, the idea that I was holding an advanced piece of DIY laser technology sounded less plausible than it had three minutes before. Then again, this was a man who knew how to melt, solder, and reshape metal and tinker around with electrical wires, not to mention that it was nearing 2020 and lasers were become increasingly passé by the day. "I mean, I don't know! It could work!" was my defense.

I figured this was likely to get me another sympatric eye raise, only he smiled at me instead, visibly enthusiastic like I was finally catching on to the larger picture. The essence of something grand. "Exactly," he agreed. "It *could*."

Those two words, "it could," hold within them the succinct summation of the incredibly complex ideology and practice of AH firearms. The ethos is one of possibility and of a reverent sort of wonder for the materials that history has produced and what everyday people have in turn produced with those materials. The notion is that the gun, above all else, exists as a material kind of text that can be "read" in order to discern a great deal about its own history and the history of its bearer. The gun exists to uphold the narrative, and the narrative exists to uphold the gun. The material object and the narrative text are one and the same, a physical object and a fantastical tale tangled together and coexisting in some middle ground compromise of reality.

The observation of the curious interplay of materiality and textuality in cosplay is not new. As Mathew Hale (2013) explored in his own ethnographic work with the steampunk community (one of the more popular subsets of the larger AH crew), the material objects produced by folk groups in general—and cosplayers in particular—are especially adept at exemplifying what he calls the "material-semiotic." Defined as the "entanglement of expressive media, where text, object, and action meet," the material-semiotic is that "often overlooked symbiotic relationship between substance and text" (Hale 2013, 31). As Hale continues, within the cosplay realm:

> Textuality and material substance are . . . inseparable. Even if a text is considered as a purely abstract form, figures and/or characters appearing within in it are imagined to have shape, form, and texture. As they progress through a given narrative arc, they interact with a world of materials; environments filled with other personas who are likewise imagined to have shape and form. Extrapolating from this hypothetical monograph, we can see that, although we tend to think of the two forces separately, the truth of the matter is that both texts and materials are always "substances-in-becoming." They are co-present and co-constitutive modes of discourse. They produce one another. (Hale 2013, 8)

Or as Hale (2013, 30–31) more simply summates, "Material is produced by its history and its accumulation of stories about how that material has been, cannot be, or might be used. . . . There are no objects without stories."

In her own work, Lamerichs (2018, 199–200) similarly supports this notion of the material-semiotic in cosplay's material performance as an "affective process," adding that despite the scholarly tendency to isolate fandom "text-driven" expressions from their physical objects, cosplay cultures "contain many material practices that use the text as a starting off point for new forms of play and productivity." As such, "The material and the textual—are not in opposition, but are, instead, both ways to understand and interpret media texts. Stuff—bodies, fabrics, plastic—allows us to tell stories. Especially in fandom, material practices support narrative inquiry and creation but also have their own aesthetic qualities as media texts." So too, in the case of Alt history gun builds, do the materials reflect and produce the narrative they want to tell. Functionality (in terms of the gun's ability to "work" in a ballistic sense) is not the point of the AH cosplay gun. Nor do most AH gun makers have any desire to make it one. There is no need for an AH gun to shoot ammunition in real life. The AH gun functions exactly as it is supposed to:

as a material object to enhance, support, and manifest the story. The gun is an object and teller of the tale. Its purpose is to be seen, read, interpreted, and admired. It informs viewers about the status of its carrier. The gun is an object and objects have histories; they have stories to tell.

"LET THE GUN DO THE TALKING": SYMBOLS, STORIES, AND "MATERIAL-SEMIOTICS" OF THE ALT HISTORY SIDEARM

Although the AH gun must follow the logic of its own story, the gun does not need to tell the entirety of its story alone. That is what its bearer is for. And like many other bearers of a community's traditions and lore, those that bear Alt history arms are exceedingly adept at performing their tales. And these performances are often done as just that—as a full immersion performance in which the bearer becomes another material manifestation of the tale. In other words, when in full cosplay, just as the agreed-upon understanding among participants is to talk of the guns as if they are "real," many of the participants commit to their persona within the scene.

Such is the case with Sebastiantine Montparnasse, who on the day in question stood idly outside the makeshift museum, awaiting the start of his afternoon panel. There are many things that stand out about Monsieur Montparnasse: his velvet waistcoat, his tall, willowy stature, and the powdered wig covering up his naturally red hair. But above all these things, it is hard not to notice the following: Sebastiantine Montparnasse carries a big gun—a grandiosity of size, pomp, and circumstance purposely designed to demarcate an even larger ego. Within the physical space of the Dragon Con scene, Montparnasse maintains character, even in the times of momentary anachronisms, such as a passing friend tossing him a bag of Cheetos from the vending machine down the hall. Sebastiantine Montparnasse remains Sebastiantine Montparnasse—an occupant of that liminal space in which his awareness of the attention called to the performative aspects of his persona do not in any way detract from it. We are all of us, after all, occupying and upholding that same tentative agreement of the Alt history space. We—his audience and fellow participants—all know "what's up." I approach him outside of a panel. Open and friendly, he takes the time to speak with me as we travel across the dull, worn carpet of the hotel hall. As we stroll, he tells me about himself and the family from which he inherited his great fortune.

Monsieur Montparnasse comes from an offset of a French timeline event in history in which the French Revolution never happened, allowing the aristocracy to reach unchecked heights of pretention and power over the lower classes. He is a man of great wealth and means. He has the weapons of his royal status secured in a hilt by his side and a pair of rose-gold-tinted spectacles that, when he is wearing them, block out anyone from his gaze who is below such an Alt history poverty line. He "sees" very few people with them on, only acknowledging other nobly dressed players as they stream down the hall.

Encrusted in "jewels" (remarkably well-tinted craft store gems hot glued to the barrel), Monsieur Montparnasse's gun is deliberately (even within the altered reality) all for show—a family heirloom meant to impress as he walks the halls among the lower classes. I discover this fact by asking him how his gun works, the kind of ammunition it is designed to fire, and in what circumstances he is inclined to draw it.

"*Mon Dieu!* I don't think this thing has fired in over a century!" he informs me, peering over his spectacles so that he might take in my less-than-noble form. Not since his great-great-great-grandfather has a member of his esteemed family had to do something so crass as fire the weapon that rests gleaming—and apparently impotent—in his hilt. I ask him what would happen, then, if he ever needed to shoot it. He's a man of stature, after all. Surely he has enemies that would wish him harm. He shudders at the thought. "Oh heavens no. That's what I have people for. They are some of the best! Incredibly discrete; I never even see them!" He leans forward, voice lowered into a stage whisper as if to conceal some grand conspiracy from any prying ears, "Could you imagine doing such dirty work? I shudder to think it; these gloves are imported imperial silk." The gloves he wears are indeed quite nice. A quality thread count of eggshell and cream; they are not meant for such stains.

For Sebastiantine Montparnasse, in a manner that would prove true for most performative participants in the scene, his gun is not simply an accessory but a *symbol*. An object meant to be read and understood as a text. In Montparnasse's case, in the recounting of his world build, his family history, and his family's position within this alternative space, the gun serves as a parody of status, wealth, impotence, inheritance, familial lineage, and kinship through its status as an inherited object. The gun is an object for show: its meaning far from subtle. Or, as Montparnasse himself summates it, "You can tell a lot about a man by the size of his *gun*, don't you think?" To which another participant, Martha Merryweather, whose velvet-handled snub nose revolver rests much more discreetly next to her tube of "honey and crimson" lipstick at her side, quickly cut in, "Yes, and it must be such a pity for you that yours doesn't work."

Not all Alt history tales contain such opulence. In stark opposition to the flashy symbology of Montparnasse's sidearm and his noble pedigree, camped out across the very same hall and waiting patiently outside one of the Sheraton's conference rooms for another panel to begin, were a band of three dystopic "Great Atomic West" survivors, also known as "The West Atomic Three." As Montparnasse and Merryweather sashay off down the hall to greet a freshly arrived acquaintance, I turn to this subset gathering of folk and they indulge me in conversation about their backgrounds as they wait. In short, the apocalypse had happened after a nuclear blast. Not an Atomic Age blast, mind you. This was no Cold War. A peculiar scientist, eccentric and overzealous, had, in the year 1952, managed to perfect his own personal time traveling device using an atomic core. Carelessly, he traveled back to the American Old West and inadvertently introduced atomic energy into the timeline a century prior to the historical cannon. The technology was circulated across the Great Plains and a few "wrong hands" later, the blast went off: 1836 and the great American West had been transformed into a nuclear wasteland. There wasn't much left outside of the lodes and ore. The metals of the earth, at least, were still out there. The gold rush still happened, only the minerals panned from the crags and streams were usually used to make weapons. The wildlife had all but dissipated, and merely living was some hard and gritty stuff. "We shoot what we can find," one said, rather cryptically.

In keeping with their harrowing tale, the trio's guns cultivate a distinct appearance from the frivolous elite. They couldn't care less about jewels and gold. Gold isn't even worth what it could have been. "Hypothetically," they told me, "if the world hadn't 'gone to shit,' maybe gold could have been used as currency or something." As it stands, gold isn't very useful in a postapocalyptic West. It's a pretty soft metal after all, which makes it pretty useless. But it still goes into the builds where it can. They might as well try to work with it. There aren't that many people left and "the stuff" (i.e., gold) is everywhere. The real challenge when it comes to wielding a weapon in the West is the visibility. "The sun's all but disappeared," No. 3 tells me. "I think they call it a *nuclear winter*, but it ain't as cold as it is dark. It's all that damn dust; it blocks out the sun." To compensate for the dark, the trio's weapons all support their own light sources, sconce pockets with drilled-in Edison bulbs that are powered by the radioscopic packs at their hilts. A far cry from the never fired, luxury sidearms of the extremely noble Frenchmen, the trio's guns (within the narrative of their alternate history) work. They can't afford for them not to. Their troop moves around too much to carry a worthless hunk of metal. All objects must contribute or be left behind.

Figure 6.4. Caledonian Railway Rifle by Tom Fowler.

Figure 6.5. Full-Automatic by Steampunk Laboratory.

Outside of the trio's nuclear narrative, the AH apocalyptic gun has a cultivated aesthetic all its own. There are many dystopic and apocalypse performances in the scene, and although the causes and time periods may change from tale to tale, different dystopic tales do tend to yield similar agreements on the resulting weapon. In times of dystopic duress, there is no time for frivolity. Firearms are welded together from whatever material can be chiseled from the land. For many dystopic-style guns in the scene, the ammunition takes on a more prominent visual space, long strands of bullets and other possible projectiles become a part of the spectacle, ready to be fed through the gears in a seemingly unending chain. The silent agreement among the dystopic set of AH narratives is that postapocalypse guns look meaner: ready to fight—to be *used*. There are no flashy jewels, no colorful paints. They are still guns for show, but what they are intending to reveal is a very different message. In these Alt history timelines, there is no question that the dystopic gun is designed to shoot, incapacitate, and kill. These guns

Figure 6.6. Sewing Machine Gatling Gun by Anthony Sumra, close up (Maker on Etsy @ LaBoutique Vapeur).

are their own warning of survival hard-earned through the upper hand, symbols of fear, power, necessity, and desperation.

The stories told by and through the AH weapons and their bearers continue on. A woman, Maggie Singer, regales me with tales of her Gatling gun, *Molly*, fashioned from the leftover body and guts of an old sewing machine. She is a pioneering feminist preparing to radicalize the poor conditions of the sweatshop factories like the one she works in. "And they say all we woman can do is sew," she stage-whispers in fervent glee. A man, Gustaf Danielsson, the great Arctic explorer, shows me his gun, the *Gustaf Glaciator*, that he had designed for hunting trolls. "It was supposed to be a freeze ray," he laments. "And it is. Only I didn't think about how, well, trolls are used to the cold, you see, so a freeze ray only really slows them down." The *Glaciator* glows from where it rests on the table, its swollen, sizeable middle glowing a pale glacial blue that stands out against its bronze encasement. "It's powered by temporally unstable alien crystals," he explained, harvested from a secret underground cache that he had found in a deep cave on one of his far northern expeditions. Secret or not, such otherworldly power crystals were not unlike the plasma blasters of Radical Rod, a Victorian Frenchman who had traveled to the moon and brought back a curious rock that now powered his steel. "It doesn't shoot with very splendid accuracy on earth," he shrugs. "I suppose it makes sense that it works better on the moon; things do shoot differently without gravity." And yet, he still felt justified in employing the strange new source of power in his gun. "It's a brand-new science!" he exclaims. "What else would a man do with such a thing if not weaponize it?" As for Tony Ballard-Smoot, a regular in the scene who has cultivated many personas and tales within the community over the years, he likes his guns subtle yet seen. "I carry my gun at all times," he says, gesturing to the sleek outlines of his pistol that visibly rests, casual and unassuming, in its holster. "My airship has a large crew; how else are they supposed to know I'm the captain?" Guns are, after all, symbols of power and he's the one that's in charge.

The meanings to be found among these narratives are often tongue in cheek, presenting the gun in a variety of ways that both celebrate and yet poke fun at the variety of ways a weapon might function for its bearer. For Singer, the gun becomes an emblem of cleverness, justice, vengeance, and the reconstruction of female empowerment in a patriarchal society. For Danielsson and Rod, the gun can be a showcase of alternative technologies (including ones that don't quite turn out as planned), a harvested display of the thin line between exploration and imperial expansion, as well as a parody, in Rod's case, of the historical tendency to weaponize any new discovery. The ignorant follies of men who use science for violent delights "just because they can."

It is throughout these performances that the meaning-making of the gun within the (alternative) reality of the cosplay and the reality of real life often begin to blur in curious and complicated ways—particularly in the cases when the Alt history guns are carried by cosplayers who themselves in some way feel unwelcome, uninterested, or uneasy about guns from canonical history. Such is the case with Tony Ballard-Smoot. In speaking later that day at a costuming panel, Ballard-Smoot further contextualized the empowerment of his choice to bear cosplay arms in an AH timeline in terms of his own racial identity as it stood within the context of canonical history, noting,

> I'm often asked why I don't just, you know, cosplay within the realms of actual history. And I'm like, well . . . because I'm black, so that doesn't work out so well for me. . . . In a steampunk verse, I can go on expeditions with guns, in diesel punk, I can be the captain of a helium airship. It's whatever I want [to be] on my terms. (Tony Ballard-Smoot, Dragon Con 2018)

Meanwhile, Maggie Singer, in speaking about her experience with gender and history, shared that before "going rogue" she had tried to participate in the Society for Creative Anachronism, a seventeenth-century historical reenactment group, which, ironically, isn't too keen on anachronisms. As such, "They weren't too keen on me putting on pants and carrying a gun around, because women didn't *do* that sort of thing during the time. Where's the fun in that?! I'm like, but I want a gun too!!" (Maggie Singer, Dragon Con 2018).

Ay-leen, another well-known participant in the scene, has sought out new ways to reclaim her identity as an Asian woman within the space of a reimagined history by subverting the weapon-bound narratives of colonial imperialism. Ay-leen's gun, *The Peacemaker*, shines as an eye-catching emblem of this endeavor. The name, more popularly associated in the American West as the nickname of the Colt .45—the "Single Army Issue revolver created in 1873 and dubbed 'the gun that won the American West'"—shares that moniker (canonically in history) with a Chinese design for a fourteenth-century handheld rocket launcher (Djeli Clark). Carried by the Chinese infantry, this model never developed into a civilian street gun. Only in Ay-leen's recreated model in an alternative time, it has—her gun becoming a narrative transformed into a "tool of conquest refitted and re-imagined from a different history and cultural context, a declaration that practically shouts: 'OH YEAH? COLONIZE THIS!'" (Djeli Clark). For Ay-leen, the draw of the cosplay gun goes beyond the mere meaning-making of the gun as a textual object to stress and encompass the people, bodies, and cultures that the canonical history of the gun has affected in troubling ways. The reworked tales serving "as a chance to rewrite the typical white, male-oriented, European-dominated past to reflect voices that have been silenced, ignored, or oppressed" (Vandermeer 2011, 148).

And this is why that, alongside the impossibility of unraveling the material from the textual, so too are the "alternative" and the "reality" forever tied within an AH cosplay performance. For it is through the consideration of what makes an Alt history gun *alternative*, that the viewer/reader comes to understand not only something about the role of the gun in its Alt history narrative, but also in the canonically understood "master history" that the AH is deviating from. The space of the Alt history cosplay allows for not only a restructuring of the aesthetic design and cultural power value of the firearm, but also reconstrues the notion of who can bear or wield it and for what purpose(s). And through the performance of this reconstruction, the weighted difference between the "alternative" and the "historical" is brought into stark relief—particularly when the AH gun is reimagined, recentered, and resituated in the hands of women, people of color, "geeks," and any others occupying bodies and identities not traditionally associated with the hypermasculinity of military gun culture.

Although the aesthetics, the pieces, the bodies, and the performances of AH gun cosplay come in incredibly diverse variations, ultimately the cumulative folk expressions of the AH gun—from its builds to its bearers—all work together to make a rather unified declarative statement: the gun, as both an object and a symbol, has throughout time left an imprint. No matter how

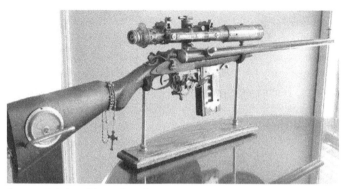

Figure 6.7. *An Industrial Weapon* by Anthony Sumrak (Etsy: La Boutique Vapeur).

alternative the materials, performative uses, or reconstructed histories, the "real world" meanings, uses, and understandings of "The Gun" underline every detail.

THE RIGHT TO BEAR ALTERNATIVE ARMS: THE REFLEXIVE RHETORIC OF "ALTERNATIVE REALITY"

These are only a few gun tales told within Alt history spaces. And yet, taken together, the accumulation of the tales, practices, and materials of the AH realms, presents a rich cacophony of manufactured traditions and lore. From tale to tale, the guns and the personas who bear them often carry an incredible amount of thought-through detail—well-worked and often retold oral histories that are freely passed around in whatever venue the cosplay is performed in. Each tale's aesthetic and build is unique, and yet they are unified, bound together by the shared agreement of performative exploration and assembly. And at the center of this performative collision of object and text, the DIY Alt history firearm occupies several important and pivotal roles within cosplay identities and customs. The material-semiotics of the AH objects and their texts at once present the AH gun as

- A physical material object of folk art, espousing the unique aesthetic values of alternative and imagined histories;
- A physical byproduct of the story and verbal creative process of both world and character building (one that, in turn, helps enforce and enhance its own tales);
- A physical synecdoche of a cosplayer's adopted identity—a distilled part, which reveals the larger identities of the bearer that holds it;

- A crucial object/tool used in the ritualistic performance of posing and/or play; and
- More abstractly, a certain kind of commentary—be it a parody, reflection, celebration, or criticism—of guns: their symbols, meanings, users, and uses throughout history

That last one is often so taken for granted in the scene that it is rarely explicitly discussed, but at the same time it is always present. It is simply inescapable. The text of *alternative history* guns and *known history* guns are two sides of the same coin, all wrapped up in the material-semiotics of The Gun. Akin to the way in which the material and the textual are inevitably inseparable constructs, the understood and agreed-upon "alternate reality" in cosplay and the reality of real life can never be fully severed from one another. After all, it is hard to have an *alternative history* without consideration of the base counterpoints to a known and canonical *history*.

On this account, although AH guns are, on the material surface, fascinating material objects as a folk art of a vibrant folk culture, at the end of the day, so too do these crystalline lasers, dystopic twists of metal, and jewel-encrusted hilts, end up, despite their fantastical encasements, having some surprisingly strong parallels in practice and meaning with guns in real life. This overlap is by and large revealed in the easy accessibility for an audience in reading the AH gun's symbolic and performative meanings. The notion that the semiotics of the Alt history gun, each occupying such widely divergent Alt history narratives as they do, are each still readily read and understood by the spectators that behold them is a telling one. That Montparnasse's gun easily flashes its heirloom status of unearned yet inherited power, dazzling in its spectacle of excess and wealth, or that the Trio's gritty mangle of ammo and scrap metal screams with a desperate force of a constantly war-ravaged land, or even that the alien twist of Gustaf's Arctic light can be instinctually understood as a weaponized threat when reconfigured into the right angles, says something about the narrative's recipient audience as much as it does its teller.

The audience can understand the meaning of an Alt history gun because they understand the meaning of *guns*. Because just like their status as material objects in the cosplay realms, guns are meaning-making objects in our known world as well. And the meanings derived from the AH tales aren't all that different from one construction of reality to another. Principally because the meanings across all times and places when it comes to the gun are many. The Alt history gun, depending on the context of the use, design, creation, community, and bearer, can symbolize power, impotence, wealth,

Figure 6.8. *Goliathon* by Esty maker Professor T. Lemetry.

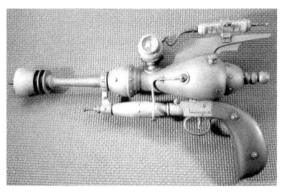

Figure 6.9. *Anti-Gravitational Blaster* by BackLotStudios.

Figure 6.10. *The Timekeeper* by Paul Baker (Etsy: Steampunk Guns UK).

poverty, status, war, greed, safety, threat, nationalism, terror, respect, occupation, masculinity, feminism, freedom, oppression, imperialism, violence, peace, political affiliation, ethnicity, desperation, pride, and the list goes on. These meanings are not foreign concepts to the known historical and present reality. The stories told through the AH gun are, at their core, familiar, even recognizable, because we have already heard their message before.

And that is why the AH guns "work" as guns. The AH gun is real within the context of its own AH world, functioning not as real-world guns do in terms of their ability to shoot but in the same way that real-world guns also act as symbolic objects that reflect the conditions and purpose of their manufacture and carry with them highly specific meanings and values to individual bearers. Overall, the performances of Alt history firearms serve as one big thought experiment on just how many different things a gun can symbolize—how many different forms of meaning a gun can bear, and the ways in which the past plays a role in the continued status, use, function, and importance of guns in the present. The thought process of the AH gun is an empathetically fascinating one not only on account of its creativity, but also in the way in which the cosplay performance in turn highlights how the underlying queries, narratives, and constructed materials might apply to our own known historical relationship with guns, which (as explored further by the authors in this very anthology) also act in their own right as a certain kind of cultural folk object which has undergone centuries of aesthetic and functional choices based on the factors of available technologies, politics, market demands, etc.

By stripping the gun of its ballistic functions to focus fully on the gun's function as a symbolic object to be read, understood, and *seen*, the Alt history performance highlights the multitude of ways that guns are indeed read, carried, and used symbolically every day, both presently, and historically, and demonstrates just how important symbology is in how firearms function in daily life. Through the open display of the Alt history gun as a material text, the gunplay of AH cosplay invites—sometimes even challenges—the spectator to consider more critically the historical narrative of their own material realities. Because above all else, the AH gun posits that guns are even more than a *symbol*—guns are *textually material*: objects deeply rooted in multiple realities as they travel through time, place, and culture. Each gun is an object culturally bound, but individually carried, and it takes on itself the burden of bearing the meaning(s) assigned by both its community and its carrier, even when the result is often a paradox. The gun *speaks*, not only as an emblem of its bearer, but further carries with it all the shadows, shine, and trappings of its own history. And with so many voices—so many *histories*—it has a lot to say. The gun is a symbol, yes, but, as the scraps of Nerf, steel, plastic and gold transformed into well-worn tales remind us, that reduction may even still be a little too simple. For, through all the weight of its symbolic burdens and celebrations, the gun is also an art, a narrative, *a story*.

Note

1. Those in the scene who make the weapons or other items such as clothing and other accessories (either for themselves, their friends, or to sell) are, appropriately enough,

referred to as "makers." It is not a requirement to be a maker to participate in the scene. Not everyone in the community makes their own wares and it is completely acceptable, if not sometimes a little encouraged, to complete one's cosplay persona with the help of other artists and makers in the scene. Outfitting a cosplayer is a group effort, one that thrives on a circular symbiotic relationship between "the makers" and "the buyers." As one participant and guest speaker explained from their perch behind a panel table on "DYI accessorizing in the scene," the Alt history track "is a world saturated with makers."

References

Cherry, Brigid. 2016. *Cult Media, Fandom, and Textiles: Handicrafting as Fan Art*. London; Oxford; New York; New Delhi; Sydney: Bloomsbury.

Djeli Clark, Phenderson. 2013. "Steampunk, Guns, and the Imperial Mission." *The Musings of a Disgruntled Haradrim*. https://disgruntledharadrim.com/2013/12/05/steampunk-guns-and-the-imperial-mission/.

Hale, Matthew. 2013. "Airship Captains, Pith Helmets, & Other Assorted Brassy Bits: Steampunk Personas and Material-Semiotic Production." *New Directions in Folklore* 11, no. 1: 3–34.

Hills, Matt. 2014. "From Dalek half balls to Daft Punk helmets: Mimetic fandom and the crafting of replicas." *Transformative Works and Cultures* 16. http://journal.transforma tiveworks.org/index.php/twc/article/view/531/448

Lamerichs, Nicolle. 2011. "Stranger Than Fiction: Fan Identity in Cosplaying." *Transformative Works and Cultures* 7.

Lamerichs, Nicolle. 2018. "Embodied Characters: The Affective Process of Cosplay." *Intermediality and Affective Reception in Fan Cultures*. Amsterdam University Press.

Menchen, Carson and Paul Froese. 2017. "Gun Culture in America." *Social Problems* 66, no. 1: 3–27.

Metzl, Johnathan. 2019. "What Guns Mean: The Symbolic Lives of Firearms." Palgrave Communications 5, no. 35: page #–#.

Okabe, Daisuke. 2012. "Cosplay, Learning, and Cultural Practice." In *Fandom Unbound: Otaku Culture in a Connected World*, edited by Mizuko Ito, Daisuke Okabe, and Izumi Tsuji, 225–49. New Haven: Yale University Press.

Scott, Suzanne. 2015. "'Cosplay Is Serious Business': Gendering Material Fan Labor on 'Heroes of Cosplay.'" *Cinema Journal* 54, no. 3: 146–154.

Stanfill, Mel, and Megan Condis. 2014. "Fandom and/as Labor." *Transformative Works and Cultures* 15.

Vall, Renée van de. 2008. *At the Edges of Vision: A Phenomenological Aesthetics of Contemporary Spectatorship, Histories of Vision*. Farnham: Ashgate.

Vandermeer, Jeff. 2011. *The Steampunk Bible*. New York: Harry N. Abrams.

Vlach, John Michael. 1980. "American Folk Art: Questions and Quandaries." *Winterthur Portfolio* 15, no. 4: 345–55.

Winge, Theresa. 2006. "Costuming the Imagination: Origins of Anime and Manga Cosplay." *Mechademia* 1: 65–76.

Chapter 7

GOD'S WARRIORS

Gunlore and Identity in the Vernacular Discourse
of a Survivalist Community

MEGAN L. ZAHAY

Shortly after rioters entered the Senate chamber of the US Capitol building on January 6, 2021, a conspiracy theorist known as the "QAnon Shaman," Jake Angeli, stood on the rostrum and began a prayer:

Thank you heavenly father for gracing us with this opportunity to stand up for our God-given inalienable rights. Thank you heavenly father for being the inspiration needed to these police officers to allow us into the building, to allow us to exercise our rights, to allow us to send a message to all the tyrants, the communists, and the globalists that this is our nation not theirs, that we will not allow the American way, of the United States of America, to go down. (*New Yorker* 2021)

As he continued this prayer, Angeli's comrades in the Capital building riot moved through the Senate chamber fumbling through desks, stealing documents, taking photographs, and even making phone calls.

Unlike most prayers performed in the Capital building, this one carried a distinctly embattled tone and war-like significance. While Angeli himself sported Norse neo-pagan tattoos, face-paint, and a now infamous horned fur Viking-style hat, many of those before him in the room and others outside it who participated in the riot that day wore much more militaristic attire: camouflage, fatigues, helmets, gloves, MOLLE belt-pouches and backpacks, even zip-tie restraints. Many of the insurrectionists carried guns (Neidig 2021) and looked similar to others who had staged armed protests at state capitols across the country in the preceding months (Censky 2020).

Angeli's prayer is only one prominent example of the religious meaning that infuses recent antigovernment demonstrations at federal and state capitols throughout the United States. Such demonstrations frame political decision-making not as a process of rational deliberation, but rather as a battle between good and evil, for the soul of the country itself. In addition to Angeli's prayer, participants at the January 6 insurrection carried other indications of their religious framing of the event: "Jesus Fish" flags waved in the crowd, some bore signs reading "Jesus Saves," and others used their signs to liken Democratic leaders to Satan (Barrett and Zapotosky 2021; Posner 2021; Schor 2021; Stelloh 2021). This marriage of apocalyptic Christianity and antigovernment sentiment is not new. From at least the 1790s until today, extremist strands of Christianity have struggled against governments they viewed as corrupt both in Europe and the United States (Aho 1996, 190). Such belief systems have framed the government as an evil or satanic force that must be defeated through such violent insurgencies.

This chapter examines a survival manual produced by one such group in the 1980s, known as "The Covenant, the Sword, and the Arm of the Lord," or CSA, who viewed themselves as God's warriors in an apocalyptic struggle against the United States government. I will attend to the ways in which the gun, as a material artifact rhetorically deployed in the manual, facilitates the vernacular performance of the CSA's religious identity and their perceived role as God's warriors. Outfitted as armed combatants, the CSA draws on a long history of gunlore in the United States to make real their divine struggle against the federal government.

In the US, the gun is a pervasive symbol of anti-institutional authority with broad cultural significance. Enshrined in the Constitution's Second Amendment, the symbol of gun has taken on varied cultural meanings that extend far beyond the specific symbolism of militia groups like the CSA. We see this significance manifested in the popularity of magazines like *Guns & Ammo*, the wide accessibility of guns for purchase at both specialty and big box stores, gun hobby groups and shooting ranges, and gun interest communities online such as *Gun and Game* and the *Firearms Forum*. Through its cultural significance the gun also carries great political weight, perhaps best demonstrated in the powerful influence of the National Rifle Association (NRA) lobbying organization. At a more granular level, the figure of the nuclear family in the United States also emerges as an important site of development for the cultural meaning associated with guns. Older generations pass on the material artifacts and shared rituals of gun use, and these sociocultural traditions yield a sense of shared identity and generational continuity. All combined, these cultural facets of gun symbolism work together to create a powerful and pervasive gunlore that can be levied to make social and political claims.

Due to its far-reaching cultural significance, the gun is a symbol that people can use to make arguments about themselves, their community, or their cause. Indeed, it is nearly impossible to pick up a gun in the United States without participating in this symbolic milieu. The gun is thus both a functional tool and a multifaceted bearer of meaning. When used for a religious cause, the gun can take on universal significance.

In what follows, I explore how artifacts like the gun enable the performance of religious identity by *materializing* beliefs about the supernatural. I examine a vernacular survival how-to manual produced by CSA that seeks to equip its readers to fight on behalf of God in the coming apocalyptic battle with the forces of Satan, often represented as the United States federal government. The CSA's presentation of the gun in their survival manual seeks to draw on its cultural salience in antigovernment lore, and, by engaging in this tradition of militaristic adornment, individuals in this community mark their shared identity as warriors in an apocalyptic battle. I argue that for the CSA, the gun materializes the religious identity of God's chosen warriors, bestowing its bearers with the prophetic authority to manifest God's will in the mundane world.

The chapter begins by situating CSA in the wider milieu of gunlore and specifically at the confluence of apocalyptic Christianity and militia culture. It then recounts the emergence of CSA's religious beliefs and turn toward violence, ultimately leading to a standoff with the FBI that would later be compared to the now legendary standoffs at Ruby Ridge and Waco. Within this context, I turn to the CSA survival manual, a vernacular document created to equip like-minded believers to face off against the US government. While such communities are often relatively closed to outsiders, this community-produced document combined with later public reflections by ex-members offers powerful insights on the role of the gun and gunlore in this community.

SITUATING THE CSA IN GUNLORE

Occupying a place within the extremist fringe of gun culture, the CSA is primarily remembered through its connections to the actions of more well-known antigovernment actors and groups. One such action is the 1995 bombing of the Alfred P. Murrah Federal building in Oklahoma City, Oklahoma. On April 19 of that year, Timothy McVeigh carried out what was at the time the deadliest domestic terrorism incident in US history (Thomas and Smothers 1995).

Though McVeigh is often presented as a "lone wolf" terrorist, there were speculations that he was connected to the underground militia movement in the US (Juergensmeyer 2003, 118). The same day as the bombing, approximately five hundred miles away in Lincoln County, Arkansas, a man named Richard Wayne Snell was executed for the shooting murder of a Black state trooper. Before his arrest and time on death row, Snell had been a leader in the CSA.

This organization's members adhered to the Christian Identity movement, a white supremacist and anti-Semitic version of Christianity which posits that white people are the true lost tribe of Israel and therefore God's chosen race. CSA believed that it was their responsibility to help bring on and fight in a race war that would signify the End Times, and they acted as the "arm of the Lord" on Earth through their religious activities along with firearms and tactical training. While the group was not successful in carrying out a major terrorist attack, their members did engage in criminal activity, sometimes violent and deadly, and harbored members of other prominent white supremacist organizations, such as the Order, within their compound.

McVeigh denied that his choice of date for the Murrah building attack was influenced by Snell's execution, though it was later learned that he had placed a phone call to a compound known as Elohim City, previously home to Snell, just a week before the deadly bombing was carried out (Michel and Herbeck 2001, 317). Adding to speculation that there was a connection between the events, Snell had reportedly seen news coverage of the Murrah bombing earlier in the day and commented ahead of his execution, "Governor Tucker, look over your shoulder; justice is coming" (*New York Times* 1995).

Undeniably, however, and by McVeigh's own admission, his actions were influenced by antigovernment sentiments nourished in the lore of religious gun culture. Instead of connecting his attack to Snell, McVeigh cited instances of what he felt were government overreach or aggression against armed religious groups. One of those incidents was another April 19 event, the 1993 standoff between Branch Davidians and FBI agents at the Mount Carmel Center in Waco, Texas. He also cited the 1992 Ruby Ridge standoff, which occurred in August of that year, as an additional aggravating factor. In addition to these stated motivations, McVeigh was found to be carrying an illustrated copy of *The Turner Diaries*, an enduringly popular 1978 white supremacist novel about a violent overthrow of the US government, in his pocket the day of the bombing (Macdonald 1978).

All these events, places, and artifacts became powerful shared symbols in discourses about governmental oppression and, in different degrees, still motivate antigovernment extremist violence in the United States to the present day. Waco and Ruby Ridge especially, both the site of deadly standoffs with the FBI, have emerged as among the most well-known antigovernment lore, particularly for their communities' religious beliefs and willingness to defend them using firearms.

While the bombing of the Murrah building has taken its place alongside Waco and Ruby Ridge within the symbolic lexicon of antigovernment activism in the United States, others, like the CSA, have nearly faded out of public memory. In such cases, groups' specific religious beliefs, particularly those that envision an apocalyptic battle, have been cited as one motivation for their antigovernment stance and tendency to stockpile weapons (Aho 1996, 192; Juergensmeyer 2003, 36; Kerstetter 2012, 133).[1] What has been less explored, however, is the extent to which the material artifacts of their daily life as they carried out preparations for the possibility of religious war—the knife, the gun, the army fatigues, the fortified compound—have themselves served as vernacular markers of religious identity. To the extent that guns function as such a marker for the CSA and other religious communities, we must understand their use as inherently religious rather than simply functional.

IDENTITY, APOCALYPTICISM, AND GUNLORE

All cultural formations participate in the construction of identity through shared sets of symbolic resources, often mobilized through folklores (Dundes 1984). Material objects, spaces, and bodies can have important constitutive functions in generating identity (Jones 2007; Otero 2020). These artifacts, as enduring human creations, reveal our experience in ways that may be unexpressed through verbal languages. For Babcock (1992), "Cultures not only create, represent, and re-create their distinctive patterns through what they say and do, but through articulations of the material world, and . . . the former not only can be but, in many cases, can only be reconstructed and 'read' through the latter" (205).

These artifacts work alongside speech and text to construct an environment that itself argues for the ontological reality of the desired subject positions (Charland 1987). Blair (2001) and Landau (2016) argue that we must account for the way that spaces and the objects within them invite or even affect particular responses in their inhabitants. The unique experience of ritual, at once discursive and material, is a space in which "the most abstract and distant of conceptions are bound to the most immediate and substantial of experiences" (Rappaport 1992, 259). For these authors, material spaces themselves construct the subject positions of participants through their suggestion of realities that invite those subjects to feel, act, and think in ways ideologically contiguous with their experience. Deployed in the context of this religious community and as presented in their survival manual, the material artifact of the gun calls up the apocalyptic narrative to manifest the identity of God's warriors. In this way, the gun and the CSA's performance of it makes the apocalyptic narrative a tangible part of the believer's reality. This is not to say that the belief is real or unreal, but rather that its manifestation is, for the believer, the reality of it, in the sense in which Eliade asserted, "Where the sacred manifests itself in space, *the real unveils itself*, the world comes into existence" (Eliade 1987, 63).

Although for Eliade the sacred is imbued with uniqueness or specialness, others have pointed out that the everyday is an even more fruitful space for the study of religious activity. Meredith McGuire (2008) observes that the actual religious practices of individuals are often only partially or loosely linked to the prescriptions of the formal religious institutions with which they identify, and that therefore analysis of those institutions tells us precious little about the reality of most religious experience. Instead, understanding "religions-as-practiced," what she calls *lived religion*, better elucidates what an individual's religion is, what it means to them, and how it interacts with their world (5). Institutions and labels of identity connected with them, such as saying, "I am Catholic," are an important way that individuals think about themselves and their religious practice, but there are significant differences in how individuals and their communities put that identity into action—practicing Catholicism in New York City vs. in Mexico City, for example. Negro and Berger (2004) caution that "the everyday" is not a static location or time, but rather a dialectical concept dependent on the viewer's perspective: "Everyday life," they explain, "is better understood as an interpretive framework" (4). For many of us, the CSA's apocalyptic religious vision and militaristic practice would not seem "everyday." However, situated within a community and a tradition of far-right apocalyptic Christianity in the United States, the CSA's practices are part of an everyday, lived experience that draws legitimacy through its distance from broadly recognized institutions.

In this space between institutionality and the everyday is where Robert Glenn Howard (2011) locates vernacular authority, drawing on Leonard Primiano's vernacular religion, which invests vernacular practices with authority via their situatedness as noninstitutional. "The term 'vernacular,'" he explains, "refers to noninstitutional beliefs and practices that exist alongside but apart from institutions" (5). Although "the 'vernacular' might support or oppose institutional power . . . it is specifically and consciously the power of not being institutional" (7). In this sense, the religious practice of the CSA is vernacular because it explicitly constructs itself against US federal and secular institutions, and it draws its legitimacy and authority from the premise of being outside of them. Importantly, however, this authority would be impossible if the CSA did not also exist alongside those institutions. Its justification of its own emergence comes from opposing the federal government on behalf of God. If there were no government to oppose, CSA's identity and organization would be fundamentally altered.

Even as CSA positions itself against and apart from the mainstream, they emerge from a broader historical trajectory. There has been a strong tradition of apocalyptic religious belief throughout the history of the United States (Sutton 2014). While it simmers always below the surface, it emerges most poignantly in times of social and political upheaval, providing rationalization of hardships as a salve to believers (Barkun 1997, 45). The apocalyptic narrative argues that there is a hidden structure ordering the world and its terrible events, and that there is a meaningful conclusion to this progression, one in which those who have believed in the hidden order will be saved (32–33). Although there are narratives within many religious traditions that can be described as apocalyptic, the genre refers especially to Christian dispensationalism. In this belief system, the apocalyptic event is seen as a final standoff between good and evil, personified in the figures of God and Satan. In this standoff, God will ultimately triumph and reward the believer who has represented his will on Earth in the final days.

For this reason, the believer's identity as saved or chosen is a key component of vernacular apocalyptic belief and practices, which often revolve around the establishment of this identity. Since God's sovereignty over historical events relies on faith and is not made readily apparent in the world, at least to those who lack proper knowledge and belief, the significance of such events must be decoded by the believer so that they can be made sensible within the apocalyptic narrative. This decoding relies upon a subject who understands themselves as saved and imbued with a special capacity to see the relationship between historical events and the prophecies of the Bible (O'Leary 1994, 52). O'Leary argues that "the authority of the prophet comes from a divine gift, a privileged vision of the realm of the sacred" (53). As this capability to see the divinely ordained nature of historical events is a gift from God, prophetic authority affirms God's sovereignty over the world while investing the prophet with the special quality of being chosen by him. The identity of the believer as chosen, and their consequent status as "in the know," is therefore singularly important to establishing their authority.

This prophetic authority constructs a worldview in which the believer is distinguished among nonbelievers, and indeed views nonbelievers as antagonists who are destructive of the world as God intended it to be. It does not, at least explicitly, allow for a plurality of beliefs or truths, but rather forwards a severe dichotomy between faith and folly, good and evil, the saved and the damned. What's more, those identified as nonbelievers are understood to pose an active threat to believers and must therefore be vanquished. For this reason, Robert Glenn Howard observes that apocalypticism "encourages believers to think of themselves as warriors in a mythic struggle against all who disagree" (Howard 2011, 15). This sense of a mythic struggle positions believers as a bulwark against the activities of Satan in the world. Investing oneself with prophetic authority thus necessitates the forwarding of a warrior identity. This identity suggests that believers should actively fight against what they perceive as Satan's influence in the world, and thus vernacular apocalyptic belief has historically inspired a range of actions, up to and including violence, buttressed by faith in the finality of God's victory (Brummett 1991, 32).

Often, these battles became tied to political ends. In its early years apocalyptic evangelicalism in the US was viewed as isolationist and apolitical, its believers waiting on the supernatural action of God to restore what they viewed as a failing social order. By the end of World War II, however, American evangelicalism had taken on an explicitly political tone, particularly in conservative fundamentalist circles. Matthew Avery Sutton (2014) observes, "By the end of the fight fundamentalists had done what just a few years earlier had seemed almost unthinkable—they had baptized Christian fundamentalism in the waters of patriotic Americanism" (266). While this political activity sought to redress a feeling of cultural disempowerment and even victimization in the postwar years by restoring traditionalist values, and often did so motivated by an apocalyptic theology, the work was carried out through electoral rather than violent channels (Shuck, 60). It was not until years later amidst their growing discontent with Vietnam that some extremist, white supremacist strains of Christian fundamentalism became explicitly tied to a project of antigovernment violence.

This was particularly the case in what became known as the militia movement. Historian Kathleen Belew (2018) argues that the white power militia movement emerged as a response to Vietnam and many of its members' experience in the military service. Participants were quite literally "bringing the war home," as suggested by her book's title, to address grievances with domestic society and government (3). Many were unhappy with discontinuities between Reagan's campaign promises and the policies he delivered, disillusioning them to mainstream conservatism. Instead, they sought to forge a new path that would ultimately lead them toward violent revolutionary action (4).

While the white power militia movement incorporated some elements of early twentieth-century Ku Klux Klan Christianity, it was also theologically distinct from it, and there remains some conflict within groups concerning their religious identity (Belew 2018, 3; Baker 2011). Belew explains that after the Cold War, some rejected Christianity and instead "adopted Odinism and other forms of neo-Pagan white supremacy that posited a shared, pan-European white cultural heritage" (6). Many of the most visible and violent white supremacist groups, however, upheld a modified version of Christianity known as "Christian Identity," in which white supremacy and violence were themselves key components of religious faith (6). In this belief, "whites were the lost tribe of Israel and . . . nonwhites and Jews were descended from Satan or from animals" (6). Descended from British-Israelism and modified to explicit anti-Semitism, today Christian Identity beliefs unite many white supremacist groups, including some segments of the Ku Klux Klan, Aryan Nations, the Aryan Republican Army, and of course the CSA.

By the mid- to late-1980s, far-right leaders were explicitly linking their gun use to their religious beliefs. Responding to federal gun-control efforts after the 1989 Stockton shooting, Pete Peters, leader of *Scriptures for America*, produced a pamphlet called *Everything You Wanted to Know (and Preachers Were Afraid to Tell You) about Gun Control*. In it, he proclaimed, "The sword of that day [Bible times] was A LEATHAL WEAPON, equivalent in our time to a pistol, a rifle, a machine gun and, yes, an assault rifle" (Burlein 2002, 96). Ann Burlein observes that "many gun owners read the Second Amendment as a sacred covenant" (96). Burlein also draws on James Gibson's view that "from this religious or mythological perspective, the semiautomatic combat rifle came to symbolize the entire American creation myth, and gun control in turn represented an abridgement of God's covenant by the forces of evil'" (97).

As public discourse surrounding gun control ignites controversy today, far-right conservatives have continued to draw on this legacy of the gun as a sacred covenant with God. Julie Ingersoll and Sarah Posner (2010), in an article for *Religion Dispatches*, report that today the militia movement benefits from its interactions with Christian Reconstructionists, who "both contend that our current civil government, most especially the federal government, is illegitimate: that it has overreached the limits of its divinely ordained authority, and that it continues to do so." Here, the legitimacy and authority of the federal government is questioned not as a political issue, but as a distinctly religious one in which government should be subject to biblical law. In Ingersoll and Posner's interview with Larry Pratt, executive director of Gun Owners of America, Pratt explained, "When we're talking about firearms, we're not really talking about a right but an obligation, as creatures of God, to protect the life that was given them" (Ingersoll and Posner 2018). So framed, the gun is a means through which God not only enables but *obliges* his people to defend themselves against what is unbiblical in society, including the federal government.

For the CSA, as I will argue below, it is likewise the case that the gun represents a sacred covenant with God. But more than a mere representation or symbol of that covenant, proficiency with firearms, in addition to other survivalist tactics, renders the bearer into an actant of God's providence, literally carrying out his will on earth as "the arm of the Lord." In this way, the Second Amendment's "right to bear arms" becomes a divine right bestowed directly upon man by God. While the Constitution, as the founding document of a country understood by CSA to be itself divinely ordained, may recognize this right, the right does not emanate from it. In the performance of bearing arms in the CSA survival manual and their activities more broadly, members materially manifest their divine identity as God's chosen people.

DEVELOPMENT OF THE CSA

While they are unique in many ways, the CSA was not a singular or exceptional organization, and despite their physical separation from society in their compound, they participated enthusiastically in the broader militia movement developing in the 1970s and 1980s. In addition to providing tactical training to likeminded groups, they created propaganda, held conferences, and networked with others to help construct the legacy of right-wing paramilitarism and apocalypticism that we see today. In the materials they produced, particularly the survival manual analyzed in this chapter, CSA helped to link the religious right with antigovernment politics through their use of the gun, which still functions as an important symbolic resource of the religious and political right.

The CSA began as a closed religious community known as Zarephath-Horeb. The Zarephath-Horeb Community Church originally followed a charismatic fundamentalist model of Christianity that focused on speaking in tongues, prophecy, and healing (Quarles 2004, 135). The man who would become its leader was James Ellison, a fundamentalist preacher in San Antonio who had a vision that he should start a community church. To do so, he purchased a plot of land previously owned by Campus Crusade for Christ near the Arkansas-Missouri border, an isolated area close to Bull Shoals Lake (FBI, 2). According to former member and elder in the church Kerry Noble, over time the group became more insular and Ellison gained greater authority, with one scholar describing this period as "more like a cult" (Quarles 2004, 136). During this time, Ellison and the church embraced Christian Identity beliefs and the compound itself went through intense fortification. Through this process, the militaristic arm of Zarephath-Horeb would come to be known as "the Covenant, the Sword, and the Arm of the Lord."

Belew (2018) suggests that it is during this time in 1979 that "violence became part of their day-to-day routine. Their homes had kerosene lanterns and wood-burning stoves, but in their workshops they built silencers, converted weapons from semi- to fully automatic, and produced hand grenades and Claymore-type land mines. They wore camouflage field fatigues and prepared to fight" (139). As they networked with other Christian Identity militia organizations, the group also began to train them in shooting and combat tactics at a facility in their compound created for this purpose, known as Silhouette City. According to FBI documents, training at the compound included:

instruction on organization, survival techniques, and para-military topics. Also taught are firearms and marksmanship, repelling, foraging for food, erection of such obstacles as punji sticks and barbed wire to detour looters, urban warfare, military field craft, national forest survival, home defense, Christian martial arts, Christian military truths, nuclear survival and tax protesting. (FBI, 3)

A poster for a conference held at their compound in 1982 to teach these skills demonstrates the range of their associations with other militia and white supremacist organizations at this time. In addition to its proclamation that "only White, Patriotic, Serious CHRISTIANS need apply" (emphasis in original), the poster announces guest speakers including Robert E. Miles, influential Christian Identity leader, founder of Mountain Church, member of Aryan Nations, and former grand dragon of the KKK (Lindsey 2019). It also included Richard Butler, founder of Aryan Nations and mentor of Ellison, as well as Col. Jack Mohr, another prominent Christian Identity leader and evangelical pastor (SPLC 2003).

The group eventually became known to local law enforcement and the FBI through the criminal activity of its leaders and members, including violent anti-Semitic attacks, transporting stolen property across state lines, and stockpiling weaponry. They were also suspected of harboring wanted members of the white supremacist group the Order, named after a secret society in *The Turner Diaries* novel (the same novel McVeigh carried the day of the Oklahoma City bombing). The FBI feared that the group could be planning an attack against a government building or official, but they also recognized that the CSA identified a range of enemies including "communists, Jews, blacks, halfbreed [sic] Mongoloid sinners, oriental, non-white, IRS, the Federal Reserve System, and the Trilateral Commission" (FBI, 3).

By 1983, the FBI was investigating the possibility of conducting a raid at the CSA compound. These efforts ramped up in July 1984, when leader Richard Wayne Snell shot and killed a Black Arkansas state police officer, and they began making new inquiries with local law enforcement about the activities of the group (9). Local officials said that the group's size had dropped considerably, from between 90 and 122 years earlier, to about sixty by 1984 (9).

This raid eventually did occur on April 20, 1985, when the FBI, ATF, and Missouri and Arkansas state police showed up in force to the compound and began negotiations with Ellison. Despite this show of force, the CSA felt well-prepared for siege by the federal government that they saw as inevitable. In his memoir, former member Kerry Noble explained their preparations:

I didn't think it wise to inform him [the FBI negotiator] that we also had an unlimited water supply, plus five years' worth of food stored at the main settlement. In addition, everyone owned several kerosene lamps, with plenty of kerosene reserves; and with wood stoves to cook on, the government could cut power and the effect would be minimal. We had been preparing for this for seven years. (Noble 2011, 20)

Despite these efforts, officials successfully secured Ellison's surrender in just two days (FBI, 12). There were also, as the FBI had suspected, several members of the Order in the compound as well, who surrendered along with Ellison (17–18). The arrests were made without any violent confrontations, no doubt aided by the large law enforcement presence surrounding the compound. Inside, officials found records of their connections to other white supremacist organizations, stolen vehicles, and a wealth of weaponry, both legal and illegal, including nearly a hundred long guns, thirty-five machine guns and sawed-off shotguns, land mines, grenades, dynamite, and other explosives, along with a 30-gallon drum of cyanide (18, 51). One official, J. W. Hicks, commented in his May 2, 1985, statement regarding the raid that, while successful, greater information about CSA's ties to other white supremacist organizations could have been gleaned by a more careful search.

He remarked that, "The discovery to two FBI fugitives, associated with the Aryan Nations group, inside the CSA compound serves to prove the association of many white hate groups in the US and indicates the necessity for an intensive, long range investigative effort" (34).

James Ellison was sentenced to twenty years in prison for racketeering and mail fraud. Richard Wayne Snell, however, was sentenced to death for shooting a state trooper, a sentence carried out on April 19, 1995, just a few hours after the Oklahoma City bombing. After serving out his prison term, Ellison moved to Elohim City, a compound in Oklahoma founded by Robert Millar, mentor to Ellison and well-known Christian Identity adherent.

Despite the peaceful conclusion of the CSA siege in 1985, the next decade would produce both the Ruby Ridge and Waco standoffs, which both resulted in violence and death. The memory of these events has fueled violent anti-government activism and helped to solidify common cause across the Christian Identity militia movement. For these and other believers, CSA, Ruby Ridge, and Waco confirm the persecution of white Christians by a federal government who usurps God's own authority. To arm themselves and their fellow believers against this persecution and the apocalyptic scenario they felt would ensue, the CSA produced a survival manual. In the next section, I will analyze how CSA used this manual and particularly the object of the gun to demonstrate their identity and authority as, literally, "the Covenant, the Sword, and the Arm of the Lord."

THE CSA SURVIVAL MANUAL

The 1982 manual is a 174-page, self-published, vernacular document that provides instructions to readers about how to prepare for a biblical apocalypse the authors feel is imminent. The document is vernacular in the sense that it does not derive authority from its affiliation with an institutional source. Rather, the manual establishes its authority through visual and textual displays of CSA's tactical and survival prowess, particularly as it draws on the wider vernacular gun culture and lore of the US. Through its textual descriptions and visual imagery of gun use, the manual argues that its authors are warriors in a supernatural battle on God's behalf.

In his memoir, Kerry Noble explains that he contributed to the manual in addition to a number of other manuscripts for CSA, both "as propaganda" and as a way to make money that could be distributed among groups and individuals who shared their ideology. Penning it alongside other CSA members, Noble states that the book "became the training manual for the

176   GUNLORE AND IDENTITY IN A SURVIVALIST COMMUNITY

right-wing, giving instructions in firearms, weapons, knives and gear; personal home defense; how to store food; natural survival; and first-aid and nuclear survival" (Noble 2011, 119). It is important that the document was intended for distribution rather than solely in-group use, as this demonstrates its performative function in establishing how the group sought to be viewed by others.

Of God and Guns

While the manual focuses throughout on the practical aspects of arms training and survival tactics, it emphasizes that these are actually religious practices. The manual opens by proclaiming, "The Lord is exalted. He dwelleth on high. The fear of the Lord is His treasure" (CSA 1982, 1; summarized from Isaiah 33:5–6). In this section, the authors differentiate the manual from that of other survivalists by emphasizing the religious rationale of their work and connecting it to a longer tradition of apocalyptic beliefs. While there are some religious institutions who proclaim apocalyptic doctrines, much apocalyptic discourse is vernacular (Howard 2011). This manual does not merely outline the physical and material preparations for "financial collapse, nuclear war, famine, riots and a host of other calamities," because "they do not reveal all the truth!" (CSA 1982, 1). Instead, the real impetus for survivalism is that "the planet earth is about to become the battleground between the forces of God, led by Jesus Christ, King of Kings, Lord of Lords and the serpent, father of deceit, Satan and his seed, the satanic blood-line Jews and those who have been deceived or bought off" (1). Apocalyptic beliefs such as this proliferate in the American consciousness and have a long history, stemming from the earliest religious traditions of the Puritans (Wojcik 1999, 6). While they are sometimes connected to particular church doctrines, most often such beliefs, like CSA's, are noninstitutional, vernacular expressions that themselves enable religious practice.

For CSA, the work of producing this manual is a divine act, given to them by God to preserve his people. Rather than the mundane effects of raising money to support their cause or distributing their beliefs to others, while certainly immediate benefits to its production, the manual frames itself as a materialization of the CSA's authoritative status as warriors of God:

> We at CSA have been called to serve Jesus, to be counted among His army, to help prepare His people. We are not in this for money or personal gain. We are here to serve. All praise to our Lord Jesus Christ! All blessings upon Him!

This manual is one of the ways that Jesus has ordained for us to raise His Standard among His people. We urge you to turn your life over to Jesus, to praise His name before all. (1)

The work is thus more than a statement of faith or a manifesto of their political beliefs. Rather, it is an explicit expression of group identity that marks the authors and their community as part of "His army" and "His people." They explain that the manual "is one of the ways that Jesus has ordained" them.

Although this excerpt does not specifically mention guns, we know from other parts of the manual and additional public records that the gun is an essential element of this ordination. In at least one public instance on a television report, "Jim Ellison [CSA's leader] could be seen raising his rifle and declaring that the rod of iron that Jesus spoke about in the book of Revelation was a gun" (Noble 2011, 120). Brandishing the gun, then, both demonstrated one's identity as a Christian warrior and the imminency of the apocalyptic battle described in Revelation.

While many survival manuals prioritize information about procuring food and building shelter, the CSA manual foregrounds firearms as the most important consideration for other would-be survivalists. Because they view this survival as predicated on successful engagement in God's ultimate battle with the forces of evil, the manual dedicates fifty pages to "Firearms, Weapons, Knives and Gear." Focusing primarily on guns, it offers advice on selecting, using, and caring for them. In this sense, gun maintenance is not only a functional practice but a spiritual and religious practice as well.

To establish the tactical authority due God's warriors, the authors of the manual take great pains to demonstrate an extensive knowledge of firearms. Decisions about the most appropriate caliber for End Times survival are made with granular detail. Considerations are given weighing the accuracy and power of each caliber, the weight of each bullet, the weight of the gun, the distance ammo may need to be carried, and the energy required to carry it (CSA 1982, 15–16). No stone is left unturned.

This fastidious attention to detail is illustrated in a section titled ".45 or 9mm?" In it, the authors describe a test they performed to determine whether the .45 or 9mm works best as a defensive weapon "against flesh" rather than for target accuracy (19). They explain their methodology: "We were able to best simulate flesh by taking magazines and soaking them in water, making sure the water penetrated between all the pages. After a while they fluffed up. We ended up with about 14 inches of spongy, flesh-like material" (19). Validity of such a flesh test notwithstanding, the authors go on to provide comparative data for the weight, velocity, energy, penetration, and expansion of each caliber's shot into the spongy magazine material. While this detail conveys the seriousness of their efforts and desire to convey those efforts to readers, it also reveals a desire to legitimate themselves as worthy bearers of the holy mission for which they are preparing. They are not merely offering advice about guns, instead they take great care to demonstrate their own dedication to and preparation for God's coming war.

In addition to establishing their authority through detail, the vernacular document also borrows the institutional authority of the US military to bolster its own, a process similar to the hybrid vernacular authority observed by Robert Glenn Howard in his study of online Christian apocalyptic discourse communities (Howard 2011). Despite their antigovernment ideology, the authors' strong appreciation of US military tactics and weaponry is clear throughout the manual and often figures as a guidepost for determining the most effective equipment.

Although the military is a federal institution and CSA positions themselves explicitly against the federal government, they align themselves with the power and capability of the US military by likening it to their own firearms proficiency and knowledge. In choosing a handgun, the authors observe that "the Colt Government .45, our first choice, is readily available and is an awesome manstopper. It has functioned as the US Service for over 70 years" (CSA 1982, 18). Here, the gun's use by the US military is forwarded as an argument for its efficacy in an End Times survival situation. As Belew (2018) notes, many white power militia members are former service members, and they undoubtedly bring this cultural experience to bear in their firearms activity. It also allows them to identify as warriors within the militia, this time fighting on behalf of the legitimate authority of God rather than the illegitimate federal government.

The Christian Warrior

In addition to selecting the most appropriate guns and regularly caring for them, the shooter's tactical comportment is key in developing oneself as a Christian warrior. The manual spends a great deal of time emphasizing the importance of the shooter's character and bodily proficiency. "Too often this essential skill is overlooked, taken for granted, or deemed unimportant," the authors note. "However, if this lesson is learned first, a Christian warrior can be used effectively in defense of his people" (CSA 1982, 25).

Here visual imagery serves the double function of demonstrating techniques to the reader and legitimating the manual's authors through a militaristic aesthetic. The section describes how to hold one's gun and oneself, how to breathe properly while shooting, and various positions for shooting effectively. It also elaborates on military fieldcraft techniques for properly supporting one's weapon on a tree trunk, improvised tripod, and other supports, each with a hand-drawn example. At the end of the section, a detailed diagram informs the reader of bullet trajectory relative to angle of shooting and demonstrates the depth of CSA's attention to shooting craft.

Thus, Christian warriors must diligently prepare their bodies and practice their craft in order to effectively carry out God's mission in the End Times. "Man or animal," the authors assert, "is killed by a good combination of rifle, cartridge, and shooter. The most important, of course, is the shooter. If the shooter cannot comfortably handle his or her rifle, then it becomes useless" (13). The shooter must also be physically fit enough to bear the weight of additional ammo in a combat situation, because if they are not, "by the time you get to your target you would be too worn out to wage war" (13). Just as with guns, the manual's section on knives encourages readers to "discount anything you have seen in the movies" (34) and learn proper techniques. This focus on the physical body and admonitions to avoid fanciful depictions of warriors illustrates the seriousness of their endeavor to prepare for holy war, but it also reveals that this supernatural task is really a material one. The trappings of war, from the gun to the warrior's body, are religious articles that inscribe the holy war in reality. They take the apocalyptic narrative and make it a tangible object of the authors' and readers' lived experience.

In addition to verbal descriptions, the manual uses visual imagery to convey the materiality of the apocalyptic narrative. The profusion of images and detailed descriptions allows the viewer to bear witness to the CSA's enactment of biblical survivalism by drawing on readers' likely associations with military clothing, weapons, and tactical exercises. In these images, armed men appear tough, stoic, and deadly. They don camo fatigues, black boots, patrol caps, and rugged fingerless gloves. They carry assault rifles and wield sharp blades in deadly positions. The images evidence the CSA's tactical prowess, and the resultant visual effect is intimidating. These literal armaments are likened to the armor of God, exemplified by a diagram and image of an ALICE[2] harness flanked by Exodus 12:18, "But God let the people about, through the way of the wilderness of the Red Sea: and the children of Israel went up harnessed out of the land of Egypt." The combination of visceral text and images works to demonstrate the reality of the group's apocalyptic narrative and reifies their identity as God's warriors within it.

The City vs. the Saved

Amidst the varied and wide-ranging gun culture in the United States, the CSA manual employs a geographic metaphor to differentiate their religious use from the gun use of others. By locating the gun as a religious object not just on the body but in space, the manual creates an *axis mundi* which connects their tactical training to its heavenly source (Eliade 1991). The safety and divine purpose of the Christian warrior's stronghold is contrasted with the chaotic danger of the city and its devilish inhabitants.

Always identified with evil, the city is styled as the seat of Satanic influence and government. While some of its residents, "the people of the cubicles (house, car, office, shopping mall)," may have simply been duped, their way of life "is the ultimate tribute to the artificial support systems that maintain the 'beast'" (CSA 1982, 73). What's more, the city is a site of "racial riots, looting, and gang crime uprising," invoking the CSA's white supremacist beliefs (73). Associated with gun use by people of color, this use of the term "gang crime" evokes a racialized image of wanton violence meant to contrast with the disciplined military training of the CSA. It establishes an "us vs. them" framework which reinforces the boundaries of the Christian warrior identity and attempts to justify armed violence that is carried out in the service of God's plan.

Contrasted with the city's lawlessness, the Christian warrior's dwelling is an orderly sanctum, comprehensively defended and imbued with the shield of its inhabitants' faith. Its physical defenses mark out a sacred space in which the gun becomes Revelation's "rod of iron." Geographically and spiritually distant from the city, this space should be "at least 100 miles distance from the nearest city of 100,000 population" (82). It should be elevated to enable a clear view of "attackers slowly trudging upward towards you" (82) and with a clear "field of fire" that "attackers must cross to approach you" (86). Even the house itself should be fortified with rocks up to the windows (82) or piled wood obtained by clearing the field of fire (86). There should also be, "ideally, three fences at various distances from your dwelling" (88). Roadblocks, sharpened posts, concealed barbed wire, and other obstacles should be placed to "aid in conquering any intruders" (91). Finally, hidden bunkers should be constructed and filled with emergency supplies (92). In short, each detail should be attended to with safety, security, and active defense in mind.

The authors are careful to note, however, that these physical defenses are only protective insofar as they emanate from the spiritual power of God. Despite the nearly one hundred pages of tactical and survival advice that precede it, an "Important Note" clarifies that, "The best personal home defense, remember, is Christ Jesus and abiding in Him. Lean upon the Scriptures for faith, knowing that faith pleases God" (97). The Note offers two pages of passages from Psalms which suggest God's primacy in Christians' defense, and ends by admonishing readers to

> Remember the word of the Lord in commandment and promise as recorded in Joshua, chapter 1, and take it to heart: ". . . Now therefore arise, go over . . . unto the land which I do give to . . . the children of Israel. Every place that the sole of your foot shall tread upon, that have I given unto you . . . I will not fail thee, nor forsake thee . . ." (98)

In this passage, the authors reaffirm their status as God's chosen people and the land itself as an extension of His covenant with them. It commands these chosen to "arise" and "go over" the land, clearly forwarded here as divine justification of armed conflict understood to be inevitable (Wojcik 1999). Throughout the manual, the authors heed this call by carefully attending to all the minutiae of preparation, from the best tactical harness set-up to the most effective way to hold a knife, the most secure arrangement of fences around a dwelling to the techniques for sprouting seeds. And of course, all these preparations are foregrounded by the construction of God's warrior, the man and his gun, inevitably fated to be guardian of God's promise and vanguard of His war.

CONCLUSION

Through careful descriptive language and evocative visual imagery, the CSA survival manual demonstrates how cultural artifacts like the gun enable the performance of religious identity by materializing beliefs about the supernatural. In it, the gun becomes a tangible manifestation of the apocalyptic narrative, identifying and reifying God's warriors in this End Times battle. It "inscribes in reality" (Eliade 1987) the divine war that they are already fighting, and its powerful symbolic associations in wider US gunlore render it meaningful and interpretable by other would-be warriors and onlookers. By identifying their weaponry and tactical training with spiritual activity, reading these practices onto their own bodies and comportment, and sacralizing a physical space in which to perform it, the CSA's manual makes real their authority and identity as God's chosen warriors.

Although it is a document of its time, much of the language of the CSA survival manual resonates with calls for antigovernment activism and violence today. Just before the end of the manual, the authors ask the reader to imagine what it will be like to be a Christian fugitive from "Communist rule or under Martial Law" (CSA 1982, 170). Similar sentiments were echoed in the crowd during the riot at the US capitol on January 6, 2021. Social media posts and news footage captured antigovernment militia activity by groups like the Oath Keepers and Three Percenters, while other participants carried the South Vietnamese flag for its anticommunist connotation (Rosenberg 2021; Wang 2021). Christian symbolism was also on prominent display. The leader of a group called Cowboys for Trump "led rioters in prayer" before they invaded the building, attendees flew "Jesus fish" flags, carried Bibles, and held signs that read "Jesus Saves," and, of course, Jake Angeli (the "QAnon Shaman") gave his prayer from the rostrum of the Senate chamber, which thanked God for allowing them to send a message to "the tyrants, the communists, and the globalists" (Barrett and Zapotosky 2021; Posner 2021; Schor 2021; Stelloh 2021). Even the Save America March just before the riot, headlined by then-President Donald Trump, opened with a prayer by Christian televangelist Paula White (Posner 2021).

After the FBI raid at their compound, the CSA ultimately disbanded. However, the group's members and the community they created continued to be an influential presence in far-right militia circles and in gun culture at large. After his release from prison, CSA's founder Jim Ellison moved to Elohim City, Oklahoma, another compound known for its Christian Identity religious tradition, paramilitary training, and white supremacist belief system. It was also home to Andreas Strassmeir, the man phoned by Timothy McVeigh just two weeks before the Oklahoma City bombing. Reporting at the time talked about McVeigh's affinity for gun shows, emphasizing that they made him feel "at home," and the novel he carried on the day of the bombing, *The Turner Diaries*, valorizes a violent overthrow of the US government (Kifner 1995).

While such groups, individuals, and actions clearly do not represent the majority of gun owners in the United States, their influence in the history of the country's gun culture should give us pause. Though the CSA has largely faded from public memory, events like the January 6 Capitol riot remind us of the enduring influence and danger of religiously charged antigovernment beliefs. Looking forward, it is important to be aware of this history and to be alert to those who would make the apocalyptic battle between good and evil a physical and violent confrontation, fought by the guns of God's warriors today.

Notes

1. As these authors discuss, there are a variety of internal and external factors beyond specific beliefs that may ultimately contribute to incidents of religious violence, including group organizational structure, media representation, public or governmental response, real or perceived persecution, among others.

2. Alice stands for "All-purpose Lightweight Individual Carrying Equipment" and is a type of equipment system previously used by the US military.

References

Aho, James. 1996. "Popular Christianity and Political Extremism in the United States." In *Disruptive Religion: The Force of Faith in Social Movement Activism*, edited by Christian Smith, 189–204. New York: Routledge.

Babcock, Barbara A. 1992. "Artifact." In *Folklore, Cultural Performances, and Popular Entertainments: A Communications-Centered Handbook*, edited by Richard Bauman, 204–16. New York: Oxford University Press.

Baker, Kelly J. 2011. *The Gospel According the Klan: The KKK's Appeal to Protestant America, 1915–1930*. Lawrence: University Press of Kansas.

Barkun, Michael. 1996. *Religion and the Racist Right: The Origins of the Christian Identity Movement*. Chapel Hill: University of North Carolina Press.

Barrett, Devlin, and Matt Zapotosky. 2021. "FBI Report Warned of 'War' at Capitol, Contradicting Claims There Was No Indication of Looming Violence." *Washington Post*, January 12, 2021. https://www.washingtonpost.com/national-security/capitol-riot-fbi-intelligence/2021/01/12/30d12748-546b-11eb-a817-e5e7f8a406d6_story.html.

Belew, Kathleen. 2018. *Bring the War Home: The White Power Movement and Paramilitary America*. Cambridge, MA: Harvard University Press.

Blair, Carol. 2001. "Reflections on Criticism and Bodies: Parables from Public Places." *Western Journal of Communication* 65, no. 3 (June): 271–94.

Brummett, Barry. 1991. *Contemporary Apocalyptic Rhetoric*. New York: Praeger, 1991.

Burlein, Ann. 2002. *Lift High the Cross: Where White Supremacy and the Christian Right Converge*. Durham, NC: Duke University Press.

Censky, Abigail. 2020. "Heavily Armed Protesters Gather Again at Michigan Capitol to Decry Stay-At-Home Order." *NPR*, May 14, 2020. https://www.npr.org/2020/05/14/855918852/heavily-armed-protesters-gather-again-at-michigans-capitol-denouncing-home-order.

Charland, Maurice. 1987. "Constitutive Rhetoric: The Case of the Peuple Quebecois." *Quarterly Journal of Speech* 73, no. 2 (June): 133–50.

CSA Survival Manual. 1982. CSA Enterprises, Inc.

Del Negro, Giovanna P., and Harris M. Berger. 2004. "New Directions in the Study of Everyday Life: Expressive Culture and the Interpretation of Practice." In *Identity and Everyday Life: Essays in the Study of Folklore, Music, and Popular Culture*, edited by Harris M. Berger and Giovanna P. Del Negro, 3–22. Middletown, CT: Wesleyan University Press.

Dundes, Alan. 1984. "Defining Identity Through Folklore." *Journal of Folklore Research* 21, no. 2/3 (May–December): 149–52.

184 GUNLORE AND IDENTITY IN A SURVIVALIST COMMUNITY

Eliade, Mircea. 1987. *The Sacred and the Profane: The Nature of Religion.* New York: Houghton Mifflin Harcourt.

Eliade, Mircea. 1991. *Images and Symbols: Studies in Religious Symbolism.* Princeton, NJ: Princeton University Press.

Federal Bureau of Investigation. *The Covenant, the Sword, the Arm of the Lord.* Report Number:100-HQ-487200. https://vault.fbi.gov/TheCovenantTheSwordTheArmoftheLord/.

Hill, T. E. 2016. "(Re)articulating Difference: Constitutive Rhetoric, Christian Identity, and Discourses of Race as Biology." *Journal of Communication and Religion* 39, no. 1 (Spring): 26–45.

Howard, Robert Glenn. 2011. *Digital Jesus: The Making of a New Christian Fundamentalist Community on the Internet.* New York: New York University Press.

Ingersoll, Julie, and Sarah Posner. 2010. "Gun Ownership: 'An Obligation to God.'" *Religion Dispatches,* July 13, 2010. https://religiondispatches.org/gun-ownership-an-obligation -to-god/.

Jones, Michael Owen. 2007. "Food Choice, Symbolism, and Identity: Bread-and-Butter Issues for Folklorists and Nutrition Studies." *Journal of American Folklore* 120, no. 476 (Spring): 129–77.

Juergensmeyer, Mark. 2003. *Terror in the Mind of God: The Global Rise of Religious Violence.* Berkeley: University of California Press.

Kerstetter, Todd M. 2012. "State Violence and the Un-American West: Mormons, American Indians, and Cults." In *From Jeremiad to Jihad: Religion, Violence, and America,* edited by John D. Carlson and Johathan H. Ebel, 127–39. Berkeley: University of California Press.

Kifner, John. 1995 "The Gun Network: McVeigh's World – A Special Report." *New York Times,* July 5, 1995. https://www.nytimes.com/1995/07/05/us/gun-network-mcveigh-s -world-special-report-bomb-suspect-felt-home-riding-gun.html.

Landau, Jamie. 2016. "Feeling Rhetorical Critics: Another Affective-Emotional Field Method for Rhetorical Studies." In *Text + Field,* edited by Sara L. McKinnon, Robert Asen, Karma R. Chavez, and Robert Glenn Howard. University Park: Pennsylvania State University Press.

Lindsey, Michael. 2019. *CSA Flyer.* Encyclopedia of Arkansas. Digital photograph. https://encyclopediaofarkansas.net/media/covenant-the-sword-and-the-arm-of -the-lord-flyer-8316/.

Macdonald, Andrew. 1980. *The Turner Diaries.* Washington, DC: National Alliance.

Michel, Lou and Dan Herbeck, 2001. *American Terrorist: Timothy McVeigh and The Oklahoma City Bombing.* New York: HarperCollins.

Neidig, Harper. 2021. "Police Seized Alarming Number of Weapons on Capitol Rioters, Court Documents Show." *The Hill,* January 16, 2021. https://thehill.com/regulation/court- battles/534329-police-seized-alarming-number-of-weapons-on-capitol-rioters-court.

The New Yorker. 2021. "A Reporter's Footage from Inside the Capitol Siege | The New Yorker." YouTube video, 12:32, January 17, 2021. https://www.youtube.com/ watch?v=270F8s5TEKY.

Noble, Kerry. 2011. *Tabernacle of Hate: Seduction into Right-Wing Extremism.* New York: Syracuse University Press.

O'Leary, Stephen D. 1994. *Arguing the Apocalypse: A Theory of Millennial Rhetoric.* New York: Oxford University Press.

Otero, Solimar. 2020. *Archives of Conjure: Stories of the Dead in Afrolatinx Cultures.* New York: Columbia University Press.

Posner, Sarah. 2021. "How the Christian Right Helped Foment Insurrection." *Rolling Stone,* January 31, 2021. https://www.rollingstone.com/culture/culture-features/capitol-christian-right-trump-1121236/.

Quarles, Chester L. 2004. *Christian Identity: The Aryan American Bloodline Religion.* Jefferson, NC: McFarland.

Rappaport, Roy A. 1992. "Ritual." In *Folklore, Cultural Performances, and Popular Entertainments: A Communications-Centered Handbook,* edited by Richard Bauman, 249–60. New York: Oxford University Press.

Rosenberg, Matthew, and Ainara Tiefenthäler. 2021. "Decoding the Far-Right Symbols at the Capitol Riot." *New York Times,* January 13, 2021. https://www.nytimes.com/2021/01/13/video/extremist-signs-symbols-capitol-riot.html.

Schor, Elana. 2021. Christianity on Display at Capitol Riot Sparks New Debate." *Associated Press,* 28 January 2021. https://apnews.com/article/christianity-capitol-riot-6f13ef0030ad7b5a6f37a1e3b7b4c898.

Shuck, Glenn. 2005. *Marks of the Beast: The Left Behind Novels and the Struggle for Evangelical Identity.* New York: New York University Press.

Southern Poverty Law Center. 2003. "Remaking the Right." *Intelligence Report,* November 12, 2003. https://www.splcenter.org/fighting-hate/intelligence-report/2003/remaking-right.

Stelloh, Tim. 2021. "Cowboys for Trump Founder Arrested After Allegedly Leading Capitol Rioters in Prayer." *NBC News,* January 17, 2021. https://www.nbcnews.com/news/us-news/cowboys-trump-founder-arrested-after-allegedly-leading-capitol-rioters-prayer-n1254559.

Sullivan, Tim, and Adam Geller. 2020. "Increasingly Normal: Guns Seen Outside Vote-Counting Centers." *Associated Press,* November 7, 2020. https://apnews.com/article/protests-vote-count-safety-concerns-653dc8f0787c9258524078548d518992.

Sutton, Matthew Avery. 2014. *American Apocalypse: A History of Modern Evangelicalism,* Cambridge, MA: Belknap Press of Harvard University Press.

Thomas, Jo, and Ronald Smothers. 1995. "Oklahoma City Building Was Target of Plot as Early as '83, Official Says." *New York Times,* May 20, 1995. https://www.nytimes.com/1995/05/20/us/oklahoma-city-building-was-target-of-plot-as-early-as-83-official-says.html.

Voll, John O. 1993. "Forward." In *The Society of the Muslim Brothers,* by Richard P. Mitchell. New York: Oxford University Press.

Wang, Claire. 2021. "Why the Defunct South Vietnam Flag Was Flown at the Capitol Riot." *NBC News,* 15 January 2021. https://www.nbcnews.com/news/asian-america/why-defunct-south-vietnam-flag-was-flown-capitol-riot-n1254306.

"White Supremacist Executed for Murdering 2 in Arkansas." *New York Times,* April 21, 1995. https://www.nytimes.com/1995/04/21/us/white-supremacist-executed-for-murdering-2-in-arkansas.html.

Wojcik, Daniel N. 1999. *The End of the World as We Know It: Faith, Fatalism, and Apocalypse in America.* New York: New York University Press.

Chapter 8

A KNACK FOR PRECISION

The Art and Science of a Gun-Making Dynasty

SANDRA BARTLETT ATWOOD

My family, the Bartletts, are to gunsmithing what the Robertsons are to duck calls, the so-called "Duckmen" of the well-known reality TV show *Duck Dynasty*. The Robertson family is portrayed as the keepers of the traditions of duck-call making. Although reality TV fame and mass sales have never been our aim, my family has been quietly perfecting our craft for generations. Why? You may ask. The answer seems to be nothing short of this: because they can.

The Bartlett family consists of my parents, my four siblings, their spouses, many grandchildren, great-grandchildren, one great-great-grandson, and me. As a folklorist interviewing my own family, this look at gunsmith culture offers the perspective of an insider as well as an outsider, employing "emic" ethnography and "etic" theoretical approaches as my method.

CONSERVATIVE AND DYNAMIC ELEMENTS OF FIREARM FOLK GROUPS

As with all folk groups and folklore, there are common core features that make the group or genre recognizable and cohesive. In the case of gunlore and gunfolk, firearms would be considered a conservative element, while the type, quality, innovation, and use of those firearms would reveal wide-ranging dynamic elements within and between firearm folk groups. Folklorist Alan Dundes famously defined a folk group as "any group of people whatsoever who share at least one common factor" (Dundes 1965, 2). He specifically noted that extended family groups could be studied as folk groups (Dundes 1980, 7). Later, folklorists Elliott Oring and Jay Mechling demonstrated the

186

richness of such small folk groups (Mechling 2006). The Bartlett family gun-making dynasty, with its unique intergenerational culture and traditions, offers an example of one such high-context but small folk group.

Although folk traditions are typically learned informally, this gunsmith-ing dynasty weaves both folk and formal art and folk and formal science together in important ways that have led to innovations and improvements while maintaining the integrity of their longstanding traditions. In fact, the most conservative, foundational tradition of the group is a commitment to *the quest for precision*. This shared value is an inherently dynamic process that necessarily changes with advances in technology. However, the group's ability to apply this technology intuitively in creative ways leads to superior firearm production and performance to what the gun industry currently produces. This consonant dance between tradition and innovation in the pursuit of increasing precision demonstrates another complex way that fire-arms as objects can become the basis for folkloric expression that is both precise and beautiful, expressive and functional. This complex dynamic will be the prevailing theme throughout this chapter.

INFORMAL TRANSFER OF TRADITIONAL KNOWLEDGE

A gunsmith is a person who engages in repairing, modifying, designing, or building guns. Gunsmithing requires a vast skill set, "an unnatural patience,"[1] and a knack for precision. Because gunsmithing necessitates distinct inherent capacities that are hard to teach, it is a craft that is not readily transferred—even from parent to offspring, often bypassing an individual or crossing fam-ily lines. This is certainly the case with my family, where, although I had no real affinity for it, my son Col possessed the natural inclination and aptitude and as such was recognized and mentored by my father, Charles, and my brother, Greg. Although most of my family enjoys shooting and reloading their own ammunition, there exists the tacit recognition of those who have the knack and those who have one or more of the skill sets (or have the skill but not the interest) but not all.

My father grew up in Tridell, Utah, at the foot of the Uinta Mountains. He learned to defend himself and put food on the table from his father who learned from *his* father, who learned from his father, Charles Claymore Bartlett (my father is his namesake). One of my uncles told me that my dad was well named because he had the same natural affinity for guns and marksmanship as his great grandfather. When I asked my father about his earliest gun memories and how he got his start, he reminisced:

Figure 8.1. The Bartlett family shooting the cannon for Charles and Judy's 60th wedding anniversary, near Smithfield, Utah.

Well, I think my first experiences was when my dad would be out sighting in a rifle and I was always kind of on his shirt tail and he'd ask if I want to shoot it and I would say sure and I would shoot his deer rifle or whatever he had. So, I kind of got interested in that. I think he found out I could shoot, so he got a kick out of watching me . . . I grew up with firearms. My dad liked them, and he didn't have a lot of money to waste on them but he kept them very well. We have in the family now, we have a .32-20 model Winchester rifle, the .32-20 colt single action pistol that were his. And when he was younger, he bought the handgun and he herded sheep for his dad and other people quite often. And he said he genuinely would sleep with that colt under his pillow, made him feel good. But I think that's where we learned our respect and to take care of them, clean them, oil them, type of thing, for firearms. Reloading, my dad used to reload his own stuff and that got me started on that.

In my interviews, shooting and gunsmithing are described as just kind of *happening*. It was never really planned or forced and often learning gunsmithing preceded learning to shoot. There was no set age or protocol, not even an expectation that one *ought* to possess the knack (although it is believed, by many, to run in the Bartlett veins). In fact, if there was a rite of passage, it was perhaps the moment of becoming aware; awakened to your innate gift and being acknowledged and mentored by members of the group in mainly unspoken ways. A mere interest in gunsmithing wasn't enough; you had to be recognized by the group as having "the knack" to be fully initiated into the group. The ritual is an unspoken one and is recognizable only

Figure 8.2. Charles Claymore Bartlett's father, Charles Owen Bartlett near Tridell, Utah.

by the master making time for the apprentice and including him or her in the process by transferring knowledge little by little, generally one-on-one. I use the term "apprentice" loosely because much of the learning is more of a guided inquiry of the inner workings of firearms that stretches the learner's capacity to think and problem solve creatively and independently.

When I asked my brother about his earliest memories of working on guns with Dad, he looked away as though reaching back in time as he recalled, "Well, I think it started when I was probably about fifteen I think when Dad let me build the, he did the metal work on a rifle for me, the Mauser. And he let the, let me do all the woodwork on it." Soon, Greg was put to work cleaning guns that were brought in for work. Noting how the parts fit together led my father to recognize he had the knack: "So, nobody really taught me how, other than gave me a few basics and told me what the business end was and where to point it and not shoot anything you didn't want to kill. But that was kind of where I got started."

Later, when interviewing my son Col, he spoke about his introduction to guns in a similar way noting that he didn't "really know of a specific start but there was always just kind of guns around."

Reflecting on his history with gunsmithing, Col gave a detailed account of his early experiences, noting, "I honestly don't remember exactly when [I started gunsmithing], but I think I was in the third or fourth grade." As he recalled these early experiences, Col began to detail the step-by-step process of his first rebuilt rifle when he was thirteen years old. His uncle Greg offered to teach him "how to build a gun" as he and his friends were looking over his Grandpa's "cool guns." Col decided to build "a precision .22 as a first-time." So, he and his uncle got to work finding the perfect base gun to rebuild: "I didn't want to build the one I already had 'cause it was nice and brand new and so we found an old one, looked online for maybe six months to find the right one." For Col, the gun he could rebuild would end up being more than anything he could buy new. As it exhibited a powerful sense of folkloristic expression, it was important to him that it not even "look new" but, instead, be built up from old parts. Further, he would make this old gun new by making it both precise and beautiful. He described in great length how he learned to make the gun more accurate. He learned to replace and tune the springs to create a custom trigger with "a two-pound pull." He spent hours shaping and carving a new stock for the gun, noting that he "got to figure out how to finish a stock in . . . all the sanding and coating and everything that is involved with that." Finally, he "matched the flutes and the barrel to the red in the stock just like, as like a little aesthetic, making it look extra cool or custom." The care and creativity Col took to rebuild this first rifle clearly illustrates the way firearms can become expressive objects that are both aesthetic and functional.

My other family members had similar experiences of their gunsmithing practices just "happening." My brother Dan noted how "growing up in the Bartlett home, firearms were everywhere and all around us." My brother Wade expressed the belief that family members ended up involved in guns less by choice than by predisposition: "You could say [my youngest son] has a Bartlett shooting gene. Dad was always the best shot, he could hit anything and I feel that we all have a little bit of that in us."

When asked what "having a knack" for gun-making entails, the common response always included a wide array of skills and the necessity of being above average at each of those skills. These skills are often described as having artistic and scientific components. Charles, for example, "People say: 'What do you need to know to be a gunsmith?' And I say well you need to be an expert machinist and a metal worker. . . . And you need to know quite a bit about metallurgy. And, you know, to be a good wood finisher helps. And a lot of common sense."

In my brother Greg's discussion of the gunsmith's skill set, he focusses on the importance of being picky, patient, and precise. He notes how a gunsmith has "to understand tolerances and where they need to be tight and where it doesn't matter." He describes himself as "nitpicky" when he engages in this "labor of love": "You just have to enjoy doing it. Because if you don't, you don't want to spend much time in it. I don't know, I just kind of enjoy the physics of the whole thing."

My brother Dan expands on this idea by emphasizing the necessity of an engineering and scientific mind: "You have to have an engineering mentality." But he continues by maintaining that this mindset is more of a talent that

Figure 8.3. My sons' first .22 rifles, received when they each turned twelve: Angus (top), Bryn (middle), Col (bottom).

Figure 8.4. Col Atwood building his first rifle with his uncle, Greg Bartlett, in Smithfield, Utah 2012.

people are born with than learned. "I think it is something that is passed down more than anything from father to son. I don't think it's something you go and learn on your own. I think it has to be something you're exposed to as a young person and you want to do it."

My son Angus also emphasized being drawn to the science process. He emphasized patience as the fundamental quality of a gun maker:

I think the first thing is patience. Because nothing about gunsmithing is fast. Like, it takes an extraordinary amount of patience [that] I do not think I have. Like Col, he has an unnatural amount of patience ... and [you need to] have a really keen eye for detail in what you're

Figure 8.5. Charles Bartlett in his basement workshop Lethbridge, Alberta, 1964, his shop in Smithfield, Utah, 2020, and the gun-stock duplicator jig that Charles and Greg Bartlett designed and built together in Smithfield, Utah, 2005.

doing. You really need to be able to focus . . . and pay attention to what you're doing 'cause if you're, like for reloading, if you reload a bullet with a wrong charge you could turn your rifle into a, into a bomb . . . We started doing the brass, reloading them and stuff.

Angus went on to recount being drawn to the science of it but also its "magic": "I remember being super fascinated by the magic and the science of it. So, it was super cool to do that kind of stuff."

When I interviewed my son Bryn, he described why he was not suited to gunsmithing by noting that the people who are "really good" at gunsmithing have a different "temperament" than him. He went on,

> I'm kind of a loud person who likes to hear my own voice and everybody that I know who is good at guns is quiet, real sort of methodical, thoughtful person. And I think it's just, it's a, not something I ever got into, not something that I had an affinity towards, but something I was always interested in.

All the interviews repeatedly mention that there was very little explicit instruction. They spoke in terms of learning by observation, practice, patience, experimentation, trial and error, competition, performance, and play.

My father described how competition could upset everything from family hierarchies to chore assignments. He described how they would often engage in family competitions. One of the things they would do was "when we would come in for lunch when it came time to do the dishes, somebody would go out and make a little blaze on a pine tree and put a charcoal mark on it and then we would shoot to see who did the dishes and I did the dishes once all summer."

In some of his stories, my brother Greg describes competition as a context for innovation and increased precision. He tells of how he rebuilt three regular rifles with "tighter chambers." These common and relatively inexpensive Ruger brand model "10/22s" rifles are not known for their precision out of the box, so when he and his friends took the modified rifles to a competition, they got noticed.

> We took gold with a rifle and all of us shooting 10/22s which made everybody kind of sit up and take notice 'cause there was some expensive rifles down there. And there was a few good shooters but there wasn't the combination of as much practice and good shooters and good rifles that we had down there because I had figured out how to make them perform like they should so the only weak link was the loose nut on the trigger which was usually the problem most of the time.

Some individuals in the group spoke about learning certain skills formally in contexts unrelated to gunsmithing and then creatively reinterpreting and transferring those skills to gunsmithing. Sometimes the skills were intentionally acquired in response to a specific need or problem, but most often the skills and the unique applications of those skills—woven together naturally with preexisting practices and mentalities—became embedded in the traditions of the group and passed down informally to subsequent apprentices in following generations. Charles described, for example, how after he left the Navy, he took classes at the university and melded that context of a university class to his desire to make guns.

> In one of my classes at Utah State University . . . an art metal class . . . I built a muzzle loading pistol and it's kind of on the style of a dueling pistol, single shot and that one I still have. I commandeered a cow horn that my father had carved some stars and moon in—it laid around the house for a long time—and made a powder horn for it.

Figure 8.6. Greg Bartlett teaching his nephews and grandsons how to shoot from standing, kneeling, sitting, and prone positions in Logan, Utah, 2013. Greg also used to compete, shooting a pistol from the Creedmoor (back or supine) position.

In a similar way, the group repurposed objects. They described using metal and wood scraps, common household items, and trinkets for their gunsmithing. These reappropriations often held both functional and aesthetic value for the gunsmith. In fact, each of the individuals I interviewed held the common practice of collecting a wide eclectic range of these items for potential future use. The group's tendency and preference to build things "from scratch" is a recurring theme as well. YouTube videos, magazines, and books were also mentioned by all three generations as a unifying source of learning and sharing with other gunsmiths and represent dynamic ways in which the group's customs have evolved over space and time. In one case, this repurposing of material objects led my father to building a "cannon."

> I had the barrel of the cannon, [one that someone] gave me, it was a line throwing gun . . . it was a gun designed to shoot a line from one ship deck across the bow of another one so they could drag an oil hose across or whatever. It was a [two-and-a-half-inch] bore. So, I built [the] cannon using that barrel and made the trail and everything out of red oak and the wheels, the whole works . . . it recoiled pretty severely for that light of a framework . . . So, I bought a piece of hydraulic tubing which if you understand hydraulics, the inside is very smooth and polished and that's where the piston goes that actually works the hydraulics. The outside was just normal size, so it was an inch and a half inside and then [two and a half] outside. Then I slid it down in the barrel of this gun and extended it to about 30 inches, reduced the diameter down to an inch and a half . . . the inch and a half worked out very well and it shot very well.

Although basic gun maintenance, repair, marksmanship, and vernacular engineering have been passed down through my family for generations, the etiology of modern gunsmithing for the group is firmly grounded in the

Figure 8.7. Picture taken of Charles Bartlett's Utah State University art metal project from 1962 in Smithfield, Utah 2020.

legendary achievements of Utah gunmaker, John Moses Browning. While everyone I've ever known or heard of looks up to my dad for his demeanor, precision, creativity, and straightforward ingenuity, my dad looks up to John Moses Browning. He represents the pinnacle of the craft. No gunsmith before or since has approached his status or influenced the world more. Notwithstanding, John M. Browning never put his name on his inventions or tried to market his own brand (Browning's sons would develop the brand later), he lived simply and his motivation, like my family's, seemed to be, "because I can" (and perhaps more accurately in his case, because *no one* else can). For my dad, "There's not much about John Moses Browning that was bad." Browning's design principles are imagined as embodiment of an ideal: "I just, I like the way he thought. Simple, straightforward, the simplest way's the best type." The ideals of precision and patience are embodied in John Browning: "He just didn't do anything the short way, but some of the stories that go along with it are amazing. He said one time if he had to issue a curse on anybody, he'd make them an inventor 'cause they just always have to be doing." For my dad, Browning's diligence in creating designs simple and clever enough to withstand any situation were captured in "his one saying, 'Anything that can happen to a gun eventually will.'"

METACOGNITION OF PROCESS

Having the mindset that anything that can happen to a gun will eventually happen, influences every aspect of design and while aesthetics is very much valued by my family, precision and utility are priority. However, precision as mere function and reliable performance are not all that interest the group. There is also precision for precision's sake. The family members make this clear when they talk about events and experiences that influenced the various paths they took in their common pursuit of precision.

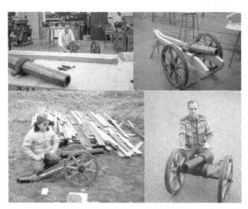

Figure 8.8. Charles Bartlett building and firing his 3" muzzle loading cannon in Lethbridge, Alberta, Canada 1970.

For example, my brother Greg talks about how winning a major competition "instilled in me to kind of wonder what makes things function as accurately as they can." This wondering increasingly became an obsession:

> I was trying to figure out how to make a rimfire shoot because you can't buy, you can't reload your own ammo for rimfire, you have to shoot what's available. Well, after some tinkering and some modification, and I bought a couple of, three different reamers and a couple of, three different barrels from different places. I tried bolt guns, I tried a number of different platforms to see if I could figure out how these things worked. And it finally got through to me what, the chamber that you cut into the end of the barrel and the way the cartridge fit to that chamber, was what made a rimfire shoot. Everything else was kind of superfluous, you know. I found that even a garbage .22 barrel, I could make shoot pretty good if you put the right chamber in it.

Later on, Greg augmented his natural aptitude and obsessive interest with experience in a high-end gun shop:

> I had a fair amount of knowledge by the time I went down to work [at a custom rifle shop] for about a year, but I learned quite a bit. I got to meet . . . some of the honest to God war heroes that would come through and you get to talk with them and chat, with some of their experiences that you just don't get to do every day . . . I got to learn a little bit about cartridge performance and what you could expect out of things. The kind of stuff we were building was pretty

Figure 8.9. John Moses Browning's gun shop in Ogden, Utah, John Moses Browning with one of his rifles, and John Moses Browning deified as "Saint John Browning, Father of the Modern Firearm, American Original Gangster 1855-1926 Do It for the Culture" by admirers at CK Gunroom Ontario, Canada.

high-performance stuff. It had to be right because you know, you'd build it incorrectly, you're gonna hurt somebody. So, we made sure everything was how it needed to be before it left the shop. We spent a lot of time on making sure the appearance of it was like you'd expect for the kind of money they were spending on a rifle. But that was a lot of fun, I got a kick out of that.

Col described how their custom work led to his focus on loading high-precision ammunition in pursuit of precision for the sake of precision:

Around that time, we started customizing our own guns [at ages fifteen and sixteen], we realized it was expensive to shoot ammo. And for precision ammo, once again, factory made is 95 percent good, but it's not, like the powder weights aren't exact. The grain of the bullets aren't exact, the brass isn't exact, the primers might be set in all funny. So, all that added up, it leads to lesser accuracy, so we decided to turn to reloading after talking to my Grandpa.

After buying expensive precision equipment to do the reloading, they lighted on the idea of saving money on the actual lead they used to make their bullets:

For that part of our life, it was hard to find reloading supplies. . . . We turned to old tire shops to get lead from the old tire weights, [they] are usually around 70 percent lead, 50 percent lead. Now they've turned zinc

198   THE ART AND SCIENCE OF A GUN-MAKING DYNASTY

usually. But the old, all the old weights that are sitting around tire shops we would melt down and cast our own bullets to solve that problem.

Dan described his obsession with precision as a life-long condition:

I'm an engineer at heart that's what I graduated in, engineering. I've worked in quality control my whole career and you know, had done a lot with engineering and construction.

And so, I love the science project that reloading is, and marksmanship is. To me it's a science project. Because you could take two guns that were manufactured from the same factory on the same line from the same day and you put the same ammunition in it, and they will shoot differently. And that's because maybe the tool that cut the chamber was a little bit duller than it was for the previous gun, you know, barrel that it was used in. There's just all kinds of variables to it. And what I love about it is for any given weapon there's probably ten of fifteen possibilities of bullets that you could use and bullets that weigh different weights. And there's also probably four or five different powders that you can use in that cartridge. Some of those powders burn differently. Some burn a little slower and some of them burn at different rates or at different, they're just constructed differently, the grains of the powders. You can seat—like how far the bullet goes into the brass cartridge—you can seat it at different lengths. You know, so all of these things you can use to what they call tune the bullet to the barrel. So, that to me is fascinating and the science project. To find which bullet and which powder produces the best results for that gun. I love that process.

For the Bartletts, everything from the tools right on up to the finished product is "custom." This play on words is intentional because not only does the group produce some of the finest custom firearms available but invention itself is actually a custom of this gunsmith folk group. Innovation is often tied to motivating factors like necessity, utility, precision, or beauty; other times, its simply because they can. I have often wondered if one reason why you can't buy a gun like my family can make, is in part because you can't buy the tools that they use to make them.

Different family members collect widgets and doodads they come across and store them away. And then take them out and repurpose them as the need arises during the gun-making process. They use these bits and pieces in everything from tools to gun parts to performance paraphernalia. Ideas too are collected and stored away for later use.

Figure 8.10. Hand cast bullets Col and Angus made from melted down wheelbase in Cardston, Alberta, Canada 2015 and Col reloading in his gunsmithing shop in the basement of our home in Cardston, Alberta, Canada 2020.

Charles, for example, described how he made cannon balls for his cannon saying, "Yeah, I made everything on the cannon. I made the mold that you make the balls with. I made the cutter to cut the hole for the mold that [I] make the balls in. So, they really don't just grow on trees."

Describing their custom of homespun inventions in the pursuit of precision, function, and beauty, Greg noted, "You need specialized tools for it and sometimes you can't just go buy them, you got to make them." Charles expanded on this by describing how they repurposed objects to make tools that were better than any they could purchase:

> If somebody had a nice Browning over-under [shotgun], they wanted a recoil pad on it, one fella used to do it, but once in a while he would make a mistake and scar that beautiful finish and that didn't go too well with the gun owners. Well, I told him I could do a couple for him and in doing so I built a device that hangs from a vertical belt grinder. And I would first mount the little, square the stock and mount the pad to the stock in its full size and then I would scribe around the stock into the pad so that the big light part of the pad would show up with the scribe mark and mount it to a little jig and set the slope of the stock so it would come out looking good on the bottom. Then I would grind the pad and put it back on the stock and I could mount recoil pads without damaging the stock at all.

Beyond molding lead or mounting pads, my father explains how the police force sought him out to develop a more effective bomb disposal device than was available on the market at that time. He describes the common objects he had laying around which he creatively and skillfully transformed in order to safely detonate bombs.

Figure 8.11. 11-ounce cannon ball and mold, capping die, punch, ring gage, 1½ inch ball, and a powder, ball, and fuse kit that Charles Bartlett made for the cannon.

Figure 8.12. Specialized gunsmithing tools designed and built over the years by Charles and Greg Bartlett: a recoil pad grinding jig that Charles made in Lethbridge, Alberta, Canada 1970, a barrel vise for unscrewing a rifle barrel, action wrenches (which slide into a rifle action, with the barrel clamped the action can be removed or torqued into place), and a headspace indicator.

While [gunsmithing, I also] taught metal or machine shop and other courses at the Lethbridge Community College. And I built a bomb, a disposal wagon. Also, before that, I built an "explosive package destroying" little water cannon which they could put 90 grains [FFG black powder] in a 12-gauge shell and then a dynamite fuse in the primer pocket and they could literally destroy an explosive package before it had time to go off. Once in a great while if it was a black powder package, it would ignite but then the powder just burned, it didn't explode. But an ammunition cannon or anything like that would just disintegrate with this water blast that would hit it. The bomb buggy, I never did get a picture of that but it was built so that it would deflect the blast. Actually, they'd carry, let's say they had a suspected bomb, they would carry it in a salmon landing net very carefully, that way there would be no jiggle, jar, or bump, and then they would hang it over the top of this hopper on the buggy, and it was a tandem wheel buggy, and drive it to some place where it could be lifted out and then destroyed. The buggy, I designed it in such a way with a pyramid at the bottom and a heavy pipe cut in half in the bottom edge like a water trough and then up the sides so that the blast would be deflected up into the air. Calgary used a dump truck loaded with sand and they would put that bomb up on top of that load of sand and haul it away. But this little buggy that I built could be pulled behind a police car. They tested it with quite a few sticks of dynamite and it worked fine but, I don't think it was ever, that I know of when I left anyway, used and had anything go off inside. Had it been so, somebody said to just leave it open at the bottom, but to me that means there is going to be gravel shrapnel going ankle high all over the place and I didn't want that. So, the way it was designed it would be deflected back up into the air and at such an angle it wouldn't hurt any bystanders or anything.

In addition to law enforcement, the family also employs new materials and sciences in creative ways to improve accuracy, efficiency, and aesthetics, in their business ventures. Greg remembers:

Dad had built [a shooting rest years ago] and it seemed to work pretty good but it was a little bit antiquated for the kind of materials and things we had to work with. So, we kind of sat down and redesigned it a little and we sold all kinds of them silly shooting rests all over the place. We were hooked up with [the major firearms retailer] Brownells for a while. Doing that, I bought some tools for the shop that are still in the shop now. That and a few shooting benches, we just figured out how to make them 'cause we were too poor to go out and buy the expensive ones so we built a few shooting benches to shoot from.

Speaking about the One-Shot Scope Sighting Jig they designed and marketed together, Charles adds:

At home my father built a plate of steel that he laid on top of an oil drum. And it had a yoke up on one end that he could lay a rifle in and help him in sighting and help with shooting basically. And while we were in Canada, I thought, well I need something like that that I can take to the range except I want it to hold a rifle completely. And so, I developed a deal that you could lay the firearm in and it would hold the butt stock which secured the rifle. And the idea was that you could with one shot, you could zero a scope rather than spending the money for a half box of shells. . . . So, now you've got a gun that's shooting where you're looking. And with one shot I demonstrated one time and I hit a penny the second round at 100 yards with a little .222 Magnum. . . . So, I think we had 1,000 boxes printed, we sold that many. And then it got a little tiring and the wholesalers wanted to pay us less and less and so I didn't make any more.

Greg illustrates perfectly the notion of custom work being a custom of this gunsmith folk group. When he talks about his custom work on gunstocks. He notes how,

Yeah, when I, I got to the point to where I wanted a stock to fit a certain way. I realized that through my rimfire work and through my position of shooting and stuff, I realized what a stock needs to feel like and how it needs to fit you in order for the stock to make you be able to shoot it a little better because you can only instill only a certain amount of accuracy in the assembly of a gun.

Dan expanded on this point talking about designing a recoil reducing muzzle device:

I got talking to Greg and Dad and a muzzle break is something that you can put on the end of a rifle that reduces the recoil of the rifle. It vents the gasses out in front of the bullet and just reduces the recoil of the rifle through different design strategies and everything. We had gone to all these gun shows, and people were claiming that they could reduce recoil by some ridiculous amounts. Well, so we kind of got snooping around and asking how do you determine that . . . There were two tests that are done, and they are really crude. One's called the "slide test" and you take a piece of carpet and you lay the rifle down on the carpet and you reach out with your finger and you fire the rifle on the carpet and it slides back a certain distance and you mark that. And then you put your muzzle break on the end and then you do it again . . . then you take the difference and decide it's only 65 percent reduction or 45 percent reduction or whatever, pretty crude test. The other one was a pendulum test where you basically put the

Figure 8.13. One of the original sighting jigs (orange) built by Charles Bartlett in 1972 and three other early One-Shot Scope Sighting Jig prototypes and the final product (bottom) in Smithfield, Utah 1993–1994.

rifle in a rope; and it hung from a central point up against a piece of plywood or a wall and again you reached up and you shot the shot and it swung up the wall and you marked where it swung up to. And then you put the muzzle break on it, and you shoot it again and it doesn't go up as far, so then you can figure out how much it was. So, I went to my Doctor, PhD guy, that was over me and I told him that I wanted to build a recoil comparator is what I was gonna call it. And I built a rail system and drilled holes in these rails and then I built a sled, a composite sled and then we mounted the rifle to the composite sled and then we piped nitrogen at high velocity into the rails and it lifted that sled up so it was resting on a cushion of nitrogen. And then with a remote-control device, we set off the rifle and as it came back, it crossed two laser beams. A start and stop laser beam and then we could accurately record the time that it took to go from point A to

204   THE ART AND SCIENCE OF A GUN-MAKING DYNASTY

point B. Then you could put the muzzle loader break on and then you could do it again. And you could do this so many times to get a standard deviation. Well, my professor was so excited about the project, it was so cool . . . Dad and Greg were pretty excited about that.

Speaking of how all these elements come together to make a gun that is both functional and beautiful, Col notes that: "The craftsmanship and the accuracy and just the uniqueness of the rifle is very cool. And I also do value aesthetic as well. I mean I always like making them cool and custom and kind of one off from everyone else." Dan expands on this saying: "Well I like tight fitting machine parts. So, if something is a little bit sloppy or rattley, I wouldn't even pick it up." Wade weighs in saying, "What appeals to me in a pretty gun is the wood of course."

THE POWER OF GUNS TO FORM RELATIONSHIPS

When considering the role guns play in the development and maintenance of identities and relationships among the group, it becomes evident that shooting and gunsmithing are more than a pastime or occupation because they help form intimate relationships between these individuals. Through both process and product, interactions surrounding guns become one primary way this family enacts its shared identity. It is a lifeway, an extension of self, a lens through which most ideas and experiences get filtered and interpreted. Theirs is a world where guns (as well as the folk who craft and care for them) enjoy the status of beloved, trusted companions. Growing up especially, and even now, quality family time usually involves talking about, working on, or shooting, guns. Birthdays, Christmases, weddings, graduations, reunions, crises and so on often include some firearm related ritual or custom. These gun traditions in connection with significant family milestones and celebrations forge and preserve relationships and create a collective identity among the group. The most meaningful gift you could get from, or give to my dad, is a gun. Aspects of gun customs are even described as being therapeutic and contributing to the general sense of wellbeing of individuals and the group.

The way guns function to form these bonds in the family are numerous. They are deeply intertwined with the celebration of customs. For example, Dan described how

at Christmas time we had all of the kids there . . . And I have been thinking about giving, you know the Contenders, the pistols,

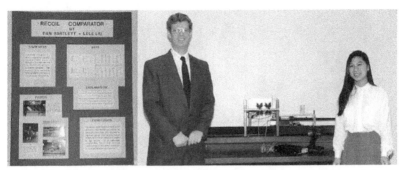

Figure 8.14. The recoil comparator designed by Dan Bartlett and Lele Liu at Utah State University, Logan, Utah 1993.

Figure 8.15. Custom rifle built by Greg Bartlett and its .283" grouping at 100 yards, Idaho Falls, Idaho 2020.

the single-shot pistols that Dad gave me and Wade and Greg at Christmas time a long, long time ago. Anyways, Christmas time this year I took Dean [Dan's son] aside and Amy [Dean's wife] and said there's something that I want you to have and I don't know if you'd be interested in and he said, "Well, what's that?" And so, I took that Contender out and I said, "I want you to have this." and I said, "Do you know what it is?" and he said, "Yeah, I know what it is. That's the gun that Grandpa gave you." And I said, "Would you be interested in that?" and Amy actually said, "Oh, yeah, Dean has talked about that before." [Dean] said, "Yeah, I would love to have it." . . . It was kind of touching that he was touched . . . [then for] Mom and Dad's 60th Anniversary, we went to the range and shot with everybody that wanted to go up and shoot . . . Dad has sights on the cannon that are much like on a rifle—open sights. So, you can look through the back sight which has a post in it and then the front sight has the little two tubes, you know, the two hills and a valley in the middle and then you put the post in the middle of that and you try to put it on your target that's out there. We were shooting at a steel target at 100 yards and hitting it with the cannon . . . Yeah, just with iron sights. And we found, and I told Dad this, I said I'm having to aim at the bottom left corner of the target to hit, to barely hit it on the right side and he's like, oh, wow, we're gonna have to work on that.

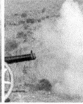

Figure 8.16. Picture frames taken from Dan and his wife, Young Suk Bartlett's video footage of the cannon firing in Richmond, Utah 2018. In the middle picture, you can see the ball exiting the barrel at approximately 1200 ft. per second.

Firearms are among my dad's most prized possessions. Often, he would buy or make a gun for my mother for her birthday, wedding anniversary, or Christmas. Although many people, including my family, joke about men buying tools and guns for their wives, for my dad, these were gifts of profound love. One Christmas morning there were five envelopes taped to the mantle of the fireplace, one for me and each of my four siblings. The letter inside from Dad said how much his rifles meant to him and that he wanted to give us something that was deeply meaningful to him. There was a list of all his rifles except the ones he had given my mother over the years. We were to choose which gun we wanted. There were some beautiful modern high-powered precision rifles on there but I knew the one I wanted, my grandfather's Winchester 92 .32-20 and when I told him, he said, "You know that one comes with the Colt .32-20 pistol, the reloading equipment and the old leather holster and scabbard my grandfather had made and used with them, they shouldn't be separated." I was speechless and I could tell he was happy that I chose that rifle; he was glad that it meant something to me.

Wade remembered other guns given as important expressions of love, saying, "For Christmas when I was in high school I asked for a Thompson Contender .22 handgun and I got it. I was probably 14 or 15, Santa Claus brought me one. I still have that today."

Angus recalled a similar experience on his 12th birthday, when he got his first gun: "My Grandpa came over for my birthday and I [unwrapped] my gun and he talked to me about gun safety. And we just did a lot of stuff like that you never put your finger in the trigger hold until you're aiming at what you want to shoot and ready to fire." For Angus and Col, these gifts quickly became a means to engage in the family rivalry that emerged into family customs:

> I do remember it becoming a little bit of unfair advantage because I remember Col getting his gun and it was far superior. I had a, what's

Figure 8.17. The Winchester 92 .32-20 and Colt .32-20 Sandra Bartlett Atwood got for Christmas in Smithfield, Utah 1992.

called a little cricket and the size was from my fingertip to my elbow as a grown adult and is a very, very tiny compact gun. Wonderful shooter though, it always performed super well but it was one of those guns that it only took a few years before I physically outgrew it. And Col's is kind of a timeless piece, upgradeable, 10 round mag that came with it, super precision, precise. So, there was a bit of jealousy about that. I was always more jealous of how good of a shot Col was. You always have brotherly rivalries and so me and Bryn were always trying to outshoot each other and it felt like Col would come and lay it down like Clint Eastwood or something. Shooting when I was fairly young, pre-teens and stuff, out at the house, very fond memories. It would be awesome when our Uncles from Canada would come down and we'd go shooting out in the backyard. Just really, really enjoyed that.

As the family faced the inevitable changes brought on by age. Angus recalled:

Another time that really stuck out to me and I had a really good time was, my Grandpa had been, I forget what, anyways, he almost died and I needed to stay down here in Utah with them for a little bit and just help out my Grandma who is suffering from dementia. And during that time, my Grandpa was like, "hey do you want to go out and shoot handguns." And I was feeling quite lonely, it was just whatever and I hadn't done a lot of handgun shooting but I remember that week I had just, I had boughten a punch card for the range and if it wasn't every day it was every other day that I went to the range and was just shooting handguns. It was just a really blissful experience

208   THE ART AND SCIENCE OF A GUN-MAKING DYNASTY

and just a really enjoyable at helping me with, cope with what was going on around me.

In another example of how guns functioned to maintain personal relationships during difficult times, Angus described how guns helped him cope with his parents' divorce:

There came a time when my brother, Col, was super interested in building firearms again and doing more stuff and he wanted to do some stuff with me . . . And I had kind of felt like since my parents had split up, me and Col had grown a little more distant so I was ecstatic that he wanted to do something with me . . . I think the first gun we built together was a 16-gauge bolt action shotgun. It was a rusty nasty old thing. A lot of people said it was a hideous mother. . . . It was just a nasty old gun that was kind of cool. So, we ended up doing a lot of sanding. I remember that was initially my job until [Col] realized that I was not that great at sanding, so he took me off that job. I hate sanding. Sanding and painting are not my thing, but for me that experience was most enrichening just spending time with my brother and learning what he was talking about 'cause honestly a lot of it, I had no idea. Like he was talking about bluing which was, intentionally rusting the barrel [to prevent rusting] which I thought was really interesting. And I think it is interesting how it correlates to other things. Like with meat, how you intentionally . . . in smoking or something you intentionally *do* something to the meat to make it so the bacteria has a harder time living. And it's kind of like a fire fights fire thing but with the guns . . . So, I thought that was really cool, the processes, and wondering how people learned what they learned.

Greg described how guns can take on powerful emotional valences because of the roles they come to play in the personal relationships in the family:

Well, there's a, I know there's one of them that I can't sell just 'cause of the sentimental value. But that was when I was working in Ogden off and on. I'd come across, I'd acquired two single-shot actions and I got one for Dad and I got one for me. And then we bought wood, we bought Dad a stock and I bought me a stock. And I had them roughed out by this guy and so we, together Dad and I, I literally assembled them for him and made sure I put them together the way I thought they needed to be. But I got the metal work ready to go. We

Figure 8.18. Charles Bartlett in the Navy Alameda, California 1956 and holding the .244 Remington, Tridell, Utah 1957.

had to do some work on the actions and silver soldered bolt handles on both, do the timing on the bolts and things but a lot of work went into making all the metal work right. But then we, Dad and I, sat down and started carving the stock and sanding them out 'cause there was quite a bit of work that needed done. He did the inletting on his and I did the inletting on mine to get them put together but I remember summertime sitting out under the willow tree sanding the stock, talking to him. We were both working on these things to where we could put some finish on them and make them shoot. That was kind of fun, so there's some sentimental value to the Mach 4 that he put together and the .20 caliber that I built on a piece of myrtle. I don't think I could get rid of that 'cause there's some sentimental value tied to that. That was kind of fun, I got a kick out of that, I got to build a gun with Dad.

These objects become, for the family, completely intertwined and inextricable from our family bonds. As Dan put it,

If you wanted to spend time with Dad you needed to go to the gun range with him or you needed to go down to the gun room where he did gunsmithing. And you could spend time with him in the evenings 'cause he spent most evenings, probably at least three days if not four or five days a week doing gun repair for the gun shops around where we lived. So, that was his part time job and like I said if you wanted to spend time with Dad then you went down in the basement and watched

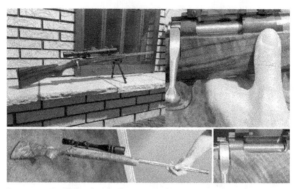

Figure 8.19. The Mach 4 that Charles Claymore Bartlett (CCB) built Smithfield, Utah 2005 and the .20 caliber Greg Charles Bartlett (GCB) built Smithfield, Utah 2005.

him repair guns and have conversations with him. Or if you wanted to go with him on Saturdays, he would have to test, you know, proof the guns I guess you could say to show that he made them better than they were. And he would shoot them before he fixed them and after he fixed them and that would usually be on Saturdays at the gun range.

Guns and my relationship with my family were so intertwined when I was a teenager that I wrote this song to describe my relationship with my father. The theme was, not surprisingly, about firearms:

> I used to sit and watch my daddy
> working with his hands
> and I believed there was nothing he couldn't do
> with a little leather steel and wood.
>
> He barely said a word to me
> but it was plain to see
> he sure liked his little girl's company
> and I love those memories.
>
> Daddy never said he loved me
> that's not the way he was
> but I always knew and I still do
> 'cause he shows me that he does.

A sense of responsibly to the family also emerged at the nexus of personal relationships and guns. This becomes clear when the family members

Figure 8.20. Charles Bartlett shooting his .222 Remington magnum in Ely, Nevada 1966.

recounted some of their customs related to gun safety, gun cleaning, gun handling. Not just practical, these customs demonstrate the groups shared values for a respect of life and nature. A sort of family etiquette, these customs seem to verge on the sacred. Greg, for example, talked about how, "There is no allowance for making mistakes there." Col noted how, "Grandpa just made sure we had proper gun etiquette: cleaning, where to point the gun, never going in front of another one's barrel." Dan said: "You know, Dad did not mess around with gun safety." The most important safety rule was, "The biggest thing is to always treat it as if it's loaded even if you know it's not loaded. The people that get shot . . . whenever a gun accident happens, it's always happened with an 'unloaded' weapon." Greg expanded:

> You got to be safe. . . . Intrinsically it means if I'm doing assembly on a gun or a rifle, something like that, you want to make sure it functions as designed and that something doesn't happen to it that is unexpected and would cause somebody some trouble. That range safety, you know, make sure that gun is unloaded, make sure you know what's behind your target. Make sure you know what the target is.

Precision and responsibility to the family also emerged around the seemingly mundane practice of gun cleaning. Learning the importance of cleaning guns was emphasized in the family from a very young age. The gun cleaning rituals themselves were repeatedly mentioned throughout the interviews. Gun maintenance practices are specifically reported as being a function of precision that emphasized taking personal responsibility. As the family says, precision guns place the ethical responsibility on the shooter by "taking the excuses out of the gun." Dan expanded on this idea saying: "You know, it was the same with cleaning the weapon. You had to keep the weapon clean, again, so it would perform the best that it could." Bryn specifically described this almost ritual act as a form of "respect": "As far as maintaining firearms, that was something with the respect of a gun that I was taught [since I was] young."

This sense of respect for the firearm clearly meshes with respect for individuals when the family speaks about the etiquette surrounding picking up a gun that is not yours. Greg spoke about it this way: "Well, it's the same as if you [don't] want that person touching your wife. It has the same criteria. You have to get permission, you know." Col expanded on this theme saying, "There's never a really good time that you would pick someone's [gun] up without their permission, definitely not without asking." Dan agreed saying, "Well, I think whenever somebody is showing you their gun, before I ever touch it, I would say, 'Do you mind if I pick it up?' . . . That is the way I was taught from Dad was you always ask for permission." Angus added the idea that because the handling of another person's gun requires permission, the giving of that permission is an expression of intimacy in a relationship:

> You never handle someone else's firearm without them being present . . . Like, 100 percent if it's somebody else's gun you just don't touch it unless they're around. And even then, I think it's really important that the offer is extended to you or that the implication of that being acceptable through, like the vibe is kind of there. Like, if they're showing you the gun and kind of like talking to you about it, if you say, "May I hold it?" that's acceptable . . . I would definitely say that it's kind of, it's one of those things that you let the person who is talking about it be the expert even if you do know more about [the gun than they do].

Dan also conveyed this idea in terms of the intimacy of a marital relationship saying, "I've heard some people say that, 'Treat your friends' gun like you would your friend's wife.' I think that's not a bad policy . . . it's a huge honor [if someone offers for you to shoot their gun] and it's almost an insult to turn it down." Angus goes on to explain in terms of the intimacy of sharing food:

> It's something that they're excited about that's precious to them and if they're extending that offer to share it to you, it's amazing. It would be

like if you went to some old grandma Mexican lady and she's making you original tacos from Mexico and you're like, "Oh, no thanks, I had McDonalds three hours ago." It's like, no, you accept what she's making. It's clearly something that she's proud of . . . My Grandpa's offered me to shoot his handguns a couple times—huge honor, huge honor. Whenever somebody offers you to shoot a gun, unless you have like, something major, I would say that it's one of those things that you accept.

This respect for other people extends itself into the natural realm as well. For my family, the process of carving a stock from wood is reminiscent of Michelangelo's statement about sculpting: "The sculpture is already complete within the marble block, before I start my work. It is already there, I just have to chisel away the superfluous material." Greg expands on this theme:

Mother Nature makes the beauty it's just a matter of the poor guy carving it out to show what Mother Nature's made. . . . There's just nothing like a pretty piece of wood and I think I probably got that from Dad 'cause Mother Nature makes some awfully pretty stuff and sometimes it's fun to see what you've got hold of by the time get it all carved out and put that first finish coat on there 'cause then it hops to life and then you know what you've got a hold of.

Charles expands on this idea of respect for nature when he describes how precision takes the form of reverence and mercy. He explains how being a good shot and using the proper gun and ammunition so that the game and varmints you shoot at don't suffer: "I don't think I've ever shot a factory round at a game animal in a long, long time because I generally reloaded everything so I knew exactly what it would do." Dan elaborated on this point saying: "That's something that Dad taught us. You never want to wound an animal. You always wanted to dispatch the animal as cleanly and quickly as possible." Dan went on to describe how his father connected that respect for the game animal to precision of the gun:

Whenever people miss an animal, they want to blame the animal or blame the gun, right? They want to blame the gun; the scope wasn't sighted in or something was wrong with the gun. It was always the gun's fault; it was never their fault. And dad taught us that that was a bunch of baloney. You should never have to blame the weapon for that. The ammo should be dialed in with the weapon that you're shooting and the weapon with the scope that you're using or the sights that

Figure 8.21. Many of Greg Bartlett's custom wood stock rifles and 17 Mach IV 100 yard test fire on small targets (casings) 1993.

you're using so that they are as perfect as you can make them. And then when you are out hunting, you miss the animal because you misjudged the yardage, how far away was the animal or, you jerked, or something happened to you. But it wasn't the weapon's fault, the weapon was perfect and that was kind of what and how we learned that. And that was the same with archery or anything. We shot and shot until we could shoot perfectly and do those things properly. And I don't, I think that's a rarity and I don't think your normal person with a gun thinks about that.

This sense of respect for nature is deeply linked to the form and function that the family takes with its guns. As Wade describes it, "To own guns, you need to be responsible for them. Not only use them safely, but care for them. Treat them good. I was taught by my Dad, with many hours seeing him work on guns and making them look good and shoot well." Bryn described it saying, "I'm a believer that, um, if you shoot it you got to eat it. . . . You don't waste things as much as possible." Angus talked about it differently by noting his dislike for killing things. Instead, he spoke about how the thing he enjoys most about guns is "the concussive force as it's going off, the anticipation as you're pulling the trigger and the way that it would hit the target, like if you shoot a brick it explodes." He went on to note the aesthetics of the sound of shooting: "If you shoot at metal, it makes a really nice ringing harmonic sound. And if you're shooting at wood, it makes a really solid thump and stuff like that." For Angus, these aesthetics of the shooting experience are what is important. For him, "respect" is found in not killing animals for sport: "For me . . . I really hate shooting live things. I've only gone gopher shooting like once or twice and for me, I find the taking of life very unnecessary. And so, in my mind I think I've separated [shooting from killing], they're not a toy and they are to be respected." Wade expanded on this idea by noting how this responsibility is connected to function by respect for animals:

A responsible gun owner knows what their gun will do and so they can be merciful when hunting and be safe when using their guns . . . That is a merciful way to hunt rabbits, with big guns, because if they were hit, they exploded and so they didn't just get injured and cry, it took care of them. They lived or they died. They weren't just wounded, and they died instantly.

This reverence for life and nature sets the group apart from many other gunfolk and is an important dynamic feature of the Bartlett gunsmithing and shooting folk group. Although the rest of the group rarely articulates this feature, I have thought about it a lot. In Western culture and science, we are accustomed to thinking of something like a firearm as an inanimate object but, the reality is that this group's experiences and relationships with firearms suggest otherwise. Many Indigenous people, such as the Blackfoot (Niitsitapi), understand and experience everything in the natural world as animate. That is to say, all things—human beings, wood, minerals, alloys, and even more abstract entities such as sounds, emotions, thoughts, words, and symbols—are believed to have existence and are considered beings. Blackfoot scholar Betty Bastien (2004) explains, "The fundamental premise of Niitsitapi ways of knowing is that all forms of creation possess consciousness." She continues, "A symbol [or object] in the Indigenous paradigm is not an abstraction or a representation of reality, but rather a medium for communicating with the cosmic forces of the universe, a spirit, and it is alive with consciousness from Ihtsipaitapiyop'a [essence of all being; creator]." The scientific field of epigenetics informs us that experiences and memories are inheritable,[2] which seems to correlate with the group's experience of feeling that they and their offspring are born with a knack for gunsmithing and marksmanship. We have seen how the group utilizes both sides of the brain to achieve precision through art and science, but precision also requires skills of the heart. As Greg explained, "It is a labor of love," and while I never inherited the knack for gunsmithing or learned how to modify and dial in a rifle to achieve maximum long-range precision like some members of the group have, I do possess my father's capacity for interspecies and interphenomenal relationships with what the world might consider inanimate or abstract things. I understand that the firearms my family creates and calibrates with inerrant precision and love, are actually part of our folk group (Kirshenblatt-Gimblett 1989; Mechling 1989, 312–23). These guns have their *own* stories to tell and when I hold my grandfather's rifle and pistol, I am literally connected to the past, *my* past.

Notes

1. Taken from my interview with Angus Claymore Atwood.
2. "Epigenics & Inheritance," Learn.Genetics. https://learn.genetics.utah.edu/content/epigenetics/inheritance/.

References

Bastien, B. 2004. *Blackfoot Ways of Knowing*. Calgary: Calgary University Press.
Dundes, Alan. 1965. *The Study of Folklore*. Upper Saddle River, PA: Prentice Hall.
Kirshenblatt-Gimblett, Barbara. 1989. "Objects of Memory: Material Culture as Life Review." In *Folk Groups and Folklore Genres: A Reader*, edited by Elliot Oring, 278–85. Logan: Utah State University Press.
Mechling, Jay R. 1989. "'Banana Cannon' and Other Folk Traditions between Human and Nonhuman Animals." *Western Folklore* 48, no. 4 (October): 312–23.
Mechling, Jay R. 2006. *Solo Folklore. Western Folklore* 65, no. 4 (Fall): 435–53.
Oring, Elliot. 1986. *Folk Groups and Folklore Genres: An Introduction*. Logan: Utah State University Press.

Chapter 9

DANGEROUS TOOLS OF EXPRESSION

The Benefits and Costs of Gunlore

ROBERT GLENN HOWARD

INTRODUCTION: YOUR MOVE, BEE

In 2012, "hollywoodleek" posted the above graphic on a website dedicated to aggregating humorous internet content. The meme couples an action movie-style one-liner with a photograph from a misleading perspective that makes it appear that a menacing pistol is aimed directly at a bumblebee. The first comment posted in response to the graphic makes a typical quip. The second comment seems to state the obvious. "Bumblebees are harmless and do not sting." The third comment, however, is unusual. Flouting the typically brief form of user commenting, "fantomen" posted 235 words that begin, "THESE LITTLE ***** [bees] ARE MASSIVE CUNTS!!! Let me tell you a story . . ." The story goes on to describe how the commenter was, as a child, stung multiple times by what she or he believes was a bumblebee. Based on my own research, I believe it is possible for bumblebees to sting, but it very rarely happens. In any case, the response concludes the story of this rare bumblebee event, exclaiming.

> And that ladies and gentlemen is an example of why bumblebees are assholes. They like to look all sweet and harmless, but on the inside they are all brutal psychos that will take every chance [they] get to harm you. (hollywoodleek 2012)

Possibly just meant as a humorous rejoinder to the post or possibly a cathartic rant about a real childhood experience, the juxtaposition of the harmless bee with the extreme power of a modern pistol creates an oddly whimsical portrayal of violence that elicits a typical internet exchange of lighthearted witticisms.

Until it doesn't.

In the midst of the silly rejoinders, a new post took the conversation in a snarkier direction by shifting the discussion from bumblebees to the handgun: "He's holding a Glock . . . I think the bee is pretty safe." Taking up the topical shift, another user posted a collage of photographs depicting twenty-two Glock pistols that appear to have cracked during use. Moving from joking attacks on the gun, another new post moves to an actual discussion of the merits of Glocks by arguing that their lighter-weight, mostly plastic frame make them harder to shoot than older, mostly steel designs: "Compared to a 1960s US army standard Colt 1911 .45 i find my aim waving all over the damn place with the glock"! Then yet another post added a little bit of gunlore: "You show your 1911 to your friends and your glock to your enemies" (hollywoodleek 2012).

How did this visual joke somehow grow into a serious discussion of handgun design and then suddenly generate what appears to be a proverb perfectly suited to the discussion? The answer to that question is obvious if you are familiar with gun culture. Some of the most common topics among gun enthusiasts are debates about which gun or gun accessory is better, and some of the most common guns compared are these two very different pistols: the Austrian-designed, mostly plastic, and modern Glock versus the US military classic, all metal, and old-school 1911. The comparison between these two pistol designs is so prevalent, in fact, that it has spawned its own community-specific gunlore such as the proverb quoted above. But like all folklore, this proverb is about more than what you see on its surface. It's about more than these two guns. It's about how the proponents of the two different pistols imagine the expressive possibilities of guns; it's not just about what the weapons do, it's about what they *mean*.

The many meanings of gunlore are folkloric in the same way that all folklore is folkloric: it emerges as an individual expression from shared practices that can be found across space and through time (Georges and Jones 1995, 1; McNiell 2013). One common way to think about folklore is that it is an aggregation of previous expression (Howard 2017). That is to say, this particular posting of the proverb is performed based on lots of other people and situations where the user heard the proverb before. This shared or emergent nature is true of online folklore just as much as it is of folklore expressed anywhere else (Blank 2009). Online, though, some of this aggregation can be easily seen in the threads of posts or in different versions of a modified

Figure 9.1. "YOUR MOVE... BEE...," at FunnyJunk.com, 2012.

meme, for example. Online and off, folklore is the aggregate expression of multiple individuals sharing similar ideas and forms across space and over time (Howard 2008; Peck 2014).

When dealing with folklore communicated through communication technologies, we should also consider how the technologies themselves influence the folkloric expression. Communication on social media platforms is enabled and constrained by the structure and features specific to each platform. Those features are made by software engineers paid by corporations to build things that meet the institutional interests of those corporations (Howard 2013). In at least these two ways, we have hybridizing forces in everyday communication online: the mixing of institutional and individual interests through the technology itself and the mixing of various individuals through the interactive and dynamic nature of communication practices that occur over time.

While all folkloric expression is an aggregation of what has come before and all online expression is a hybridization of institutional and individual expression, folklore about guns presents us with a particular tension. In the case of gunlore generally, and this proverb in particular, the individual using the existing shared understandings of these handguns is also forwarding the institutional interests of arms manufacturers. Each expression of this proverb is advertising (even promoting) the purchase of these institutional objects.

For individuals, there is a trade off in this. Because of the immense power inherent in firearms, immense power is also emergent from symbolic expressions about them. The person who engages in individual expression about firearms harnesses a little bit of this power. Whether they are sharing a sense of beauty seen in the gun's design or a connection with history or a sense of personal safety or something else entirely, each individual expression of meaning is empowered by the gun. So gunlore empowers it users. But the vast majority of guns are manufactured and sold by powerful corporations. In exchange for their empowered expression, individuals further the aims of the arms manufacturers they are promoting. While this is true of all sorts of objects, guns are particularly powerful, and promoting them and their manufactures raises complicated questions about how we as individuals benefit and disbenefit from talk about these weapons. And, of course, this is not just true of this proverb but of all expressive performances about guns, of all gunlore.

I define "gunlore" as *folklore about guns*. Since folklore is expressive forms that innovate on shared norms, gunlore is expressive forms that innovate on shared norms about guns. These expressive forms are as widely varied as any human expressive practices: from stories about hunting or shooting to techniques for making, customizing, and using guns and from beliefs about how to properly act around guns to songs containing references to guns. In any of this gunlore, the actual guns involved are dangerous human technologies that demand careful control. As a result of the power of these objects, the expressive forms that derive their power from these objects are also dangerous, dangerous tools of expression.

DOCUMENTING GUNLORE ONLINE

In the case of the deployment of the proverb above, we are looking at internet-mediated communication events. We can conceptualize each network-mediated communication event as emerging at the end of a chain of previous individual, diverse, and potentially quite different events. These previous events (taken together) constitute the new event as it emerges from the previous actions and actors. Those actors each had their own intentions, and each made their own choice to communicate. As a result, each new event is born of the heterogeneous volition of many actors over time. So-called "digital folklore" is one category of such events in which this heterogeneity is particularly clear (Howard 2017).

What we usually think of as "netlore" or digital folklore is a form of vernacular discourse (Dundes and Pagter 1975; Blank 2013). In this usage, "discourse" refers to communication about a particular thing, and "vernacular" refers to discourse that is noninstitutional. "Vernacular discourse," then, includes any communication event that is marked as distinct from any institution. An institution, in this sense, is something that has been instituted. Typically, institutions are instituted by a linguistic act such as signing a contract or making an oath. Once instituted, institutions exert very real power even if they are only our communally imagined social constructions.

Similarly, vernacular discourse exerts power. Specifically, it carries with it vernacular authority. Vernacular authority is authority that is generated by the perceived quality of being noninstitutional. The most familiar form of this sort of authority is informally shared knowledge that we typically imagine as traditional. We seek the "correct" or "authentic" song, dish, dance, or other practice, imagining there is some particular traditional way of enacting that practice (Howard 2013).

Maybe the most distilled form of vernacular authority emerges in the performance of proverbial speech. Often offered as a sort of evidentiary or explanative claim, proverbs are authoritative specifically because they are part of a shared common knowledge that exists beyond institutions. Even when an institution or an institutional actor uses a proverb, that user is seeking authority from the proverb's sense of traditional or common knowledge in addition to their position as part of an institution. The difference between vernacular and institutional authority is that institutional status is conferred onto people or things by the highly charged and high-profile act or acts of instituting. Vernacular authority, by contrast, emerges out of the imagined aggregate of many low-profile everyday individual expressions like the myriad of repetitions that render any common proverb, apparently, wise. Online or off, appeals to vernacular authority are appeals to that which we all already know, and today there is very little discourse that can be performed in both online and face-to-face contexts (sometimes at the same time). Everyday discourse online, however, tends to be fairly publicly visible, and it tends to persist for longer periods of time than face-to-face discourse. As a result, large amounts of vernacular discourse can be looked at online.

To take advantage of this large amount of vernacular expression about guns, I used a combination of computational analysis and close textual analysis to locate four major topical categories of online vernacular firearms discourse on a moderately sized mainstream internet forum dedicated to recreational gun use. I chose to use computational analysis in this medium because it provides an excellent source for the necessary data. Forums offer a large volume of vernacular communication in a relatively normalized and easily translatable format. Because forum software uses specific HTML code to create the webpages that compose it, scripting software can use those tags to extract information and place it into database fields. Creating a database allows me to generate network graphs of the discourse that then allow me to look at a huge volume of online gun discourse fairly quickly.[1]

I chose to use the Guns and Ammo Forum because it is, in many ways, a typical gun forum. It is part of the *Guns & Ammo* magazine website. The magazine that was first published in 1958 offers a largely United States audience "content covering the complete spectrum of firearms, accessories and related products." It claims to be "the most respected media brand in the firearms field" (Outdoor Sportsman Group 2015). Its online forum appears to have started in 2011. The forum is moderately sized compared to other gun forums I have documented, with about seven thousand members and just over half a million posts as of the summer of 2016. Other forums have more narrowly defined audiences, such as those that are geographically specific like Calguns.net. Calguns focuses on California gun users and has 92,697 members. Other forums narrow their users by focusing on a specific gun model like GlockTalk.com. GlockTalk focuses on the Glock brand of handguns and has 191,992 users. Based on a nationally marketed magazine, Guns and Ammo Forum gives a view into a moderate-sized forum with a broad cross section of online gun discourse.

To locate the most active users of the Guns and Ammo Forum, I created graphs that show which individuals most often speak to each other in responding forum posts or "threads." Noting individuals who interact often and individuals who interact less often, I located all the posts by different users and compared the topics being discussed in those posts.

To create these network graphs, I worked with computer programmers to write Perl[2] computer language scripts that download an entire forum and then place its contents into a SQL[3] database. As of 2016, I had downloaded fifteen gun forums for a total of 34,105,654 individual posts. The Guns and Ammo Forum alone contains 525,219 posts. If I were to spend one minute reading each of these posts on just the Guns and Ammo Forum, it would take me 364 days with no breaks. To get a good overview of the data on just this one forum is simply not possible without a computational approach. A computational approach, however, cannot replace close analysis. While numerical representations of human expression can direct the researchers' attention to important or interesting content, only close analysis brings the subtlety and nuance of individual everyday communications to light (Howard 2015). Combining close reading with the overall perspective provided by computational analysis, I can better understand the topics of discussion that define the discourse.

To locate these topics, I generated graphs that visualize which individual users post in the same threads. Using these graphs, I gain a large-scale view of the discourse on the forum even though I could not possibly have read all the posts. I can tell which individuals speak most and who they most often speak to because the more times each linked pair of individuals posted in the same forum thread, the redder and thicker the lines between them on the graph become. At the same time, the more each user posted overall, the bigger the red dot representing their location in the network becomes. To really see what these individuals are discussing, I could now search the database for all the posts posted by a particular user or users and read them. Picking the most interesting of the top ten users, I searched for and read the last hundred posts that user posted on the forum. In cases where an interesting discussion emerged, I would locate and read the entire thread where that post appeared.

ONLINE GUN DISCOURSE

By looking at what was being talked about by these users in the Guns and Ammo Forum, three clear topics of discussion become clear: "How to . . ."; "Politics"; and "Which is better?" Posts that I categorize as part of the "How to . . ." topic generally feature individuals discussing specific techniques associated with recreational firearm use including hunting techniques, gun maintenance practices, and so on. "Politics" focuses on discussions and predictions about changes to gun laws. "Which is better?" generally features individuals discussing which guns and which gun accessories they like most. In these discussions, intense debates sometimes emerge about which item is best.

Most of these discussions do not end with individuals stating that they have decided which product is finally best or which product they will now purchase. Instead, much of this discourse is what I have previously termed "ritual deliberation." Ritual deliberation occurs when individuals engage in what appears to be a debate. However, the terms on which that debate is engaged preclude any final decision being made. This sort of deliberation serves the ritual purpose of enacting shared competency in a discourse in order to demonstrate group identity (Howard 2011, 58–65).

Among the common topics in this discourse, the "How to . . ." topic serves the least ritual purpose. When engaging this topic, individuals seem most often to be genuinely seeking information about how to do things. The individuals most often engaging in this topic tend to be less inclined to speak to the same individuals about the same things. The "Politics" topic, on the other hand, is engaged by a relatively small group of people who post disproportionally more than other users. There is seldom real dissent in this topic. No one is calling for stronger gun-control measures, for example. However, engaging in these debates seems to be a way for individuals to inspire each other to political action and there are sometimes specific corrective exchanges where ideas are forwarded and then abandoned (or at least quieted) as the debate moves forward (Howard 2017).

Like the "How to . . ." topic, the "Which is better?" topic often emerges when individuals are genuinely seeking advice about guns or accessories to buy and use. However, specific discussions about particular products have inspired enough discourse to become notorious in the online gun community, such as the debate about whether the Glock or the 1911 handgun design is better. These debates function more as ritual deliberation than deliberative decision making because they seem to continue without any hope of resolution, and they seem to inspire intense identification by some individuals in the community.

Along with debates that compare the AR-15 to the AKM family of assault rifles and those that compare the .45 ACP cartridge to the 9mm cartridge, the comparison between the 1911 and the Glock inspire some of the most intense debate. "Glock Perfection" is the self-appraising slogan of the Glock weapons manufacturing company, and those who seem too fully convinced of this claim have been derisively dubbed "Glock fanboys" by the larger gun community. The very different handgun design of the 1911 also has a large following.

In the next section, I will look at how individuals use these two mass-produced commercial handguns as a resource to enact their own identities in the online gun community. As they do this, they harness the perennial symbolic power of the gun while at the same time forwarding the interests of institutional arms manufacturers.

VERNACULAR AUTHORITY SPEAKS FOR THE GLOCK

"Show your 1911 to your friends, show your Glock to your enemies" qualifies as a proverb based on Wolfgang Mieder's accepted definition because it is a fixed and memorizable form that contains generally known wisdom (Mieder 1993, 5). The wisdom here is, on the literal level, that the Glock is an effective firearm. On a more metaphoric level, the wisdom is that function is more important than form. In both registers, this kind of folk speech is also an endorsement of a specific commercial product: the Glock line of pistols.

Here, individual expression comes infused not only with the communal wisdom of a proverb but also charged with the inherent power of the gun to make meaning. As with the other topics documented in these forums, individuals perform this saying online to mark themselves as part of a shared identity in the online community. But they do so at the price of supporting commercial interests by asserting the superiority of the weapons that the corporation manufactures and sells.

Searching the words "show your 1911 to your friends, show your Glock to your enemies" on the Google search engine resulted in 43,800 results. I cataloged the first hundred results that were clear performances of this proverb. The performance of the proverb constitutes a sort of gunlore practice because its repeated performances create a community of gun owners who recognize it. The proverb exhibits continuities and consistencies, and these continuities and consistencies are magnified by digital technologies because individuals can access websites where other gun-lovers congregate and share the knowledge that defines this specific community.

Going to these sites, in turn, further increases their exposure to the continuities and consistencies. For these individuals, this proverb is one of many resources they can deploy to enact their identity as firearms enthusiasts, and this proverb is one of myriad ways to deploy the gun as an expressive tool. However, individuals expressing their identities online are not the only ones impowered by using this proverb. The Glock corporation has made the proverb possible, contributed to defining the value of function over form in the community, and, in the end, Glock benefits from the practice of repeatedly performing this proverb as individuals produce an enormous amount of free or nearly free publicity for the company's products.

The appearance of the specific brand name "Glock" is an institutional element that gives rise to the vernacular performance. Glock is the registered trademark of Glock Ges.m.b.H., an Austrian weapons manufacturer. Its founder, Gaston Glock, designed the mostly plastic pistol and patented it in 1982 as part of a competition for the Austrian military's primary handgun contract. Winning the contract, the very popular series of Glock handguns has gone on to become one of the most common and widely used pistols worldwide; adopted by over fifty national militaries and law enforcement agencies from Sweden and the United Kingdom to Malaysia and Israel. At one point, Glock reportedly had 65 percent of the US law enforcement market contracts (Glock Ges.m.b.H. 2016). The Glock model 19 is often described as one of the most effective pistols ever produced. However, when the Atlanta police department adopted the Glock, the local newspaper reported, "New Gun 'Ugly,' But Effective, Police Say" (cited in Barrett 2013, 282). Reporting on a mass shooting in 1991, the *Houston Chronicle* noted, "'Ugly' Gun Can Fire 16–20 Shots" (cited in Barrett 2013, 284). Even the gun's first major US importer, when first seeing the new high-tech pistol, commented: "Jeez, that's ugly" (quoted in Barrett 2013, 52).

In gun discourse, the Glock design is imagined as emphasizing function and not aesthetics. Glock's own marketing slogan promotes this ethos by suggesting that simplicity (both in words and in form) gives the user confidence: "Safe. Simple. Fast. = Confidence." (Glock Ges.m.b.H. 2010).

Though the term "1911" in the proverb is not a registered trademark, it still refers to a specific gun design that one of several companies actively markets to US civilians as well as military and law enforcement agencies. The 1911 is a much older design that is, arguably, less reliable but more aesthetically appealing. Originally designed by John Browning for the American firearms manufacturer Colt's Manufacturing Company, the "M1911" designation was given to the gun when it was adopted by the US military as its standard military sidearm in the year 1911. Used for the next seventy-five years, the gun has taken on an iconic status. Invoking this status in their 2016 marketing materials, Colt suggests that the owner of one of its modern versions of the pistol becomes connected to its historic users through the "faithful" reproduction from "blueprints."

Colt 1911 pistols and their descendants were in the hands of confident World War I, World War II, Korean War and Vietnam-era servicemen. Colt customers today can purchase reproductions of these weapons, each faithfully manufactured to the original specifications from factory blueprints. (Colt's Manufacturing Company LLC 2016)

Instead of emphasizing its modern design, materials, or manufacturing process, Colt emphasizes that its pistols "offer enthusiasts an opportunity to own a handcrafted 1911 type pistol" (Colt's Manufacturing Company LLC 2016).

Understanding the sorts of ethos these two pistol designs have helps clarify why individuals might use them to define their identities in this community. It also helps clarify the meaning of the proverb. One might show a 1911 to their friends because though the design is not as modern or as functional as the Austrian Glock pistol, it offers a powerful sense of connection to US history and, after all, it is considered nice to look at. It has what well-known gun blogger Nutnfancy has famously dubbed a "second kind of cool." As Nutnfancy describes it, an "item actually has TWO KINDS OF COOL: [1] PERFORMANCE within its category and [2] the intrinsic ENJOYMENT it provides its owner" (Nutnfancy 2008). If the 1911 markets itself as offering its users the "intrinsic enjoyment" of being connected to a rich history of users, the Glock claims to offer pure performance in the form of "confidence" that it will work effectively. By all accounts, however, both pistols are extremely deadly, and both have functioned effectively for individual users and large militaries for decades.

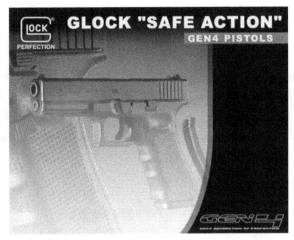

Figure 9.2. Front cover of an online brochure for the "Gen4" variant of Glock pistols introduced in 2010.

Based on this understanding of the ethos of the two guns, the meaning of the proverb in the gun community can be rendered as something like, "It is more important that the weapon work well than that it look good." To put it even more bluntly, the assertion of the proverb at the literal level is really that the Glock is the more effective weapon. The proverb is, ultimately, making a claim about which of these two commercial products is better, and that places it squarely in the common online gun discourse topic of "Which is better?"

All such discourse participates in what social network marketers call "brand communities" (Jenkins 2013, 163). These communities are a combination of the efforts of individuals who have developed a passionate attachment to a product and the careful facilitation, encouragement, and even augmentation of those communities by marketing professionals. As a result, the discourse in these communities is a hybrid of volitional actions that include both everyday actors and commercial corporate actors. In most cases, this hybrid of effort is probably not being harnessed to very serious ends. Brand communities are most associated with fan culture around media franchises like Star Trek or Harry Potter (Jenkins 1992; Bacon-Smith 1991; and Hinck 2016). But they are also common among users of specific forms of durable recreational products like motorcycles, guitars, and guns.

In a post on the California-oriented Calguns gun forum, "Travis590A1" invited other users to state which was their favorite handgun using the .45 ACP pistol round, a round that is the traditional cartridge of the 1911 and immediately associated with it by members of the gun community. Travis590A1 made his opinion provocatively clear: "Mine is a Glock."

Figure 9.3. Colt's marketing website for the 1911 pistol, 2016.

A day later, "AeroEngi" posted, "You guys would seriously pick a Glock over a 1911 in the .45 category? I'd without a doubt go with a 1911." And a long discussion of the relative merits of the two guns began. Several posts in, one user noted,

> I love shooting my 1911, but it's had jamming issues, been back to the factory twice for repairs. My Glock G30's [Glock handguns using the same cartridge as the 1911] have never jammed, not once in many thousands of rounds... I don't know the originator of this quote, but I like it: "You show your 1911 to your friends, you show your Glock to your enemies." (Travis590A1 2012)

Here the user establishes vernacular authority for his support of the Glock by portraying the saying as being commonly held wisdom, as is typical of proverbial speech: "I don't know the originator of this, but..."

After the proverb was invoked, the next 157 posts in the thread include 129 individuals sharing sixty-one pictures of their own favorite .45 caliber handguns. This flood of photos is a good example of the emic genre of "gun porn."

Amateur gun porn is the practice of taking and sharing pictures of one's own guns. While there is professional gun photography made for advertising or other purposes, amateur gun porn is not primarily interested in selling guns. Instead, it functions to assert one's identity as a member of one subgroup or another in the larger recreational gun-user community. The identification with the Glock branding community is strong enough and the community is large enough that well-known YouTube gun celebrity Colion Noir offers a two minute and twenty-nine second YouTube video titled "You Know You're A GLOCK FANBOY When..." (Noir 2012). The discourse also includes advocates like the well-known online gun magazine editorial: "Glock Fanboy Makes His Case" (Tim 2012). In another example, an amateur forum poster on the gun-friendly forum survivalistboards.com

Figure 9.4. Glock Amateur Gun Porn, 2012.

started a thread titled "I'm a Glock fanboy . . ." in which he wrote, "I know its not the popular things to say but I have to go with what works. Now glock needs to make a 1911 and all will be right in the world. . . . Okay, flame on . . ." (Uglyfish 2012). His anticipation of a coming "flame" or rush of incoming negative comments to his post reveals both the widespread nature of the Glock vs. 1911 debate and the apparent disinterest in actually coming to any new conclusions based on the debate. A 2010 thread on the ar15.com gun forum titled "Which Firearms Related Fanboys Are the Worst?" shows an overwhelming number of users believe Glocks have the worst "fanboys." One user summed up the statement well, writing, "Glock by a mile. Its design is about as exciting as a honda civic yet people worship it." Another use agreed:

> I would have to go with glock. They always have to do some ridiculous assed thing to prove (prove to who, we're not sure) how great their choice in a handgun is.
>
> Fanboy #1: I shot mine underwater.
> Fanboy #2: I shot mine in a bowl of jellow.
> Fanboy #3: I shot mine in battery acid.
> Etc. (ArmyInfantryVet 2010)

In the "Which Firearms Related Fanboys Are the Worst?" thread, the 1911 also has a large showing. The more austere nature of the gun and the stereotype of the owners that identify with it bubble to the surface in one post when a user asserts that 1911 fans are less open to joking about their gun than others: "Come on, we all know it's the 1911 fanboys. . . . They actually and seriously get offended if you talk mean to a 1911" (ArmyInfantryVet 2010).

These kinds of exchanges certainly are debates about which guns are better, and some participants probably are deciding on which handgun to use or purchase. However, these discussions most often function primarily to express one's opinion, display competence in gun discourse, and thus display membership in the gun community. Whichever brand an individual favors, there are no resolutions to these debates, nor would there usually be any real consequences of a resolution if one were to be found. Instead, these online celebrations and denigrations of particular guns allow individuals to participate in the community by expressing their preference.

Threads like the one from Calguns above inviting people to post pictures of their guns are very much meant to invite the forum users to perform their identity in the repetition of well-known arguments and opinions—and, of course, post pictures. In the 129 posts in that thread, most of the comments were affirmations of the poster's pictures, like, "+1 for my Glock." There were also positive comments made about the photographic skill of the gun owners. The photo below seemed to be the group favorite in this thread, and the dramatic lighting, reflection, and composition with liquor bottles in the background render this photograph more technically sophisticated than most. The rather bland and low-resolution Glock photo above is much more typical.

Taking and sharing these photographs is certainly a form of vernacular artistic expression, a practice that serves as means for these individuals to connect as a community. At the same time, this expressive practice could only arise as it has after the successful design and sale of these particular handguns. Further, these weapons manufacturers necessarily benefit from the development and expansion of the branding community as its members repeatedly extend the online presence of and advocate for the companies' products at little or no cost to the company.

In another example, however, we can see most clearly how the performance of this proverb offers its uses expressive power at the cost of forwarding commercial interests. On February 20, 2015, a user posted a link to an article on the "left wing gun nuts" Facebook group page. The article was from a well-known industry magazine called *Military.com* and was titled: "Marines Allow Operators to Choose Glocks over MARSOC .45s." After the link to the article, the poster noted, "You show your 1911 off to your friends and your Glock off to your enemies" (Left Wing Gun Nuts 2015).

The article he was posting as part of this proverb performance offered a short news report on the partial adoption of the Glock pistol as a replacement for a highly specialized version of the 1911 pistol in limited use by the US military. The article referenced a larger institutional debate about which gun the US military should purchase for its standard sidearm. The US military

Figure 9.5. 1911 Gun Porn, 2012.

first called for arms manufactures to offer new pistol designs for an overall pistol contract in 2011, but the contract wasn't awarded until 2018. As a result, there were long-running public debates in the online gun community about which company should be awarded the contract until it was finally decided. Arming the entire US military would be a very lucrative contract for any weapons maker, and Glock was certainly a frontrunner in the competition. On the Facebook page, that debate about what new pistol the US should purchase in the future emerged at the vernacular level.

Supporting the Glock's famously simple design over the more traditional hammer fired design of the 1911, "Dave" posted, "Choose a striker fired weapon [the Glock]!" Another user responded, "The 1911 is slick, but a Glock 19 is faster, lighter, [and] cheaper." Then yet another poster sarcastically suggested that Glocks were incapably of killing at all, writing, "'Show off your 1911 to your friends and your glock to your enemies'? Why? To hope they die laughing?" A Glock supporter rejoined quite seriously, "Personally, I love Glock. My G19 and G27 were without any doubt some of the best pistols you could buy." Then a 1911 supporter retorted, "I believe the article when it points out 'lack of enough training' . . . was part of the issue." And then still another user, "Jon," referenced the original poster's use of the proverb. So doing, he brought the vernacular authority of the proverb to bear even more resolutely by reposting a variant of it in the form of an image macro–style meme with the comment, "That is my new favorite quote" (Left Wing Gun Nuts 2015).

The deployment of this proverb here on Facebook expresses its support for the US military's adoption of the Glock in an informal exchange, and this initial contract offered significant financial rewards for Glock. It would increase sales and prestige, and it could even become a stepping-stone toward the larger and more lucrative contracts still undecided at that time.

In January of 2017, however, Army leadership did not choose the Glock from the competitive bids it received. Instead, coming in far cheaper, the Sig Sauer P320 was chosen to replace the US Army's aging stock of M9 handguns (Cox and Hope 2017). Designed by Beretta, a private Italian weapons manufacturing company, the M9s have been in use since 1985 and were widely considered to be out-of-date, worn out, and in need of replacement (White 2016). A general contract with the US Army could have been worth as much as $98.1 million (Cox 2016). Typically, follow-on contracts would be expected with all the other branches of the US military, which could be worth as much as $160 million. Further, adoption by the US military would have certainly boosted civilian sales of the pistols because its usage by the military would be seen as a stamp of approval. The amount of money at stake for Glock was significant, and Glock disputed the Army decision in civil court. Though Glock lost the contract to a strong competitor, Sig Sauer's pistol immediately displayed significant safety and reliability problems. As those problems became widely reported, the voices of Glock aficionados responded with loud I-told-you-so's (Dabbs 2017). While the participation of vernacular authority in the public debates about the decision is not quantifiable, the vernacular authority of this proverb is clearly speaking for Glock.

THE BENEFITS AND COSTS OF GUNLORE

In the example of the "show your 1911 to your friends, show your Glock to your enemies" proverb, a bit of gunlore empowers everyday people to express themselves through the symbol of guns. For these individuals, this is a benefit: to express themselves in ways that connect them to a community. In most cases, I think, this expression takes forms more like the rush of gun porn or the debate following the rant against bumblebees. If not most often than very often, the gun proverb is used like a lot of gunlore is used: as a means to express a shared community identity by repeating well-known opinions and ideas using the words and ideas associated with firearms.

Like all branding community discourse, however, these acts of communication also promote the intentions of the product manufacturers. Glock and all the other corporations that produce these guns make this vernacular expression of identity possible by making the objects, the guns, that are the basis for that identity expression. One potential cost of this expression, then, is that the expressor is selling the products of the arms manufacturers and

Figure 9.6. The "Show your 1911 to your friends, show your Glock to your enemies" proverb as an internet meme, 2015.

thus putting money in the coffers of these large corporations. In this way, the symbolic expression of these individuals is creating very real material benefits for other individuals. What if the arms manufactures and the person performing proverb have different material needs? What if they inhabit different positions of power?

These questions raise complicated critical issues. At the very least, each deployment of any sort of gunlore imagines and maybe even promotes a world in which guns exist. And that is not just limited to folklore about guns but, probably to a much greater extent, portrayals of guns in mass media. Product placements show us that a world with guns is an exciting world we can live in if we choose (in the US at least) by buying more guns. TV shows like *The Walking Dead*, movies like *Die Hard*, and a wide variety of popular music, all encourage us to live in a world filled with guns. While most of us probably don't have a lot of control over the entertainment industry, what about gun imagery like exhorting our colleagues to "keep our powder dry" before the contentious meeting starts or suggesting our rather unpredictable friend has stalked off "half cocked"? If enough people around me at the dinner table would know that when I said, "Well, you show your Glock to your enemies after all, right?" I meant you should privilege function over aesthetics in important situations, I might well say it. But in saying it, I would be framing that context (a family dinner for example) in terms of particular kind of power, and I would be, at the same time, putting in a plug for Glock.

Maybe that is OK for many of us. Maybe living in an action movie world seems harmless or even attractive. Maybe firearms are an unfortunate necessity for us, or maybe they enable us to do our job, or maybe they are a way for us to express our identity as empowered and confident members of a community. Any way we view it and however it is we relate to guns, the repetition of these performances reshares the idea that guns are in our world and that idea, in turn, encourages more performances of our valuation. As more performances are performed, more individuals are invited to imagine a world that includes guns. Even if in a very small way, each of these performances shares some responsibility for the normalization of guns into our shared world. In the case of this proverb in particular, its users are normalizing a specific arms manufacturer as part of our world.

This is nothing new, of course. Institutional actors have appealed to constituents by deploying proverbial speech long before the advent of social media through grassroots fan clubs and hobbyist communities that emerged around commercial products. There never was some golden age where vernacular expression was pure. Expressive communication is always a product of empowerment and a means to empower. This is true of all symbols, mundane or extraordinary. Ghosts, gods, or guns, these symbols are powerful precisely because we have repeatedly preformed them over time.

In the case of gunlore, though, the power of the gun itself further ladens the expression about guns with a real gravity that comes from the potential danger associated with the objects they reference. We can scare each other by imagining a world filled with ghosts, or we can comfort each other by imaging a world governed by a benevolent god, but when we imagine a world filled with Glocks, we normalize a very material and very attainable (in the US at least) place. There is no debate that Glocks are prevalent in the United States today and that they are extremely powerful objects. Piggybacking a bit of our own expressive power off that very material power of the gun necessarily furthers a world filled with guns. Are the benefits of making that expressive choice worth the costs (Gencarella 2009)?

It's not an empty question because some people right now are imagining a world free of guns as a dream to be pursued. At the same time, other people are imagining such a gun-free world as one we must actively seek to avoid. For many people there is unquestionable joy associated with shooting guns. For many there are perceived advantages for gun ownership, from procuring meat to self-defense. For many there are social advantages to guns, from expressing identity to artistic or similar self-expression through gun building and customization. For those who value guns, performing gunlore forwards interests they already have anyway.

In the great debate about guns in the United States today, the discussion between gun advocates and detractors must be one about the costs and benefits of owning guns. It centers on concrete questions of value, such as if the specific benefits of personal self-defense are worth more than attempting to reduce gun deaths through gun bans. And different individuals will necessarily imagine that equation based on different life experiences and from different social positions. Wherever a person falls out on debates like that, both sides should acknowledge that human expression about guns is very powerful indeed, and it is inextricably intertwined with the actual realities (good or bad) of guns being in our shared world. The power of gunlore goes both ways: the real power of guns renders our talk about them more exciting and empowering, and, at the same time, our talk about guns imagines and reimagines a world filled with these very real and very powerful objects. For better or worse, gunlore is a dangerous tool of expression, and, like any dangerous tool, we need to pay attention to what we are doing and follow sensible safety rules when we use it.

Notes

1. For more on my methods, please see my 2015 book chapter in *Research Methods for Reading Digital Data in the Digital Humanities.*

2. Perl is a general-purpose computer language commonly used to automate simple computer network tasks.

3. SQL or "Structure Query Language" is a special purpose computer programming language designed for managing data in relational database systems.

References

ArmyInfantryVet. 2010. "Which Firearms Related Fanboys Are the Worst?" January 2, 2010, http://www.ar15.com/archive/topic.html?b=1&f=5&t=978375.

Bacon-Smith, Camille. 1991. *Enterprising Women: Television Fandom and the Creation of Popular Myth*. Philadelphia: University of Pennsylvania Press.

Barrett, Paul M. 2012. *Glock: The Rise of America's Gun*. New York: Random House.

Blank, Trevor J. 2009. *Folklore and the Internet: Vernacular Expression in a Digital World.* Logan: Utah State University Press.

Blank, Trevor J. 2013. *The Last Laugh: Folk Humor, Celebrity Culture, and Mass-Mediated Disasters in the Digital Age.* Madison: University of Wisconsin Press.

Colt's Manufacturing Company LLC. 2016. "Catalog." January 1, 2016, http://www.colt .com/Catalog/Pistols.

Cox, Mathew. 2015. "Marines Allow Operators to Choose Glocks over MARSOC .45s." February 2, 2015. http://www.military.com/daily-news/2015/02/19/marines-allow -operators-to-choose-glocks-over-marsoc-45.html.

Cox, Mathew. 2016. "Army Chief Eyeing Glock Pistol as Service's Next Sidearm." March 21, 2016. http://www.military.com/daily-news/2016/03/21/army-chief-eyeing-glock -pistol-as-services-next-sidearm.html.

236 DANGEROUS TOOLS OF EXPRESSION: BENEFITS AND COSTS OF GUNLORE

Cox, Mathew, and Hope Hodge Seck. 2017. "Army Picks Sig Sauer's P320 Handgun to Replace M9 Service Pistol." January 18, 2017. https://www.military.com/daily -news/2017/01/19/army-picks-sig-sauer-replace-m9-service-pistol.html.

Dabbs, Will. 2017. "Glock vs Sig: The 'World War III' for Pistol Fanboys." August 16, 2017. https://www.tactical-life.com/firearms/handguns/glock-vs-sig-fanboys/.

Dundes, Alan, and Carl R. Pagter. 1975. *Urban Folklore from the Paperwork Empire.* Austin, TX: American Folklore Society.

Gencarella, Stephen Olbrys. 2009. "Constituting Folklore: A Case for Critical Folklore Studies." *Journal of American Folklore* 122 (484): 172–96.

Georges, Robert A., and Michael Owen Jones. 1995. *Folkloristics: An Introduction.* Bloomington: University of Indiana Press.

Glock Ges.m.b.H. 2010. "Glock 'Safe Action' GEN4 Pistols." January 1, 2010. https:// us.glock.com/documents/BG_Gen4_6_2010_EN_MAIL.pdf.

Glock Ges.m.b.H. 2016. "Glock Law Enforcement." January 1, 2016. https://us.glock.com/ products/sector/law-enforcement.

Hinck, Ashley. 2016. "Ethical Frameworks and Ethical Modalities: Theorizing Communication and Citizenship in a Fluid World." *Communication Theory* 26, no. 1 (February): 1–20.

Hollywoodleek. 2012. "You Move Bee . . .," November 27, 2012. http://www.funnyjunk. com/funny_pictures/4262807/Your+move+bee/.

Howard, Robert Glenn. 2011. *Digital Jesus: The Making of a New Christian Fundamentalist Community on the Internet.* New York: New York University Press.

Howard, Robert Glenn. 2013. "Vernacular Authority: Critically Engaging 'Tradition.'" In *Tradition in the 21st Century: Locating the Role of the Past in the Present*, edited by Trevor J. Blank and Robert Glenn Howard, 72–99. Logan: Utah State University Press.

Howard, Robert Glenn. 2015. "Digital Network Analysis: Understanding Everyday Online Discourse Micro- and Macroscopically." In *Research Methods for Reading Digital Data in the Digital Humanities*, edited by Gabriele Griffin and Matt Hayler. 165–83. Edinburgh: Edinburgh University Press.

Howard, Robert Glenn. 2017. "GunNets: Why a Theory of Heterogeneous Volition Is Necessary in the Study of Digital Communication." *Cultural Analysis* 16, no. 1: 116–33.

Left Wing Gun Nuts. 2015. "When I Posted . . ." 20 February 2015. https://www.facebook .com/LeftWingGunNuts/.

McNeill, Lynne S. 2013. *Folklore Rules! A Fun, Quick, and Useful Introduction to the Field of Academic Folklore Studies.* Logan, UT: University of Colorado Press.

Mieder, Wolfgang. 1993. Proverbs Are Never Out of Season: Popular Wisdom in the Modern Age. Oxford: Oxford University Press.

Jenkins, Henry. 1992. *Textual Poachers: Television Fans and Participatory Culture.* New York: Routlege, Chapman, and Hall.

Jenkins, Henry, Sam Ford, and Joshua Green. 2013. *Spreadable Media: Creating Value and Meaning in a Networked Culture.* New York: NUY Press.

Noir, Colion. 2012. "You Know You're A GLOCK FANBOY When . . ." August 23, 2012. https://www.youtube.com/watch?v=UsyY5ecNs4k.

Nutnfancy. 2008. "Two Kinds of Cool." November 25, 2008. http://www.youtube.com/v/yGsNeUQZ1fo?fs=1&rel=0.

Outdoor Sportsman Group. 2015. "Guns & Ammo." January 1, 2015. http://www.outdoorsg.com/brands/shooting/gunsandammo/.

Peck, Andrew M. 2014. "A Laugh Riot: Photoshopping as Vernacular Discursive Practice." *International Journal of Communication* 8, 1638–62. http://ijoc.org/index.php/ijoc/article/view/2692.

Peck, Andrew M. 2015. "Tall, Dark, and Loathsome: The Emergence of a Legend Cycle in the Digital Age." *Journal of American Folklore* 128, no. 509: 333–48.

Tim. 2012. "Glock Fanboy Makes His Case." September 6, 2012. http://www.thetruthaboutguns.com/2012/09/tim-harmsen/striker-fired-pistols-mines-a-glock/.

Travis590A1. 2012. "Whats Your Favorite 45 Caliber Handgun?" November 29, 2012. http://www.calguns.net/calgunforum/archive/index.php/t-650560.html.

Uglyfish. 2012. "I'm a Glock Fanboy . . ." September 24, 2012. http://www.survivalistboards.com/showthread.php?t=259414.

White, Andrew. 2016. "US Army Moves Ahead with Handgun Replacement Programme." May 31, 2016. http://www.janes.com/article/60814 us-army-moves-ahead-with-handgun-replacement-programme.

Chapter 10

GUN PLAY AS VERNACULAR
RELIGIOUS EXPERIENCE

JAY MECHLING

In 2008 I published an article, "Gun Play" (Mechling 2008), exploring many forms of play with guns and offering what Clifford Geertz (1973c) calls a "thick description," rather than a "thin description," of such play. Born and raised in Miami Beach, my only experience with real guns (I owned a BB gun) was at Boy Scout camp, where we learned firearms safety and shot .22 short rounds from single-shot bolt action rifles at targets. I was a pretty good shot and earned the Marksmanship merit badge (Mechling 2014). Although I am not a hunter, like some in my extended family, I became interested in hunting while teaching and writing about animals in American culture, from pets to wildlife films to zoos to hunting (Mechling 2004).

Returning to the topic of gun play after more than a decade, and thinking that I probably had nothing new to say about the topic, I realized three things. First, for some reason I cannot recall now, the snapshots of gun play I originally wanted to include in the 2008 published essay were not published, and looking again through my collection of snapshots of gunplay has given me some new ideas. Second, my work on folklore in the male military group (Mechling 2012; Wallis and Mechling 2019; Wallis and Mechling 2020; Mechling 2021) led me to think some more about guns, deep play (Geertz 1973a), and our imagining of our own deaths. More on this issue below. And third, my writing and teaching about religion in American lives (e.g., Mechling 2010) made me consider the unlikeliest idea of all, one that had not occurred to me in 2008—namely, that gun play is a vernacular religious practice.

When I use the word "gun" in this essay, I have in mind handguns and rifles because they are the two sorts of firearms I most associate with "gun play" (Mechling 2008). I know that people go to shooting ranges and open spaces to "play" shooting automatic weapons at targets and other objects,

238

but hoping a drill instructor does not come down on me for calling a rifle a "gun," I will use that word with the understanding that I am including rifles. As the famous boot camp chant has it, "This is my rifle [touching the rifle at rest on the shoulder], this is my gun [grabbing the penis]" (Burns 2003). More on guns and sex below.

"Play" is the other word in the phrase "gun play," and here, as always, I rely on Gregory Bateson's (1972) frame theory of play and fantasy. Briefly, Bateson showed curiosity about and amazement at the ability of mammals to communicate in ways in which the messages exchanged do not mean what they would mean outside what he calls "the play frame." Playfighting was the prime example that set Bateson thinking about the "paradox" of play, how the actions and their messages in the play frame—"the nip that is not a nip," watching dogs playfight, for example—do not mean what they would mean in the frame "this is a fight." The key was seeing that the mammals exchanged a metamessage, a message about the messages in the frame, creating the agreed-upon "reality" during the space and time of that interaction.

As I move this essay toward specifics about my wanting us to think about gun play as a vernacular religious experience, I need to note that play and ritual are, as one anthropologist puts it, "complementary frames of meta-communication" (Handelman 1977). Both are framed events outside of ordinary time and space. Both the play and ritual frame are social constructions through the exchange and agreement to a metamessage, "this is play" in one case and "this is ritual" in the other. Both frames are fragile, easily broken, and if the frame matters to the participants, they repair it as quickly as possible.

The play and ritual frames do differ in some respects. The ritual frame asserts and affirms the natural order of things, endorsing that facticity. The play frame, in contrast, is in the subjunctive "what if?" mode, opening up an alternative possible world where nonsense comments on sense (Stewart 1979) and the normal order of things is reversed (Babcock 1977).

When I define religion below, we will encounter Geertz's point that one important function of religion is to tame chaos, bringing order to disorder. Ritual is comforting. Another way to define religion, however, is by looking at it through the lens of play. The ancient Greeks understood this, imagining both Apollonian and Dionysian approaches to religious experience (Nietzsche 1872). I do not have to look back that far, though, for the idea that play can be as much a religious experience as is ritual. William James's discussion of mysticism (James 1902, 379–429) and Mihaly Csikszentmihalyi's (1975) concept of "flow" will help make clear how play with guns can be a vernacular religious experience.

240 GUN PLAY AS VERNACULAR RELIGIOUS EXPERIENCE

Both ritual and play are about power. Both can be magical, which means that guns can be experienced as magical objects. I will return to this below.

Before I define religion, I should say a few things about the snapshots I present in this essay. I have collected vernacular photographs (amateur snapshots) over many years and have used them in my scholarship about American culture (Mechling 2004; Mechling 2005; Mechling 2012; Mechling 2016b; Mechling 2021). I do not offer snapshots as mere illustrations; rather, I treat them as visual evidence of practices not always revealed in other evidence, written or oral. I use the snapshots that way in this essay.

FORMAL RELIGION AND VERNACULAR RELIGION

Scholars in religious studies commonly distinguish between substantive definitions of religion and functional definitions of religion (Mechling 2010). The former defines religions by the particularities of their beliefs and customs, mostly ritual customs. A functional definition of religion, on the other hand, tries to describe *religious experience* and examines cultural activities and practices that share at least some, not necessarily all, of the elements that make up religious experience. This functional approach, for example, can describe sports—especially American football (Novak 1976)—as a religious experience, just as that approach can see in visits (pilgrimages) to awesome natural sites, such as Yosemite Valley in California, a religious experience (Robertson 1984; Sears 1989; Robertson 1997).

I elect to use here the phrase "vernacular religion" rather than "folk religion" for reasons apart from the conversation among folklorists (e.g., Yoder 1974; Primiano 1995; Clements 2019), a conversation mainly having to do with groups and individuals. That conversation mainly is about the everyday religious practices of people apart from the formal beliefs and ritual customs, but practices still understood by the practitioners as small group or even personal variations on the formal religion's beliefs and customs. As should be clear from this essay, the term "vernacular" is more appropriate for writing about practices that fit a functional, rather than a substantive, definition of religion (Mechling 2010).

I also prefer "vernacular religion" to "folk religion" for writing about gun play because the scholarly tradition of the anthropology of experience (e.g., Turner and Bruner 1986), from which Geertz (1973b) composes his definition of religion as a cultural system, emphasizes emotions and the experience of feelings grounded in those physiological emotions. Elsewhere I argue that we should look at vernacular (folk, if you wish)

Figure 10.1.

practices as ways we both display and manage our feelings (Mechling 2019b). As we will see shortly, Geertz puts "mood and motivations," not beliefs, at the center of his definition of religion (Geertz 1973b, 96–97, 118). This emphasis on moods and feelings serves well our thinking about the range of vernacular experiences we want to understand as "religious," including gun play.

Geertz provides a good starting place with his essay, "Religion as a Cultural System" (Geertz 1973b). Religion, writes Geertz, is

(1) a system of symbols which acts to (2) establish powerful, pervasive, and long-lasting mood and motivations in men [sic] by (3) formulating conceptions of a general order of existence and (4) clothing these conceptions with such an aura of factuality that (5) the moods and motivations seem uniquely realistic. (Geertz 1973b, 90)

Notice that in Geertz' definition of religion there is no mention of a supernatural being (William James will add that) or of formal religious dogma or rituals. Geertz sees as most important the function of religion as a system of experiences, beliefs, and practices that attempt to bring order (and the comfort of order) to the potential chaos of everyday life. Religion, as a cultural system, must "affirm something," must impose order on the chaos of everyday existence (1973b, 99). Chaos threatens not just interpretations of reality but the *interpretability* of everyday reality (1973b, 100). Religion invokes *ritual* to create order and affirm truths in the face of disorder, chaos. "In a ritual," writes Geertz, "the world as lived and the world as imagined, fused under the agency of a single set of symbolic forms, turn out to be the same world" (1973b, 112).

One class of threat to meaning we encounter in our everyday lives is suffering and death (Geertz 1973b, 103–5). The explanation a religion has for human evil, suffering, and death is its theodicy (Berger 1967). This is not a trivial function of religion, and (as we will see) thinking about death is one of the functions of a folk religion with guns at its center.

Most formal, established religions can be seen easily in Geertz's description of a religion as a patterned set of symbols and rituals meant to bring order to everyday life, to assure and comfort people, and to affirm what is good. Geertz aims to steer us away from the organized institutions of religion to consider the informal *religious experience*, which is precisely what interests folklorists in the orientations they practice, focusing on the communal, the common, the informal, the marginal, the personal, the traditional, the aesthetic, and the ideological aspects of small group cultures (Oring 1986, 17–18). Most established religions have a vernacular aspect to their practice (Yoder 1974; Danielson 1986; Primiano 1995; Clements 2019). While the Roman Catholic Church has official dogma and practices, it takes a folklorist or other ethnographer to distinguish, for example, how different ethnic communities actually practice their Catholic faith, how an African American Catholic congregation might differ from an Italian or Latino one (Bales 2005).

What I am attempting to understand here, therefore, is how the experience of playing with a gun resembles a vernacular religious experience, creating even an island of order in a world of chaos. Before I look at particular instances of play with guns, however, I need to add two more pieces to the theoretical mosaic. Our guides are William James and Mihaly Csikszentmihalyi.

WILLIAM JAMES (MYSTICISM) AND CSIKSZENTMIHALYI (FLOW)

I have long argued that American Pragmatism provides the most useful set of ideas for the study of folklore (Mechling 1985). Other folklorists whose work I use often also work out of that tradition, including Roger Abrahams's (2011) approach to everyday life and Simon Bronner's construction of a "practical" approach (praxis, practice) to the study of folklore (Bronner 2016). James's classic work, *The Varieties of Religious Experience* (1902), can guide the next step in my inquiry here.

What I like most about the Jamesian, pragmatic approach, of course, is his privileging of experience, and his definition of religion highlights that focus. Religion, he writes, "shall mean for us the feelings, acts, and experiences of individual men in their solitude, so far as they apprehend themselves to stand in relation to whatever they may consider the divine" (James 1902, 31). Folklorists take as a given that they are studying communication of ideas and moods between people in a group, but James's focus on the experiences of the individual is not incompatible with the interests of folklorists.

James's chapter on mysticism provides some clues about how we might consider gun play a form of vernacular religious experience. James opens his discussion of mysticism with the notion that "personal religious experience has its root and centre in mystical states of consciousness" (379). That state of consciousness is apart from the consciousness of everyday life. The qualities of mystical experience include ineffability ("defies expression"), "noetic quality" (a "state of insight"), transiency, and passivity (James 1902, 380–82). Mystical experience, James says, is an "ecstatic experience" (from the Greek "ekstasis," meaning standing outside of ordinary experience). In mysticism this ecstatic state is often considered a trance, and James catalogs the sorts of religious experience that can induce a state of ecstatic consciousness, trance. Those include the use of intoxicants and anesthetics, experience in nature, and a range of religious practices including the use of music, dance, prayer, fasting, and self-flagellation. James accepts the view that mystic experiences give us access to cosmic truths not accessible in everyday experience (James 1902, 398). Already we can see the seeds of trance in play with guns.

The last concept I invoke here to understand how we might understand gun play as vernacular religious experience is Csikszentmihalyi's (1975) notion of "flow." Dissatisfied with the Western binary opposition of play and work, Csikszentmihalyi examines the state of consciousness one can experience in a range of activities, from traditional play to rock climbing to brain surgery. To show what these experiences of engrossment share, Csikszentmihalyi asks us to consider two elements of an activity—the degree of difficulty of the task and the skill of the person performing the task. If the task is too simple for the person's skills, then the person experiences boredom. On the other hand, if the challenge of the task exceeds the person's skills, the person experiences anxiety. Somewhere there is a balance between the challenge and skill, a zone in which the person experiences "flow," a total engrossment in the task, an engrossment that takes the person out of everyday consciousness into a state unaware of time and place, a state of ecstasy.

NEUROSCIENCE, RELIGION, AND GUNS

William James was a scientist, one of the fathers of American scientific psychology, as well as a philosopher. He published *The Varieties of Religious*

Experience in 1902, which is the same year two English scientists, E. H. Starling and W. M. Bayliss, discovered the first hormone, and within a few years they understood the role of chemical regulation in human physiology (Cawadias 1940). James must have understood the biological basis for the varieties of religious experience, even though he would not have advantage of the full picture of the role of hormones in the experiences. Charles Darwin paved the way for James to understand the role of instincts and biology in human behavior, and when G. Stanley Hall (a second father of American scientific psychology) published his two-volume work on *Adolescence* in 1904, he noted how the hormones involved with male puberty inclined the young man to spiritual and religious thoughts and impulses, like altruism (Meching 2016a).

I see some puzzle pieces from neuroscience that fit together now for us to speculate on the neuroscience of guns and religious experience. The first piece is the finding that when oxytocin, a hormone "critically involved in social bonding," was administered to a sample of middle-aged men, the test subjects showed an increased spirituality, "which is the belief in a meaningful life imbued with a sense of connection to a Higher Power and/or the world," while those subjects taking placebos did not experience that same increase in spirituality (Van Cappellen, Way, Isgett, and Fredrickson 2016). The second piece of the puzzle is the research on what happens to the endocrine system when a person shoots a gun (Wade 2011; Kotler 2012; Linehan 2017; Mosher 2017). Fitting these pieces together takes some speculation that needs more research, but some of the research shows possible links in the endocrinological consequences of shooting a gun and experiencing greater spirituality.

The foregoing discussion may seem like a long warmup to the main point of this essay, but my claim is so unusual that I want the reader to see how all these ideas fit together—play frames and ritual frames, vernacular religious experience versus formal religious experiences, magic, ecstasy, flow, and even the physiological aspects of the experiences. Before I get into the concrete examples, though, I want to discuss one other realm of culture where we find religious narratives that enter the folk religious experiences. I mean "national religion" as found in public culture, including mass-mediated, popular culture.

GUNS AND NATIONAL RELIGION

Having established definitions of formal and informal (vernacular) religious experiences, this would be the point in this essay where I should begin examining aspects of play with guns that I see as deserving the label "vernacular religion." I will get to those connections shortly. I pause here, though, to deal with a third, important realm of American religious experience, the American Civil Religion, sometimes called "public religion," out of my hunch (call it a hypothesis) that there are vernacular religious dimensions to the place of the gun in the national public sphere.

The sociologist Robert Bellah (1967) saw in public events and ceremonies, from the Kennedy inaugural address to Lincoln's second inaugural address to the Super Bowl, a national, public religion that fuses classical British liberal political theory with American Protestant religions. The American studies scholar can't help recognizing in public discourse about guns and gun rights elements of the American Civil Religion. I will resist the temptation to launch into a detailed rhetorical analysis of the gun-rights debate and say simply that if the American rights guaranteed in the Bill of Rights derive from the God-given rights mentioned in the Declaration of Independence, then the right to own a gun is a religious right and the practice of shooting a gun at inanimate targets or at animals is a religious practice. Many gun-rights advocates consider gun ownership a "sacred right." And in the public debate about gun ownership, one does not have to go far to find rhetorical claims that we are a nation of guns and gun violence (Courtwright 1998).

This excursus into guns and the national religion may not be as strange a detour as it might seem. American vernacular religion does not exist in a bubble separated from national public discourse. Our examination of the folklore of and about guns in the United States really must take into account the fact that guns have a unique place in American culture and mythology compared with cultures outside the United States. Put differently, the everyday understanding of the meanings of guns and their use and care develops within the contexts of a national public culture and its discourse about guns. What Alan Dundes calls "folk ideas" (Mechling 2019a) reflected in folklore can be applied to gunlore. Certainly the rights debate about guns and violence is a source of folk ideas, such as the idea that guns are tools for self-reliance, a strong value in American culture (Mechling 2019a).

American mass-mediated culture, popular culture, is the locale for the most pervasive and most powerful narratives putting guns into larger stories about the meanings of everyday life in colonial and postcolonial United States. This essay is not the place to launch a full analysis of guns in American popular culture, but the larger narratives worthy of the label "mythologies" carry ideas that show up as folk ideas. The work by historian Richard Slotkin (1973; 1985; 1992) and by religious studies scholars Robert Jewett and John Shelton Lawrence (1973; also Lawrence and Jewett 2002) make the case that Americans view gun violence as acceptable if the violence is in the service of redemption, of countering a wrong to make it right. Redemption, of course,

Figure 10.2.

is a religious concept, so the notion of "redemptive violence" is also a religious concept and might enter play with guns.

If we now think we will know a vernacular religious experience when we see it, we must engage, finally, the nature of the experience of playing with a gun. War and policing are two realms where the act of killing with a gun is deadly serious, but (of course) I would exclude these from the realm of play and, therefore, from the possibility that those uses of guns are a form of vernacular religion. My focus here is upon two play activities: pretending to kill and actually killing nonhuman animals.

First let us consider the meanings of killing and then move on to the play forms of killing with guns.

ON KILLING

Holding a gun in your hands, even a toy gun, opens up an array of feelings and thoughts. We know that guns are dangerous. They are tools designed for killing a living animal, including human animals. As Dave Grossman (2009) points out, humans have an aversion to killing other humans, an aversion military training aims at extinguishing. So real guns bestow power on the individual. Many war veterans write memoirs testifying to the feeling of a god-like power of life and death in combat. The experience of power inherent in holding a gun already suggests to us that the gun induces a frame apart from everyday experience, a nascent ecstatic experience, at least in the imagining. As I stated earlier, the gun in our hands can carry the same symbolic power as magical artifacts in mythologies and folklore. Realizing that brings us partway toward understanding how the experience of power holding a gun, much less using it, might transport the gun owner into a state of mind resembling a folk religious experience.

Both pretending to kill and actual killing (hunting) make the gun user think about death. Death is the ultimate chaos threating the interpretability of our lives. Sigmund Freud initially thought he could explain the psyche and human behavior by positing a pleasure instinct, but eventually Freud realized he needed to posit a death instinct, as well (Freud 1961 [1920]). The *danse macabre* between Eros and Thanatos drives our thoughts and behavior.

It is easy to go through the routines of everyday life without thinking much about death. Family members and friends deal with fatal maladies and even die; we might deal with the death of a beloved pet; if we pay attention to the news we learn of deaths on both a small and large scale. A child might ask a parent, "What happens when you die?" and that question from a child often prompts parents to offer something like a religious or spiritual answer, a variety of a theodicy.

In general, though, we mentally healthy people do not dwell on death. A gun, real or toy, forces the issue of death into some level of our consciousness. We imagine killing with the gun in our hands, and we might even imagine our own deaths while imagining the death of a human or nonhuman animal at our hands. In short, play with guns heightens our awareness of death and demands of us some thoughts about what happens after death.

In my 2008 article on gun play, I discuss "pretending to die" as a curious pleasure (fun) in kids' playfights with toy guns, and then I called this "the Tom Sawyer effect," referring to the scene in Mark Twain's 1876 novel, *The Adventures of Tom Sawyer*, where Tom and Huck are in the unused church gallery watching their own funeral, imagining how their families and friends feel about their deaths. It turns out that some philosophers and psychologists actually see benefits in our imagining our own deaths. Reviving a very old idea from the Stoic philosophers, William Irvine argues that "the [Stoic] philosophy offers a recipe for happiness, in part by thinking about bad things that might happen to you. The big one, obviously, is death—both yours and that of people you love" (Beck 2015). Along these lines, "terror-management theory" emerged in social psychology to explain the strategies people use to "quell their fear of death" (Beck 2015), practices meant to give a person a sense of symbolic immortality.

John Wallis and I (2019, 119–38) elaborate the argument by philosophers and psychologists (Beck 2015) when considering the meanings of what Geertz (1973a) calls "deep play." More on that below.

This ends the warmup. Now let us consider pretending to kill and actually killing in the play frame.

248   GUN PLAY AS VERNACULAR RELIGIOUS EXPERIENCE

PRETENDING TO KILL AND PRETENDING TO DIE

Playing with guns fuels fantasies of killing and of being killed. Remember that Bateson's original article presents his frame theory as a "theory of play and fantasy" (1972), and the fantasy (especially) taps unconscious drives and motives, including the mysterious death instinct formulated by Freud and explored by many, including Ernest Becker (1966; also Becker 1973), and the inspiration for Sheldon Solomon's formulation of "terror-management theory" (Solomon, Greenberg, and Pyszczynski 2015).

Death certainly is the ultimate disturber of order and meaning, and an important function of culture and, especially, of religion as a cultural system, is the fashioning of ideas and rituals meant to counter the chaos of death and death's assault on not only interpretations of the meaning of life but, as Geertz notes, also on "interpretability" itself. Barbara Babcock-Abrahams (1975), drawing on Mary Douglas's work on pollution and taboo (Douglas 1966), shows the alternative ritual strategies cultures devise to counter the threat to meaning posed by anomalous (disordering) events. Cultural rituals can ignore or otherwise minimize the threat of the anomaly, but some cultures choose to tame the threat by putting the anomaly at the center of rituals. This is precisely what play with guns does in the everyday, vernacular practices of Americans. Play with guns brings heightened attention to the matter of our deaths and the deaths of those near to us.

It is not necessary that kids who are playing with guns, pretending to shoot each other, think about real death when they point a finger, a stick, or a toy gun and say "bang, you're dead." Kids know that this is fantasy play (Jones 2002), just as the grown men (and some women) who play at paintball know that the "killing" is not real (Gibson 1994).

Of course, this fantasy play tames our fear of death because it actually offers the immortality Becker and others (e.g., Lifton 1987) say we seek. We don't really die. Pretend killing leads to pretend dying and pretend coming back to life, resurrection.

In surveying military male folk practices that seemed to us to bear strong resemblance to formal therapy for posttraumatic stress disorder (PTSD), such that the folklore of the military group functions as immediate "psychological first-aid" in the field, Wallis and I devoted a chapter to the playing of first-person shooter (FPS) videogames (Wallis and Mechling 2019, 89–103). Everything we might say about playfighting with toy guns or their equivalent we can say about playfighting in FPS videogames. In the case of soldiers in combat zones, one of the paradoxes of the video game play is that the soldiers may be using the play as a way of "coming down" from the excitement and terror experienced an hour earlier in actual combat or other activities in the combat zone.

Wallis makes much of two features of some FPS games—the ability to change perspective and watch your own death, and the regeneration of the player's avatar after death to continue the fighting. We mention only in passing the religious echoes in the two events in the fantasy world of the games, but it is worth noting here the resemblance to "pretending to die" in children's fantasy play fighting. Again, there may be psychological and spiritual value in contemplating one's own death and resurrection.

The elements of play with guns resembling vernacular religious practices are lining up—elements of magic, of flow, and the forced contemplation, even if unconscious, of the meaning of death, which then makes us reflect on the meaning of life. Let me turn now to some other vernacular religious elements in gun play.

Let us note at the outset that a child's acquisition of a toy gun usually occurs as part of a festive event, notably Christmas and birthdays.

The snapshots of kids with guns make this point. Many of the snapshots are of boys receiving guns as longed-for and cherished presents, but the gun manufacturers and the National Rifle Association began after World War II making rifles integral objects in the celebration of postwar family life, even making the case for mothers' and sisters' joining in on the family fun of shooting guns for sport and recreation (Mechling 2014). So we do have snapshots of girls with guns at Christmas.

I mentioned in my introductory remarks that I am including snapshots of play with guns and that in most cases the snapshots are more than mere illustrations of points made in the written or oral evidence. Some snapshots actually should be "read" as texts revealing something not obvious in other evidence. Take, for example, figures 10.4 and 10.5.

These are only a few of the many snapshots in my collection of boys (and sometimes girls) pointing real or toy guns at the photographer. In figure 10.4 two teen boys (on the back someone wrote, "Buddy aprox 13") are in a field pointing rifles at the photographer, and in figure 10.5 we see four boys pointing pistols at the photographer, and we know from the writing on the front and back that these boys are at "Camp Hemlock" and the date is August 12, 1939.

In my view a "thick description" of these snapshots and of others like them needs to explain why the boys are pointing their guns at the photographer, who might be an adult or (in most cases) another boy. Some pose with guns at their sides, and a few point the gun at an imaginary target off camera (figures 10.1 and 10.2). The boys (almost always boys) who point their

Figure 10.3.

Figure 10.4.

Figure 10.5.

pistols and rifles at the person taking the picture are not showing threat or aggression but agency. Play with guns is play with power (Jones 2002). And play with magic.

Freud often began a lecture or book chapter with the warning, "What follows is speculation, often far-fetched speculation," in an attempt "to follow out an idea consistently, out of curiosity to see where it will lead" (Freud 1961 [1920]), and I find myself issuing the same warning working on the surprising and seemingly unlikely idea that play with guns is a form of vernacular religious practice. There is another genre of snapshots that lead me to a highly speculative connection to vernacular religion. Consider figures 10.6 and 10.7.

The first snapshot is me (age four or so) dressed as a cowboy, and the second is me dressed ready for Sunday school (roughly the same age, almost five). The first snapshot is common, easy to find, and sometimes it is girls who are dressed as cowboys and, like me, pointing the toy pistol at the camera. The second snapshot is of me dressed to go to Sunday school and church on Easter Sunday, 1950. Again, that snapshot represents thousands of others, some of which are traditional first communion snapshots of boys and girls dressed for that important religious ritual (I am not Catholic, so the Presbyterian Sunday school photo will have to suffice).

I juxtapose these two snapshots, as representatives of thousands, probably millions of snapshots like them in both genres, to speculate on their resemblance. In both snapshots the boy is wearing a costume creating a frame apart from everyday experience. In the first I am dressed for a fantasy experience imagining myself a cowboy and playing with a gun. In the second I am dressed for religious ritual. Same boy, different costumes; same experiences of play and ritual away from the frame of everyday life. Note that on Easter Sunday the "topic" of the rituals in Sunday school and then in the church service is death and resurrection, precisely the experience of play fighting with guns. Death and resurrection.

We are used to understanding the important role of costume in religious ritual. We should consider the costumes young people put on for their gunplay as part of the invocation of magic, flow, and ecstasy we attribute to vernacular religious experiences.

Costume play (cosplay, as it is now called) is a common and important ritual "prop" for creating the frame (play frame in one case, ritual frame in the other). The fact that so many of the snapshots of children with guns show them dressed as "cowboys and Indians," or, in some cases, as Davy Crockett or Daniel Boone, reminds us that folk practices often appropriate narratives and images from popular culture. For the baby boomers (born 1946–64), the costumes for their gunplay were military or drawn from narratives of the American West. Television in the 1950s and 1960s was filled with WWII movies and made-for-television war stories. The Davy Crockett "craze" was a product of the Disney movies in the mid-1950s (King 1995), and "cowboy and Indian" movies were standard fare in theatres and on television in the 1950s into the 1960s. The subsequent generations added to army and cowboy costumes an array, including Star Wars characters.

So far I have been discussing playfighting with play guns; sometimes, though, people playfight with real guns. In my collection of vintage snapshots of soldiers, sailors, marines, and aviators are several picturing men playfighting with real guns, both pistols and rifles (Mechling 2012; Mechling

Figure 10.6.   Figure 10.7.

2021). These are instances of "deep play," a concept Geertz borrows from the Utilitarian philosopher Jeremy Bentham to describe play with stakes so high that it is irrational to play the game (Geertz 1973a, 432). The other forms of playfighting with toy guns and their equivalents merely imagine the death the play can bring. Playfighting with actual weapons elevates the play into deep play. Deep play with weapons and the possibility of sudden death is play with ultimate meaning, and that can be a spiritual experience if not a vernacular religious one.

Pretending to kill and pretending to die share with religious experiences elements of play, ritual, and fantasy. By making death the symbolic subject of the play, the play helps tame our fears of death. Actually killing a living thing with a gun can also be a religious experience. I have read enough war memoirs to know that killing another person is a very moving experience for most people, making the warrior think about ultimate questions of life, death, and chance. Fate. Why does one person die and another not? Being a warrior in the combat zone demands a theodicy.

Killing in war is not play with guns. Killing nonhuman animals, though, is play with guns, so that is the second realm of religious-like experiences with guns I will discuss.

Figure 10.8.   Figure 10.9.

KILLING NONHUMAN ANIMALS: HUNTING

Seeing the elements of the practice of a vernacular religion in playfighting with guns is far more difficult than seeing the elements of the practice of a folk religion in the folk customs of hunting nonhuman animals. Many hunters write about the sport in terms and images similar to those one might use to describe religious experience (Mechling 2004). A few folklorists, most notably Bronner (2008), provide us with detailed ethnographic accounts of hunting customs, and Bronner's description and analysis of both the conscious and unconscious meanings of the "blood rituals" used to initiate the novice hunter into the group make very clear the resemblance between hunting customs and religious customs.

Figure 10.10 is one I also used in my article on the vernacular photography by hunters (Mechling 2004), and I reproduce it here because of all the snapshots of hunting I have in my collection, this one is the one that most invokes hunting and killing animals as a vernacular religious experience, a set of meanings I did not fully explore in the 2004 essay. In my view this is a remarkable and remarkably moving snapshot. We presume the young man killed the moose; he holds the rifle by his side. The angular tree trunk, a visual line that artistically complicates the composition of the photograph (in contrast to the vertical lines of the other tree trunks) functions to hold the dead moose's head up and toward the camera. The effect is for the boy's gaze and the moose's gaze to be in the same direction.

The boy's posture and face convey a solemn mood, one much in contrast to other hunting photographs where the trophy animals are displayed among smiling hunters. The boy's eyes appear to be closed. Perhaps they are closed merely because he was blinking at the split second of the camera's exposure. But perhaps he is in prayer or at least spiritual contemplation, recognizing the weight of the act of taking a life. In some episodes of the popular television show "Naked and Afraid" (a program interesting for its showing us how two strangers, a male and a female, naked and afraid in a harsh wilderness, develop a functional or sometimes dysfunctional relationship in their struggles to survive), one of the players sometimes is successful in killing an animal for food. In many of those cases, more often for birds or mammals than for snakes, the hunter pauses after the kill to gently touch the dead animal and thank it for the sacrifice of its life for the survival of the two people. One could say that this gesture is the result of days of hunger and discomfort, but even comfortable hunters often pause to thank the spirit of the animal they have killed. This is a vernacular religious ritual.

The actual killing of the nonhuman animal is one of those elements of play and ritual with guns that forces the individual to think about death. Hunting has additional elements further suggesting the folk religious experience. The hunting trip, for example, resembles the religious pilgrimage.

A religious pilgrimage usually is a journey from one's home place to a place of religious importance, such as a shrine or other holy place. Many formal religions have traditions of pilgrimage. Stories of religious pilgrimage fill oral and written literature. Some pilgrimages are spiritual rather than formally religious, but they serve the same functions as a more formal religious pilgrimage. Thus, those who study tourism as a cultural practice often note the resemblance of that activity to religious pilgrimage (Robertson 1984; Sears 1989; Robertson 1997).

The primary function of a religious or spiritual pilgrimage is to collect "an experience." The religious or spiritual pilgrim and the tourist all might "collect" an object at the destination—a religious relic or a souvenir—and carry the object back home as an object to stimulate memories of the experience. Hunting trophies and snapshots of the hunting trophies are the souvenirs of those experiences (see the snapshots in Mechling 2004). While some pilgrims undertake the journey because it is expected by the community, a more powerful driver of the pilgrimage experience is what Propp (1968) calls the "lack" that impels the folk narrative. A central character in the story lacks something and embarks on the journey in order to fill that need, to find something that clarifies the meaning of life.

The most important thing "collected" is the experience, and the most important experience is "awe." The scholars who see the religious pilgrimage as the model for nature tourism often name "awe" as the experience sought

Figure 10.10.

and delivered by places such as Niagara Falls and Yosemite Valley. The feeling of awe in the presence of a religious site—the birthplace of a founder or saint, a Gothic cathedral—and the feeling of awe in Yosemite Valley are, for many people, the sort of "ecstatic" experience that interested William James and Csikszentmihalyi, as we saw above. The feeling of awe transports the individual from the frame of taken-for-granted everyday reality into another reality, even briefly.

If hunting is a vernacular religious practice, we might think of guns as religious objects. Material artifacts interest folklorists not only for their role in vernacular practices (the rifle is an artifact in the vernacular practice of hunting), but also for their symbolic value, a function particularly relevant to seeing the rifle as a religious symbol.

Colleen McDannell's analysis of religion and popular culture includes detailed, ethnographic attention to the use of religious objects as home decor, especially when a family constructs what is in essence a religious shrine in the home (McDannell 1996). Similarly, Santería practitioners often create shrines in their homes. If we consider the gun a sacred object, then the display of guns in the home surely counts as the display akin to religious shrines. The gun case on display in the home, the rifle mounted on a wall, and perhaps even the gun safe tucked away in a less visible space, are places set aside in the home for the sacred object.

To talk of the gun as a sacred object implies that it shares qualities with other sacred objects in religions. One of those qualities, and a quite significant one, is magical power.

A gun is magical because it causes things to happen at a distance. The sword in western mythology symbolizes strength, virtue, and redemptive violence. In video games, guns join swords as instruments used by heroes to right wrongs. Redemptive violence is at the heart of American western mythology, and the gun plays a key role in the ability of the hero to return the community into chaos to a state of paradise.

Still on the topic of real guns as magical objects, I think the intimate knowledge a person has of his or her gun and the care the gun owner gives to the gun has echoes of spiritual experience. I know from reading war memoirs, watching documentaries offering close looks at the everyday lives of warriors, and from conversations with Wallis (who, after all, is a Marine veteran with two tours in Iraq) that an important activity of using a gun is caring for it after it is used. Returning from a mission "outside the wire," away from the safety of one's outpost, warriors engage in what can only be called a ritual. Before really relaxing, the solder must secure the firearm, empty it of rounds, and engage in some level of disassembling and cleaning and reassembling the weapon. From the testimony of veterans I would say that this process is something of an exercise in Zen meditation, including (for some) entering a state of flow while engrossed entirely on the task of caring for an object your life depends on.

I promised earlier in this essay (in the discussion of the "this is my rife, this is my gun" military cadence) that I would return to the provocative issue of the relationship between guns and sex. One does not have to be a Freudian to know that shooting a gun is an experience, for many men, very much like sex, especially the orgasm. We do not need Freud to make this connection because the men themselves tell us about the sexual pleasure of firing a gun (e.g., Grossman 2009). I trust that I have set the stage for this final discussion of the ways the sex-like experience of shooting a gun resembles the sex-like experience of religious ecstasy. Ecstasy is the experience linking sex, shooting a gun, and religion.

Close to my discussion of Csikszentmihalyi's idea of flow I presented a too-brief discussion of the neuroscience of what happens when a person shoots a gun. The point there was that endocrinologists have discovered that oxytocin is the hormone linking religion and the firing of guns, and it turns out that oxytocin is also the hormone deeply involved with sexual experience, especially the orgasm in both men and women (Wallis and Mechling 2019, 106). Religious experience, shooting guns, having an orgasm—all linked by oxytocin. One more unexpected way play with guns can be seen as a vernacular religious experience.

CONCLUSION

In a passage in Alexis de Tocqueville's classic 1835 report, *Democracy in America* (1899), on his travels to the United States to study the prison system for the French government, the author recounts his coming across an isolated cabin on the frontier. The American pioneer family invites him into their humble home, and he notices on a shelf two volumes—the collected works of Shakespeare and the King James translation of the Bible. In attempting to understand American culture, which is the goal of everything I write, one could do worse than see the culture through the lenses of Shakespeare and the Bible, the sources for so many of the mythological narratives about the United States. Although Tocqueville does not mention a rifle, we can assume that this frontier family had at least one rifle for hunting and protection. The King James Bible permeates both the tragedies and histories among Shakespeare's plays, and together they establish the elements of the mythology of redemptive violence discussed above. So in my mind's eye the tableau I picture as Tocqueville looks around the cabin is a musket on the wall above the bookshelf, a very meaningful trio of objects for that family and in many ways the sort of domestic religious shrine McDannell (1996) found in Christian homes and folklorists find in other homes honoring other religions, such as Santería.

If cultures are the interconnected systems we think they are, we should be able to muster our interdisciplinary ragbag of ideas and methods in order to move from the part to the whole, from an individual object to larger generalizations about the culture. This chapter has amounted to a thought experiment of that sort, thinking about the gun as a cultural object and about its playful and ritual uses and the meanings in those uses. Aside from whatever validity and value my interpretations have here, I also mean this chapter to stand as a model for the interdisciplinary study of an object or text or practice.

My intent also has been to show how the search for ecstatic experiences is a major motivation for and result of many vernacular practices, notably ritual and play. Adopting Geertz's (1973b) emphasis on the "moods and motivations" (not beliefs) related to religious experiences significantly expands our view of what counts as religious experience, and I trust I have made a persuasive case for gun play as a vernacular religious experience. For understandable reasons, folklorists have emphasized "belief" in their study of "folk/vernacular religion," but the pragmatic approach to the anthropology of experience would put emotions and their expression in feelings at the center or our understanding of the psychological and social functions of vernacular practices.

References

Abrahams, Roger D. 2011. *Everyday Life: A Poetics of Vernacular Practices*. Philadelphia: University of Pennsylvania Press.

Babcock, Barbara A., ed. 1977. *The Reversible World: Symbolic Inversion on Art and Society*. Ithaca, NY: Cornell University Press.

Babcock-Abrahams, Barbara. 1975. "Why Frogs Are Good to Think and Dirt Is Good to Reflect On." *Soundings* 58, no. 2: 167–81.

Bales, Susan Ridgely 2005. *When I Was a Child: Children's Interpretations of First Communion*. Chapel Hill: University of North Carolina Press.

Bateson, Gregory. 1972 [1955]. "A Theory of Play and Fantasy." In *Steps to an Ecology of Mind*, 177–93. New York: Ballantine.

Beck, Julie. 2015. "What Good Is Thinking About Death?" *The Atlantic*, May 28, 2015. https://www.theatlantic.com/health/archive/2015/05/what-good-is-thinking-about -death/394151/.

Becker, Ernest. 1966. *The Birth and Death of Meaning*. New York: Free Press.

Becker, Ernest. 1973. *The Denial of Death*. New York: Free Press.

Bellah, Robert N. 1967. "Civil Religion in America." *Daedalus* 96, no. 1: 1–21.

Berger, Peter L. 1967. *The Sacred Canopy: Elements of a Sociological Theory of Religion*. Garden City, NJ: Doubleday.

Bronner, Simon J. 2008. *Killing Tradition: Inside Hunting and Animal Rights Controversies*. Lexington: University Press of Kentucky.

Bronner, Simon J. 2016. *Folklore: The Basics*. New York: Routledge.

Burns, Richard Allen. 2003. "'This Is My Rifle, This Is My Gun . . .': Gunlore in the Military." *New Directions of Folklore* 7. https://scholarworks.iu.edu/journals/index .php/ndif/article/view/19886.

Cawadias, A. P. 1940. "The History of Endocrinology." *Proceedings of the Royal Society of Medicine* 34: 303–8.

Clements, William M. 2019. "Folklore and Folklife of American Religious Communities." In *The Oxford Handbook of American Folklore and Folklife Studies*, ed. Simon J. Bronner, 806–24. New York: Oxford University Press.

Courtwright, David T. 1998. *Violent Land: Single Men and Social Disorder from the Frontier to the Inner City*. Cambridge, MA: Harvard University Press.

Csikszentmihalyi, Mihaly. 1975. *Beyond Boredom and Anxiety: Experiencing Flow in Work and Play*. New York: Josey-Bass Publishers.

Danielson, Larry. 1986. "Religious Folklore." In *Folk Groups and Folklore Genres*, ed. Elliott Oring. 45–69. Logan: Utah State University Press.

Douglas, Mary. 1966. *Purity and Danger: An Analysis of Concepts of Pollution and Taboo*. London: Routledge and Kegan Paul.

Freud, Sigmund. 1961 [1920]. *Beyond the Pleasure Principle*. Translated and edited by James Strachey. New York: Norton.

Geertz, Clifford. 1973a. "Deep Play: Notes on the Balinese Cockfight." In *The Interpretation of Cultures*, 412–53. New York: Basic Books.

Geertz, Clifford. 1973b. "Religion as a Cultural System." In *The Interpretation of Cultures*, 87–125. New York: Basic Books.

Geertz, Clifford. 1973c. "Thick Description: Toward an Interpretive Theory of Culture." In *The Interpretation of Cultures*, 3–30. New York: Basic Books.

Gibson, James William. 1994. *Warrior Dreams: Violence and Manhood in Post-Vietnam America*. New York: Hill and Wang.

Grossman, Dave. 2009. *On Killing: The Psychological Cost of Learning to Kill in War and Society*. New York: Back Bay Books.

Hall, G. Stanley. 1904. *Adolescence*. New York: D. Appleton & Co.

Handelman, Don. 1977. "Play and Ritual: Complementary Frames of Meta-Communication. In *It's a Funny Thing, Humour*, edited by A. J. Chapman and H. Foot, 185–92. New York: Pergamon.

James, William. 1902. *The Varieties of Religious Experience: A Study in Human Nature*. London: Longmans, Green & Co.

Jewett, Robert, and John Shelton Lawrence. 1977. *The American Monomyth*. Garden City, NY: Anchor Press/Doubleday.

Jones, Gerard. 2002. *Killing Monsters: Why Children Need Fantasy, Super-heroes, and Make-Believe Violence*. New York: Basic Books.

King, Jonathan. 1995. "The Crockett Craze." *Los Angeles Times*, February 27, 1995. https://www.latimes.com/archives/la-xpm-1995-02-27-ls-36630-story.html.

Kotler, Steven. 2012. "Addicted to Bang: The Neuroscience of the Gun." *Forbes*, December 18, 2012. https://www.forbes.com/sites/stevenkotler/2012/12/18/addicted-to-bang-the-neuroscience-of-the-gun/#8ebeebf7eedd.

Lawrence, John Shelton, and Robert Jewett. 2002. *The Myth of the American Superhero*. Grand Rapids, MI: William B. Eerdmans Publishing Company.

Lifton, Robert Jay. 1987. *The Future of Immortality and Other Essays for the Nuclear Age*. New York: Basic Books.

Linehan, Adam. 2017. "Here's What Happens to the Brain and Body When You Shoot a Gun." *Task & Purpose*, January 30, 2017. https://taskandpurpose.com/heres-what-happens-to-the-brain-and-body-when-you-shoot-a-gun.

McDannell, Colleen. 1996. *Material Christianity: Religion and Popular Culture in America*. New Haven, CT: Yale University Press.

Mechling, Jay. 1985. "Introduction: William James and the Philosophical Foundations for the Study of Everyday Life." *Western Folklore* 44: 303–10.

Mechling, Jay. 2004. "Picturing Hunting." *Western Folklore* 63: 51–78.

Mechling, Jay. 2005. "Found Photographs and Children's Folklore." *Children's Folklore Review* 27: 7–31.

Mechling, Jay. 2008. "Gun Play." *American Journal of Play* 1: 192–209.

Mechling, Jay. 2010. "Religious Studies." In *A Concise Companion to American Studies*, edited by John Carlos Rowe, 92–123. West Sussex, UK: Wiley-Blackwell.

Mechling, Jay. 2012. "Soldier Snaps." In *Warrior Ways: Explorations in Modern Military Folklore*, edited by Eric A. Eliason and Tad Tuleja, 222–47. Logan: Utah State University Press.

Mechling, Jay. 2014. "Boy Scouts, the National Rifle Association, and the Domestication of Rifle Shooting." *American Studies* 53: 5–25.

Mechling, Jay. 2016a. "The Erotics of Adolescent Male Altruism." *Boyhood Studies* 9, no. 2: 92–115.

Mechling, Jay. 2016b. "Sandwork." *American Journal of Play* 9, no. 1: 19–40.

Mechling, Jay. 2019a. "American Folk Ideas, Themes, and Worldview." In *The Oxford Handbook of American Folklore and Folklore Studies*, ed. Simon J. Bronner, 59–74. New York: Oxford University Press.

Mechling, Jay. 2019b. "Folklore and the Emotional Brain." In *Contexts of Folklore: Festschrift for Dan Ben-Amos*, edited by Simon J. Bronner and Wolfgang Mieder, 27–28. New York: Peter Lang.

Mechling, Jay. 2021. *Soldier Snapshots: Masculinity, Play, and Friendship in the Everyday Photographs of Men in the American Military*. Lawrence: University Press of Kansas.

Mosher, Dave. 2017. "Here's What Can Happen to Your Brain When You Shoot a Gun." *Business Insider*, October 10, 2017. https://www.businessinsider.com/firing-gun-brain-chemistry-neuroscience-2017-10.

Nietzsche, Friedrich. 1872. *The Birth of Tragedy*. Leipzig: E. W. Fritzsch.

Novak, Michael. 1976. *The Joy of Sports: Endzones, Bases, Baskets, Balls, and the Consecration of the American Spirit*. New York: Basic Books.

Oring, Elliott. 1986. "On the Concept of Folklore." In *Folk Groups and Folklore Genres*, edited by Elliott Oring, 1–22. Logan: Utah State University Press.

Primiano, Leonard Norman. 1995. "Vernacular Religion and the Search for Method in Religious Folklife." *Western Folklore* 54: 37–56.

Propp, Vladimir. 1968. *Morphology of the Folktale*. 2nd ed. Austin: University of Texas Press.

Robertson, David. 1984. *West of Eden: A History of the Art and Literature of Yosemite*. Berkeley, CA: Yosemite Natural History Association and Wilderness Press.

Robertson, David. 1997. *Real Matter*. Salt Lake City: University of Utah Press.

Sears, John F. 1989. *Sacred Places: American Tourist Attractions in the Nineteenth Century*. New York: Oxford University Press.

Slotkin, Richard. 1973. *Regeneration through Violence: The Mythology of the American Frontier, 1600–1860*. Wesleyan University Press.

Slotkin, Richard. 1985. *The Fatal Environment: The Myth of the Frontier in the Age of Industrialization, 1800–1890*. New York: Macmillan.

Slotkin, Richard. 1992. *Gunfighter Nation: The Myth of the Frontier in Twentieth-Century America*. New York: Atheneum.

Solomon, Shelson, Jeff Greenberg, and Tom Pyszczynski. 2015. *The Worm at the Core: On the Role of Death in Life*. New York: Random House

Stewart, Susan. 1979. *Nonsense: Aspects of Intertextuality in Folklore and Literature*. Baltimore, MD: Johns Hopkins University Press.

Tocqueville, Alexis de. 1899. *Democracy in America*, vol. 1. Translated by Henry Reeve. New York: D. Appleton and Company.

Turner, Victor W., and Edward M. Bruner, eds. 1986. *The Anthropology of Experience*. Urbana: University of Illinois Press.

Van Cappellen, P., B. M. Way, S. F. Isgett, and B. L. Fredrickson. 2016. "Effects of Ocytocin Administration on Spiritualty and Emotional Responses to Meditation." *Social Cognitive and Affective Neuroscience* 11, no. 10: 1579–87.

Wade, Nicholas. 2011. "Depth of the Kindness Hormone Appears to Know Some Bounds." *New York Times*, January 10, 2011. https://www.nytimes.com/2011/01/11/science/11hormone.html. Last accessed June 9, 2023.

Wallis, John Paul, and Jay Mechling. 2019. *PTSD and Folk Therapy: Everyday Practices of American Masculinity in the Combat Zone*. Lanham, MD: Roman/Lexington.

Wallis, John Paul, and Jay Mechling. 2020. "Warriors' Bodies as Sites of Microresistance in the American Military." In *Different Drummers: Military Cohesion and Its Discontents*, edited by Tad Tuleja. Logan: Utah State University Press.

Yoder, Don. 1974. "Toward a Definition of Folk Religion." *Western Folklore* 33: 2–15.

Chapter 11

SYMBOLS AND THINGS

A Reflection on *Gunlore*

TOK THOMPSON

INTRODUCTION

The various case studies contained in this book illustrate the diverse gun cultures in the United States, and in doing so complexify the oft-heard singular appellation of American gun culture. These case studies all display the strong cultural roles played by guns, in a panoply of contexts—from blues songs to legends to craft to cosplaying, and in a variety of American cultural settings. I was struck by the diverse perspectives, diverse groups, giving insight into all these different communities through the role played by the strong and varied symbolisms and significations given to guns.

I was also struck by the perception that none of the chapters had much to say about how guns were treated where I grew up, which gave me pause for thought. I was born and raised in a remote area of Alaska, in the subsistence lifestyle, where gun ownership was nearly ubiquitous (Kalesan et al. 2015). In this concluding chapter, then, I will attempt to weave both my own auto-ethnographic perspective, along with a synopsis and overview of the other chapters, into some concluding thoughts about the issues raised.

As a state, Alaska is one of the highest guns-per-capita, with guns in over 62 percent of households. Alaska also leads the nation in gun-related deaths, although this is not particularly due to homicide: homicide rates for Alaska are not exceptionally high (for 2019, the CDC rates are 10.8 per 100,000 people: Mississippi, the highest, had a rate of 15.4). Rather, the high gun-related-mortality rate is related more to the very high suicide rate (for 2019, the rate was 28.5, surpassed only by Wyoming).[1] Outside of urban areas, guns are even more widespread, and woven into the fabric of daily life.

This is the aspect I'd like to foreground from this perspective: that guns as a mundane, everyday item, largely *not* focused on human-to-human violence, play a very different cultural role. In these contexts, national debates about gun control often seem completely disconnected with the lived experiences of the community. Times have changed, somewhat, particularly in more urban areas, as guns are brought under heightened scrutiny.

A recent article in the *Anchorage Daily News* detailed the genre of "truck guns," for example, stating that

> when I was old enough to drive and bought my first truck, it had a gun rack in the back window, and the slots were always occupied by guns of some sort while it sat in the high school parking lot. Most trucks in those days had a gun rack, and there was a rifle of some sort and often a fishing rod nestled in the rack's cradles. It was as normal as wearing clothes.[2]

The more rural one gets, and the more towards subsistence communities, the more the ubiquity grows. In settings such as these, guns carried very little symbolism, being viewed more as a tool to procure meat—a noisy, dangerous tool, pretty much in the same cognitive category of the chainsaw (see Frandy in this volume as he touches on this perspective in some of his examples from northern Wisconsin). Chainsaws are noisy, dangerous tools that bring in fuel for the fire, while guns are noisy, dangerous tools that bring in meat. Except for chainsaws and guns, rural Alaska is very, very quiet. You hear the birds, the burbling of the creek, the footsteps of animals in the forest. The sonic interruptions of chainsaws and guns always seem out of place, scaring animals, and disturbing the quiet. They were necessary for our lifestyle, it seemed, but people far preferred the silence.

I mused on these thoughts during the COVID-19 pandemic, as I temporarily relocated back to my home in Alaska. I thought about this book, and my concluding chapter, as I ambled along my four-mile walk each morning. Spruce grouse appear along the road at this time of day, and some days I would witness over thirty clustered along the road. As I approach, the male often challenges me with a brilliant display of tail feathers. Sooner or later, though, as I walk through, they take to flight—awkwardly, as spruce grouse are lousy fliers: they just manage enough lift to alight clumsily in the lowest branches. The grouse brought back memories of childhood: as a boy, I regularly hunted spruce grouse, along with my brother (two years my senior), and we would bring home a steady supply to our mother, who was both encouraging and patient with our efforts and a maestro at turning them into delicious meals for the family.

My brother and I came of age deep in the backwoods. The older men of my family brought back salmon, moose, and occasionally other things as well. Being restricted closer to home, my brother and I spent a great deal of our free time, after school and chores, in procuring protein, mostly trout, arctic hares, and spruce grouse. We honed our techniques over endless hours of practice. My own experience with guns stems from this time: at first we hunted the grouse with rocks—thrown, and with slingshots. But we desperately wanted to improve our capabilities, and so, at a very early age, we made our own guns. These guns we made out of various pipes surreptitiously gleaned from my father's homestead supply. We emptied out our supply of firecrackers for gunpowder and twisted the fuses together. Then, with a carefully selected rock as our bullet, one of us would aim and the other would light the fuse with a supply of paper matches. It was all very dramatic, and resulted in some terrific bangs, but was not terribly great at striking spruce grouse. My dad caught us red-handed and promptly confiscated our homemade guns. Soon thereafter my brother and I both received our own .22 rifles as Christmas presents—my dad decided that to be the safer path, rather than leaving us to our own reckless devices. I still have the .22, and it still works perfectly.

Most people living subsistence lifestyles depend heavily on food resources procured through hunting and fishing: subsistence, in a word.[3] When I was four years old, my family moved full time from the village into the deep backwoods, miles away from anyone. There was not much of any income, apart from a few dollars earned in the summer commercial fishing season. Which is to say, we were dirt poor. Or perhaps better: we had little money. My folks were busy trying to carve out a life and living, and our domicile at that time was little more than a plywood shack—or rather, two or three plywood shacks tacked quickly together. It was hard to keep warm, as a barrel stove was our only source of heat, and the temperatures could at times be miserably low. The shack was far from airtight, and cold, bitter winds would find their way to swirl around inside. Most winter mornings found the temperatures inside to be far below freezing, and I remember how difficult it was as a young impatient boy to wait in bed until my father got the fire going, and we could get dressed, run out, and huddle by the barrel stove as our shack gradually warmed.

There was a decided lack of money, but we wouldn't have used the word "poor." We felt sorry for city slickers as we soaked in the beauty and quiet of the natural world surrounding us. Like many subsistence-oriented families in Alaska, both Native and not, we gauged our well-being on other things than monetary income (Boraas 2013, 2018). Our primary sources of meat came from fishing and hunting: mostly salmon and moose. For a while we raised chickens for eggs and meat, but it was difficult—all sorts of predators found their way to our chickens, and we engaged in a long and mostly losing battle with them over the years. Eventually, we gave up the chickens. Likewise, for a couple years we tried to raise goats for fresh milk, but this, too, was difficult, especially with bears. We kept dogs for guardians, but about half of our dogs were killed by the local wolves.

One of my more vibrant memories is of a summer day when my brother (age eleven) and I (age nine) were alone at the house. A dog started barking and we quickly realized a very large black bear was trying to attack our goats. My father had secured all the large firearms away from us (wisely, I suppose, especially considering the homemade-guns incident), and we were left with little at our disposal—my brother had a .22 rifle, and I grabbed some pots and pans. The plan, as we hatched it, would be to come up behind the bear, and then rush at it screaming, banging pots, and firing into the air (we knew it would be foolish to fire *at* a bear with a .22). We followed the plan and began our charge a mere thirty feet or so away from the bear. At first, the bear was nonplussed, and I remember considering that we had never developed a plan B, but as we got within ten feet, screaming and banging and firing .22 shots in the air, the bear had had enough, and with one casual paw stroke broke through our log fence and strolled into the woods.

We knew all about bears' hunting practices, observing their kills, and sometimes watching them in action. One time when a bear had successfully separated a mother moose from one of her twins, and then bore down on the calf, tearing into it, the calf was screaming in agony as the bear began to casually eat it, and the mother and the other calf looked on. Nature was cruel. Bears needed food, and they hunted to get it. Bears hunted moose, our goats, and at times us. We were often aware of being tracked and could later follow the prints that had been following ours. Growing up in this environment made hunting more or less a state of being, one that enjoyed endless cultural fascination and elaboration. Bear stories would be regularly regaled, and in general people strove to understand them as fully as possible. Each year in Alaska people would die from bear attacks. We were aware that the others were hunting us, too.

Bears weren't the only hunters besides us, of course: the predatory eagles are master hunters, terrorizing the lake denizens in the summer; the wolf packs as well are master carnivores, capable of taking down full-grown moose. We'd hear them call out to each other on cold winter nights. Both my brother and I had at times been surrounded by the pack, a dozen or so very large, very healthy wolves with fangs and claws and perfectly able to tear us apart. We accorded them respect, and we personally never felt threatened.

The last moose I shot was some twenty years ago—it was winter, and a starving moose had been struggling through the snow, pursued leisurely by the wolf pack. The snow was deep, and the moose made it near our house (for protection?) before collapsing. The wolves were coming closer, and the moose was clearly dying. I took out my father's old .30-06 and, after asking for forgiveness, shot the moose. With a friend, I removed the hide, then we dragged the body as best we could out onto the frozen lake, for the wolves to eat.

And that Winchester .306: For many years that tool procured food for our family, especially moose. My dad had purchased that rifle when he first went to Alaska, right after WWII had ended. He purchased it in San Francisco, on his way, and it was already an old rifle: the date of manufacture is 1907. Guns, if properly manufactured and cared for, could last indefinitely.

The subsistence community depends on solid, dependable gear. Repair shops are far, far away, and things need to last. Guns, if taken care of, last. There is a maxim in subsistence lifestyles: KISS, *Keep it simple, stupid.* Items need to be durable, and the more complex the machine, the more there is to go wrong. In discussing guns used for subsistence lifestyles, the themes would emphasize reliability and durability.

DANGEROUS TOOLS

Guns in subsistence communities are mostly used for hunting. However, guns are frequently employed in a defensive manner as well, particularly as protection against bears. Many activities, such as berry-picking or hiking, would often include guns as a protective tool, just in case. Besides actually targeting a bear, guns were perhaps more useful for their loud noise, to scare bears away. Recently, "bear spray" (specially formulated aerosol cans of pepper spray for bears) has also become popular for defensive safety. It has several advantages, including being light weight and less dangerous, but also disadvantages, especially perhaps its lack of a warning capability.

Guns, then, were relegated to a subsidiary role, to subsistence itself. Guns were a part of the whole subsistence game: the game of mending fishing nets, and keeping track of the animal tracks, and of knowing how to be out in the woods. One of my neighbors kept up this lifestyle, long after I had gone away to college and beyond. He supplemented his subsistence income with trapping, and with guiding sport hunters who would often fly up to Alaska from "the lower forty-eight." His clients often remarked on his simple equipment and simple gun, contrasting this with their own excellent tools and technologically improved marksmanship. My friend's stock reply was, "I don't have to be a good shot. I can get close enough to a moose without him noticing me that it'd be impossible for me to miss." The same friend often remarked on the differences between sports hunters and subsistence hunters, and the same sentiment pervaded the community where I lived: there was no sport to subsistence hunting, no joy at killing: it was sad work, and we were sorry to do it. There was a certain thrill of the chase, the adrenaline of the hunt, of course, but in the end, it was always sad. As my friend stated, "once I'm out hunting, they (the animals) all know what the game is, they know what's going on." Comparatively, when asked by another friend to help butcher a few chickens: "the chickens, in my arms, they were trusting me. I couldn't do it."

Not only were the wilderness and wild game respected, they were followed with avid enthusiasm. Any reports of wildlife sightings, or even tracks or scat, would be important topics of conversations, whether it was rabbits, lynx, wolverines, muskrats, wolves, or any of the other many denizens. Endless conversations on the weather, the snowpack, the various interactions of the natural environment and its inhabitants, would fill the long, dark winter evenings.

Guns, then, were viewed as part and parcel of this world. Valued for their ability to procure subsistence, and to protect against bears, guns were a necessary investment in the meager toolkit of the subsistence lifestyle. As the above introduction tried to point out, subsistence use of guns highlights their utility in food procurement, and hence guns become a utilitarian, very mundane sort of object, eliciting neither fervent support nor fervent opposition, but rather an accepted part of daily life.

OTHER GUNLORES

We see this aspect of food procurement featured heavily in Frandy's chapter "Between the Forest and the Freezer: Visual Culture and Hunting Weapons in the Upper Midwest," where he notes various types of hunters, all engaged in guns via hunting.

Frandy notes the varieties of hunting types, including Ashinabee hunters, trophy hunters, sports hunters, and more. Frandy's careful auto-ethnography also reveals his own background: "My family was perhaps somewhat different from many hunting families in the United States. Or, at least, I felt it to be a little different when I heard others talk about the ways they hunted. We weren't interested in blood sport, nor in hunting to ritualize some kind of conquest of nature" (Harrison 1992, 69). We didn't hunt to perform masculinities, nor to escape women. And we certainly didn't hunt "for fun," "for sport," "to bond," or "to make memories" (cf. Bronner 2004; Frandy, chapter 3 of this volume). Frandy traces his family's "difference" to his mixed Sámi and Finnish ancestry, including the linguistics links to hunting as an interspecial category. The ethos of subsistence hunting continues, it seems, in parts of the United States, as many people supplement meager incomes with valuable protein, procured with guns.

With this important background, Frandy then moves on to illustrate the various ways that people display, and embellish and beautify, their guns, as well as the changing perceptions over time. These once-remote areas are now increasingly in the same gun-drenched media world of the United States, and gun cabinets once proudly displayed are now tucked away, hidden from public view. Frandy draws our attention to the fact that one can learn a lot about a group, and that group's relationship with guns, in the visual display of guns. Such visual displays are overt signing of multiple meanings, symbolically rich communicative devices.

Thinking back to my own background, the lack of much signification given to the visual display of guns seems to confirm Frandy's hypothesis: a lack of visual signification is mirrored by a general silence, a lack of signification, on guns themselves, in spite of their relative ubiquity. Further, Frandy comments on how the contemporary displays of guns increasingly emphasize their nonutilitarian uses, a trajectory he sees as unhealthy, as guns become entwined more deeply with symbolic aspects of people's identity, connected to increasingly national, and even global, discourses.

This concern is easy to witness in Zahay's "God's Warriors: Gunlore and Identity in the Vernacular Discourse of a Survivalist Community." While the chapter focuses on a particular group in the 1980s, the larger cultural identities and symbolic matrices are still very much present in the United States some forty years later. For these groups, and many others, the gun has become a religious symbol, essential to their identity as "soldiers for Christ," which many see as fulfilling biblical prophecies in contemporary times. Interestingly, not only was an absolute dichotomy made between those following God and those misled by Satan, but this dichotomy was mapped onto the rural-urban divide, with the city (and government) being envisioned as a place of evil as opposed to the godly rural dwellers.

Such discourses are reflected in many more mainstream beliefs and groups that frequently locate a complex binary system of rural, godly good guys versus the urban, ungodly bad guys. While guns often do serve pragmatic purposes for rural people, it is also clear that for some rural dwellers, inspired by various antigovernment religious movements, guns serve primarily as symbols of violence, encapsulating, as the author puts it, their "religiously charged anti-government beliefs." Zahay's analysis reminds us of the long history of such movements, and the continued violent danger that they pose. Even as one group disbands or is broken apart, other groups coalesce along similar symbolic lines, with the image of the gun as weapon playing a predominant role.

The theme of vernacular religious aspects of the gun is taken up again in Mechling's "Gun Play as Vernacular Religious Experience." Here the role of play, and ritual actions, surrounding guns are highlighted to show the way that such routines are a part of much of American (particularly male) childhood, and, once again, visually displayed in various ways. Mechling is interested in the way that such matrices of meanings construct ways for people to act and engage with others, organizing society. Here his interest in religious aspects is primarily interested in this symbolic structuring of society, rather than explicit appeals to beliefs in supernatural deities, although (as per Zahay) it is clear that they often overlap. Mechling's insights into the important development stages of childhood play show how such symbolic meanings are enculturated in youth, becoming a naturalized (if highly symbolic) part of the world around them. The child often plays at dying, and at killing, and at all sorts of adult activities, including with perennial items such as toy guns, and gun-toting costumes, building the culturally gun-linked categories of the cowboy, the soldier, the bad guy. In examining these traditions, we can observe them being formed long before adulthood, all with their different significations. Mechling traces the iconic roles and differing significations of the soldier, who uses guns for combat, as well as the sport hunter, who uses guns to kill nonhuman animals. These roles create pathways of identity for American children, who use the gun as a multivalent symbol and real object with which to construct their adult identities. For Mechling, the gun is a "magical" object, due to its highly charged symbolism, and its connection with death, for the groups he details.

The roles of well-made tools and procurers of meat, alongside notions of family heritage, are further brought out in Atwood's "A Knack for Precision: The Art and Science of a Gun-Making Dynasty." Atwood, offering an auto-ethnographic account of her own family's gunsmithing traditions, paints a portrait using many common themes: rural living, hunting, and family traditions. For Atwood's family, gun use is intimately tied with a family heritage of gunsmithing, a craft of hand making durable, well-made tools. The making of guns, the knowledge of guns, the giving and receiving of handmade guns, creates a strong sense of identity for the family, enmeshed in the larger rural, hunting community. For several members, this was not only an avocation, but at times a vocation as well. The major role of the gun for these individuals, Atwood notes, is the gun's ability to create bonds, through shared knowledge, experiences, memories, gifts, and the like, and to construct a family identity based on a material craft.

The gun's symbolic roles in both gunsmithing and heritage are brought up again, but on more general and historical scale, in Bender's work "Percussioned Flintlocks: A Nineteenth-Century Folk Art." The remarkable historical developments of the gun in the last two hundred years create another kind of lore, one more interested in the stories of the past than the latest technological developments. This deeply diachronic view is a reminder of the gun's time-depth as an important symbol in building American culture and American history. Bender also notes the desire to recreate particular eras in gun manufacturing, and even the reconversion of percussion-firing mechanisms back to their original flintlocks. This is perhaps a comment on heritage itself, when the author notes that these reconversions are for the most part show pieces, rather than usable, the symbolic in such nostalgia overshadowing the functional.

The effects of such symbolisms continue among many groups, and Summerville, in his "Young Guns: Folklore and the Fetishization of Guns Among Juveniles at an all-Male Correctional Facility in Tucson Arizona," usefully employs the idea of the *fetish* to help understand the symbolic power accorded to guns. The fetish is a material object imbued by the believer with great status and spiritual power, bestowing a sense of empowerment to the owner. For this group of incarcerated African American male juveniles, guns are far removed from hunting, or handcrafts, and instead highlight in particular a perceived need for self-protection.

Summerville traces the American history as entwined with the gun, in such episodes of the national mythology as the American Revolution and subsequent wars of conquest against Native Americans (or, "How the West Was Won" in common parlance). Tracing the role of guns as a motif in the national origin story allows a fuller view of its cultural impacts on all sorts of various groups, including the incarcerated African American juveniles detailed by Summerville. Besides self-protection, guns were also seen as currency and exchange items, feminine objects to possess ("she's a beauty!"), and intricately involved in human death, particularly homicides. Summerville notes that many discuss the exchange value as one providing both monetary and social bonds, as in the idea of "holding a gun" for someone. These widespread themes frequently take the form of folk narratives, often reflecting ethnic identity, as in the folk legend of Stagolee, or the more contemporary representation in rap and hip-hop. Guns thus become welded once again to essentialized notions of identity, of belonging, of being. Summerville shows how particular formative narratives (myths) can help shape ongoing symbolic understandings of guns, with very real, and often problematic, implications.

The role of symbolic communications in shaping communal experience is taken to a further height in the Eliason and Eliason chapter "4chan, Firearm, and Folklore," where the "communities" are all online communities, following various traditions of displaying real firearms online. The highly detailed group-specific traditions, and even group-specific jargon, seems similar to those found in tight-knit communities, yet these groups are not particularly geographically located, but rather dispersed on a potentially near-global scale. With this essential deterritorialization, the varieties of visual display of real guns becomes the defining quality of much of the group's traditions and even identity. Without being there, guns are adrift from any practical purpose (you can't shoot someone over the internet), and thus the symbolic communications rely largely on the visual signifier, the computer screen, to mark group—and self—identities.

In Robert Glenn Howard's investigation of internet gunlore, the cultural exchanges are not restricted to images alone, but also verbal as well, such as his well-evinced proverb, "You show your 1911 to your friends and your glock to your enemies" (Howard, chapter 9 of this volume). Such verbal traditions travel both online and offline, and display the complicated relationship between assumed vernacular discourses, and the more institutional, corporate world of internet platforms and gun manufacturers. In participating in traditional speech featuring guns, the speaker fashions a cultural place and particular understanding for guns, both online and offline, highlighting the connections between symbolic behaviors and real-world consequences.

The move to pure signification is achieved in the realm of cosplay, where groups are formed around the idea of "play guns" rather than real guns. As Brickley investigates in "Nerf Punk: The Firearm Folklife of 'Alternative History' Cosplay," historical stories and overall symbolic attributes are not confined to real-world concerns but can indeed be completely separated, moving into a play frame of make-believe. The notion of adult play is perhaps a bit different than childhood or developmental play as explored by Mechling. In Mechling's analysis, childhood gun games were a way of preparing for real guns, whereas for Brickley's group, the play *is* the final product. Gun play, then, can be seen as inherently symbolic, and removed from the real, yet linked to the real in various and diverse ways. Even in make-believe communities about make-believe guns, the gun remains a powerful organizing symbol, showing how the outer world's roles of guns inform and impinge on the play realm.

Other aspects, outside of the function of guns, carry over in interesting ways—for example, the emphasis on handcrafting is apparent in the cosplay groups, with a great deal of emphasis put on craft skills. Here, too, we can see the effects when the symbol fully disengages from the actual thing: the point of handcrafting in the cosplay community is for the gun as a part of the overall costume, meant purely for display and theatrical purposes, whereas in other handcrafting, although aesthetics clearly plays a role, the ultimate purpose was to produce a working tool. It is interesting that we can note the overlaps with heritage here, as with those reconversions of percussion flintlocks to the original firing mechanism: these were also meant for show, and not so much for usability. The elevation of an object to heritage, it seems, can bring with it the strong symbolic qualities quite separated from mundane usage.

CONCLUSION

The chapters in this book have emphasized the symbolic role of guns for a wide variety of groups that employ them as part of their cultural repertoire. Guns are both a real thing and a highly charged semiotic symbol with a wide variety of overlapping themes and meanings. Very often the symbolic nature of guns can appear to outweigh their pragmatic functions. For those seeking to understand America's "love affair with guns," or to engage in meaningful debates regarding the proper legal regulations of firearms, it may be helpful to listen closely to the various chapters in this work, and to the cultural and symbolic manifestations of guns in the various communities that make up the nation, in order to better understand what guns signify, differently, to different groups.

Symbols have, ultimately, real effects, and with guns in American culture, we witness the deadly manifestations of these symbolic constructions on a daily basis, ranging from murders and mass shootings to suicides and accidents. America's "love affair with guns" is a love affair with a powerful tool made for killing. For many Americans, this "love affair" is a scourge of the wider society, and for many the symbolism of guns is unequivocally negative, and the exalted symbolic role that guns play in other groups is likewise viewed as deeply problematic. Guns are a deeply polarizing issue in the contemporary US, with profoundly different sets of significations in different groups.

So, in the end, what *can* a gun signify? As shown in the gun cultures displayed in this book, they can signify a great deal, and are used as communicative devices, symbols, and motifs, proclaiming various viewpoints and lifeways. The various overlapping and at times contrasting significations of guns reveal a complex fabric that weaves through much of American society, including those who are anti-gun, at times virulently so. These groups, perhaps especially the fervent anti-gun groups, also have their own highly symbolic roles for guns in their own community discourses and identities. All this is a part of gunlore.

My own background in Alaska is, in some ways, the odd one out: as I noted, guns are ubiquitous in Alaskan subsistence communities, but seem to lack a great deal of signification found in the other groups. It may be helpful here to consider that silence, too, can be full of meaning. De Saussure, in setting up the basic approaches of semiotics and interpersonal communication, pointed out that silence is often a signifier. We tend to think of silence as an absence of communication, but that is not always the case: think, for example, of being asked to observe a moment of silence for some tragedy or human loss: in these contexts, silence *is* what is being performed, and the absence of silence (e.g., the colleagues who continue to chat during the called-for moment of silence) reveals a failure to act appropriately. *When* silence is significant, then, in what contexts and among what groups, becomes the more operative question (see, for example, Ephratt 2018).

I think it notable that all the other chapters deal with guns' very active signification: guns are loud, and the discourse about guns is, in the US anyway, a very noisy discourse indeed. Yet for the community I grew up in, while the actual guns (and chainsaws) were blaringly loud, the symbolic discourse about guns was almost completely silent. This is, I suggest, largely because guns are so ubiquitous, and used in an everyday manner for mundane, mostly food-procuring, tasks. When the practical tasks are routine, and every day, focused on utilitarian aspects of procuring meat, there may be no particular need for an ethos of symbolic guns. I will even go so far as to propose a sort of equation, where the further removed from actual, mundane use the semiotic object travels, the more it is likely to be encoded with symbolic associations, held up by appeals to history, to religion, to myth, and to tradition.

This formula is hinted at towards the end of Frandy's chapter on guns in northern Wisconsin and exemplified in Brickley's display of the strong role of make-believe guns in the cosplayer communities. The further away from mundane use the gun travels, the more symbolic the discourses seem to become.

During my childhood in the woods, on many nights just before bedtime my mother would have my brother and me curl up under wool army blankets out on our porch and "listen to the evening sounds": the quiet hoots and distant howls, the splash of the occasional jumping fish out on the lake, the various nocturnal chats of the subarctic forest. We were warned to be completely still, completely quiet, to better listen to the faint and uncommon disruptions of pure quiet. And during the day, hiking through the forest, my father would commonly remind us of this as well: observe silence if you want to hear, if you want to learn.

It would be easy to overlook the sounds of silence in the vociferous gun debate, but in my own home community, this silence is very loud indeed. In this conclusion I have tried to employ it as a particular vantage point from which to observe the rather noisy presence of guns elsewhere in the United States, where their symbolic value seems far stronger and far more active than anything practical, pragmatic, or mundane. It seems that, in America at least, guns exist primarily in symbolic form, spread throughout the national culture in a variety of means and manifestations: in our songs, our crafts, our stories, our groups, our families, our play . . . and that guns, as cultural objects deeply enmeshed with many facets of American identity, can never truly be separated from gunlore.

Notes

1. https://www.cdc.gov/nchs/pressroom/states/alaska/ak.htm.

2. "Truck Guns" by Steve Meyer. *Anchorage Daily News*. 2020/1/11.

3. The word "subsistence" contains pejorative connotations in contemporary English—"just subsisting"—while for many Native peoples in Alaska, and a few non-Natives, is a treasured and far-preferred way of life.

References

Boraas, Alan, with Catherine Knott. 2018. "The Indigenous Salmon Cultures of the Bristol Bay Watersheds" in *Bristol Bay Alaska, Natural Resources of the Aquatic and Terrestrial Ecosystems*, edited by Carol Ann Woody, 3–28. Jupiter, FL: J. Ross.

Boraas, Alan, with Catherine Knott. 2013. "Traditional Ecological Knowledge and Cultural Characterization of the Nushagak and Kvichak Watersheds, Alaska." *Environmental Protection Agency Bristol Bay Assessment*, vol. 2, Appendix D, 144 pages. http://cfpub .epa.gov/ncea/bristolbay/recordisplay.cfm?deid=242810#Download.

Ephratt, Michal. 2018. Iconic Silence: A Semiotic Paradox or a Semiotic Paragon? *Semiotica* 221: 239–59.

Kalesan, Bindu, Marcos D. Villarreal, Katherine M. Keyes, and Sandro Galea. 2015. "Gun Ownership and Social Gun Culture." *Journal of Injury Prevention* 0: 1–5. http://dx.doi .org/10.1136/injuryprev-2015-041586.

ABOUT THE CONTRIBUTORS

Sandra Bartlett Atwood holds an MS in American studies/folklore with an emphasis in worldview, belief, and creation narratives, and a PhD in environment and society with an emphasis in Indigenous ecological knowledge (IEK) or Indigenous ways of knowing and being (IWKB). Atwood is currently a Professor of Indigenous Studies at Ohkotoki'aahkkoiyiiniimaan (Stone Pipe) or Lethbridge College, which is located on the unceded lands of the Blackfoot Confederacy. She recently coauthored a paper "Níksókowaawák as Axiom: The Indispensability of Comprehensive Relational Animacy in Blackfoot Ways of Knowing, Being, and Doing," published in *Society and Natural Resources* and awarded Publication of the Year by Utah State University's Quinney College of Natural Resources.

Nathan E. Bender is a special collections librarian/archivist at the McCracken Research Library, Buffalo Bill Center of the West, Cody, Wyoming. He has authored numerous peer-reviewed articles and book chapters on western history, folklore, and firearms history, including the book *The Art of the English Trade Gun in North America*. Currently an editor for *The Rocky Mountain Fur Trade Journal*, his published research includes a history of the Hawken rifles and the mountain man John "Liver-Eating" Johnston.

London Brickley earned a PhD in folklore and biotechnology from the University of Missouri–Columbia. Her primary research interests and publications focus on the intersections and interplay between folklore, science, and popular culture.

Eric A. Eliason is a professor and teaches folklore and the Bible as literature at Brigham Young University in Provo, Utah. His previous publications include *Wild Games: Hunting and Fishing Traditions in North America* (with Dennis Cutchins); *Warrior Ways: Explorations in Modern Military Folklore* (with Tad Tuleja); *The Island of Lace: Drawn Threadwork on Saba in the Dutch*

Caribbean (with Scott Squire); and *Black Velvet Art* (with Scott Squire); as well as, recently, *The Bible and the Latter-day Saint Tradition* (with Taylor Petrey and Cory Crawford). Hachette publishing's *Hammerhead Six* features chaplain Eliason's service work during the deployment of the 19th Special Force Group (Airborne) to Afghanistan in 2004.

Noah D. Eliason graduated from Brigham Young University in 2022 and currently works as an electrical engineer designing industrial control panels in Woods Cross, Utah. This finances his hobby as a DYI firearms enthusiast.

Tim Frandy is a folklorist, an assistant professor of Nordic studies at the University of British Columbia, and part of the Sámi American community. Frandy's work centers on Indigenous communities, decolonization, education, and environments. Frandy's translation of *Inari Sámi Folklore* is the first polyvocal anthology of Sámi oral tradition published in English, and Frandy's and B. Marcus Cederström's coedited volume *Culture Work: Folklore for the Public Good*—recognized by *Smithsonian Magazine* as one of the best academic books of 2022—explores community-engaged public folklore praxis today. Frandy works extensively with members of the Lac du Flambeau Anishinaabe community to revitalize traditional arts and practices, from birchbark canoe building to the snowsnake game, through culturally responsive curricula.

Robert Glenn Howard is founder and director of digital studies and designlab and professor of communication in the Department of Communication Arts at the University of Wisconsin–Madison where he teaches courses on everyday communication, digital media, religion, and folklore studies. He has published numerous articles and book chapters and has authored five books including *Digital Jesus: The Making of a New Christian Fundamentalist Community on the Internet* and *Tradition in the Twenty-First Century: Locating the Role of the Past in the Present* (with Trevor J. Blank). Most broadly, his research seeks to uncover the possibilities and limits of empowerment through everyday expression in social media by focusing on the intersection of individual human agency and participatory performance.

Jay Mechling is professor emeritus of American studies at the University of California, Davis. He is a Fellow of the Americana Folklore Society. He is a past president of the Western States Folklore Society, editing that society's journal, *Western Folklore*, for five years. He is author of three books on masculinity, including *On My Honor: Boy Scouts and the Making of American*

Youth, and over one hundred forty journal articles, book chapters, and encyclopedia articles.

Annamarie O'Brien Morel is an independent folklorist who works in museums and for nonprofits. She currently works for Folkstreams as the communications manager and Treasure Island Museum. Morel received her PhD in American studies from Penn State University, with a certificate in ethnography and folklife and concentrations in popular and folk culture, and media studies and visual culture.

Raymond Summerville earned his PhD in English with a concentration in folklore, oral tradition, and culture from the University of Missouri–Columbia. He has published work in *Proverbium: Yearbook of International Proverb Scholarship* and the *Journal of American Folklore*. He is author of *Proverb Masters: Shaping the Civil Rights Movement*, which explores intersections among folklore, history, and social justice. He teaches at Fayetteville State University in North Carolina in the Department of English: Literature, Teaching, Pre-Law, and Creative and Professional Writing.

Tok Thompson is professor of anthropology and communications at the University of Southern California. Thompson has published numerous book chapters, scholarly journal articles, and books including *Posthuman Folklore and the Truth of Myth* (with Gregory Schrempp). He has taught folklore as a visiting professor at universities in Northern Ireland, Iceland, and Ethiopia. While in graduate school, he cofounded and coedited for fifteen years the open access journal *Cultural Analysis: An Interdisciplinary Forum on Folklore and Popular Culture*. From 2013 to 2017 he was editor for *Western Folklore*. He currently coedits a series on world mythology for Oxford University Press.

Megan L. Zahay is a PhD candidate in the Department of Communication Arts at the University of Wisconsin–Madison. An interdisciplinary scholar, her work appears in journals such as *Media and Communication, Journalism & Mass Communication Quarterly*, and *Journalism Practice*, as well as the *Oxford Handbook of Christian Fundamentalism*. Her research explores how digital platforms enable online communities to mainstream outsider political messages and built trust with their audiences and the broader public.

INDEX

Page numbers in *italics* refer to illustrations.

4chan website, 110, *111*, *112*, 113–14, 121, 271
.22 rifle, *195*, 264–65
.32-20 Winchester, 188, 206, 266
.44 Magnum, 10

accidental deaths, 11, 116
activity-based gun communities, 22–24, 28, 30, 33, 116; air gunning, 33–34, 42; airsoft culture, 34, 137; cowboy action shooting, 24–26, *25*, 33, 251, 269; DIY gun modification, 18, 26, 142, 145, 158; flint and cap clubs, 26, 128; hunting, 3, 18, 22, 247, 264–69; paintball markers, 34, 248; personal defense, 21, 27, 30; physical competitions, 23–25, 30, 34, 192; preppers, 28, 172
AK-47, 7–8, *8*, 11
Alaska, 98, 101, 262–63, 273
alternative history (AH): community, 142, 144; cosplay, 137–39, *140*, *141*, 150, 157, 271; costume designing, 142–43; guns, 139–40, *145*, 145–48, 151, 159, *160*, 161; museum, 144, 147; symbols, 159–61; weapons, *154*, 155
American Civil Religion ("public religion"), 245
"American Momma," 66
American Revolution, 26, 43, 270
Angeli, Jake, 163–64, 182
antigovernment activism, 164–67, 172, 175, 178, 182, 269
apocalypticism, 164–70, 176, 179, 181

AR-15, 7–8, *8*, 18–19, 27, 94, *95*
armed genders: men, 179; protests, 32, 163–64; religious groups, 166; security guards, 49; women, 63–64, 67, 73, 82, 86
artifacts, 165, 167, 181, 246, 255
automatic assault weapons, 8, 14, 33, *154*, 238

background checks, 5
Baldwin, Alec, 12
Bartlett, Charles, 187–88, *189*, *192*, *196*, *209*, *211*
bee meme, 217–18, *219*
Bellesiles, Michael A., 6
Bennett, Kaitlin, 17, 30, *31*, 64–65, *65*, 86
biathlons, 24
Biden, Joe, 5
Bill of Rights, 245
Black America: gun culture in, 14, 32–33, 58, 270; gun violence in, 44–45, 167, 174; and young males, 41–42, 57, 60
Black Panthers, 32–33
Branch Davidians, 166
"brandishing," 19, 177
Browder, Laura, 63–65, 72, 82, 86
Brown, Jeffrey, 71, 79
Browning, John Moses, 195, *197*, 226
Buffalo Bill, 25
bullseye shooting, 23–24
buttstock, 8

Calguns.net, 222
carrying a concealed weapon (CCW), 20, 89
Catalina Mountain School, 48, 51

Christianity, 164–67, 171–72; and dispensationalism, 169; fundamentalism of, 170–71; Identity movement, 166, 171, 173, 175, 182; warriors for, 177–80

civil rights movement, 6, 33

Civil War (American), 26, 43, 133, 140, 245

Coalition to Stop Gun Violence, 33

Cold War, 7, 153, 171

Colt .45, 157

Colt 1911 pistols, 9–10, 218, 226, 228; vs. Glock, 224, 229

concealed-carry accessories, 77–79, 137, 139–40, 144, 222–24

concealed-carry community, 20, 27, 82, 88; permits and instructors, 19, 20–21; photos and selfies, 66–67, *67*, *68*, 73, *74*, 75–77, *80*, *84*, 90; posts, 64, *65*, 75, 83–85, *87*, 90; weapons, 66, 74

conservatives: commentators, 65; and family values, 73, 89; and guns, 19, 29, 64; politics, 86, 170; women with firearms, 63–64, 82, 85, 89

Constitution (US), 142; Second Amendment, 43, 66, 81, 85, 164, 171

costume play (cosplay), 70, 139–42, 150–51, 156, 251, 271; and guns, 138–41, 147, 150, 157. *See also* alternative history (AH)

"Covenant, the Sword, and the Arm of the Lord, The" (CSA), 164–67, 169, 172, 173, 174–78; siege in 1985, 174–75, 179, 182; survival manual, 165, 175–77, 180–82

cowboy action shooting, 24, *25*, 26, 33, 251, 269

Cramer, Clayton E., 6

criminal activity, 3, 5, 14–16, 45, 49, 59, 166, 173; fear of, 82–83, 85; "gang," 14, 180; urban, 82, 87

Custer, George Armstrong, 25

Dalai Lama, 19, *20*, 21

Davy Crockett "craze," 251

death, thoughts of, 44, 48, 242, 247–49, 251–52

Declaration of Independence, 245

DeConde, Alexander, 42–44

Department of Defense, 30

Die Hard, 233

Dragon Con, 138, 143–44, 148, 151, 156

Eliason, Eric, 9–11, 271

Ellison, James, 172–75, 177, 182

"Everyday Carry" community (EDC), 33, 66

fantasy play, 143, 248–49, 251–52. *See also* costume play (cosplay)

Federal Bureau of Investigation (FBI), 165–67, 173–75, 182

fetishisms, 41–42, 46–48, 56

firearms: advertisements, 72, 77, 86, 219, 228; and AH, 148–49, 154, 161; antiques, 26, 97; artistry and modification, 17, 26, 33, 41, 104; and black powder flintlock ignition systems, 126–27, *127*; enthusiasts, 10, 28, 33, 116, 225; as expressions of love, 110, 206, 215; and folk groups, 7, 186; history, 105, 126, 131–33; manufacturers of, 105, 113, 219, 225–26, 232; marketing, 41, 72, 86; nineteenth-century advances of, 126, 129; ownership, 3, 16, 32; and percussion-ignition systems, 126–27, *128*; as protection, 3, 10, 51, 83, 86, 257; in rural areas, 17, 97–98, 100, 263, 268–70; safety, 12, 118, 238, 272; for self-defense, 10, 167; as tools, 30, 97–98, 110, 178; training, 19, 28, 177; women and, 64, 66, *74*, 81, 85, 88

first-person shooter (FPS) videogames, 248–49

flintlocks, processioned, 127–33, *127*, *128*, *129*, *130*, *131*, *132*, 272

flow, 242–43

folk artistry, 7, 17, 113, 126, 138–39, 158; on percussion hammers, 129, *130*, *131*

folk groups, 7, 111, 121–22, 186, 196, 202, 215; expressions of, 3, 137, 157; speech about guns, 3–5, 113, 116, 224; traditions of, 58, 138, 187

INDEX

folklore, 58–59, 123, 186, 242–43; aggregation of previous expression, 218–19, *219*; gun genre, 3, 5, 41, 117, 119–21, 186, 245

Frandy, Bill, *103*, 104–5

Frandy, John, 106

Frandy, Tim, 263, 267–68, 278

Frandy, Tom and Patty, 98–100

Freud, Sigmund, 46, 247–48, 256

"gangster" culture, 14, 53

Geertz, Clifford, 238, 240–42, 247, 252

Global War on Terror, 34

Glock, *227*, 230–32; fanboy, 224, 228–31; proverb, 10, 218, 224–25, *227*, *233*, 271; vs. Colt 1911, 224, 229

GlockTalk, 222

Good, the Bad and the Ugly, The, 14

gun communities: activities in, 22–24, 33; on daily carrying, 27, 33; on ethnic or racial identifications, 22, 44; "fudds," 10; on gender and sexuality, 22, 30, 32; online, 224, 227, 231; on politics or advocacy, 22; on "prepping," 28; SHTF situations in, 28

gun control, 85, 171, 263

Gun Control Act of 1968, 33

gun culture, 17, 34; American, 6, 21, 42, 262, 273; and anti-institutional authority, 164; family photos in, 113, 121, *188*; jokes, 14, 73, 110; meanings about, 34, 94, 101, 159, 161, 164–65, 220, 224; military, 157; modern, 60, 69, 218; online, 83, 164, 224, 237; proverbs, 10, 218, 224–25; religious, 164, 165–66, 171–72, 180; rural communities, 98; in US, 6, 10, 22, 42, 182, 262; women's, 30, 60, 89; youths' lust for, 52–54. *See also* "gunfolk"; gunlore

gun enthusiasts, 19

gun laws, 11, 15, 45, 49, 223

gun ownership: advantages of, 234–35, 245, 263; in politics, 64; in rural America, 17, 262–63; in US, 5, 16, 32; women, 64, 69, 89; in the world, 16

gun play, 238–39, 249–51, 272

"gun porn," 70–71, 74, 113–15, 228, *231*

gun rights, 29; vs. gun control, 6, 234, 245, 274

gun violence, 5–6, 16, 44–45, 88, 165, 175, 256; against women, 69, 80, 83, 86; among male youth, 41–42, 45, 49, 57; in US, 44, 109, 167, 245, 269

gun-control advocates, 6, 64, 85

"gunfolk," 3, 7, 11–12, 17, 21, 29–30, 33, 186, 215

gunlore, 3–7, 21, 35, 220; expressions, 139, 176; genres, 11, 101, 147, 165, 181, 245, 273–74; online, 217–20, 232–35, 271

gun-related activities: biathlons, 24; competitions, 23–25, 34, 182; cosplay, 142; hunting, 22, 98; paintball, 34, 248; plinking, 12, 23

gun-rights: advocates, 6, 63, 85, 245; "Covenant," 171–72, 177; family values, 64, 73, 164; fear, 51, 82, 155; group identification, 56, 102, 271; masculinity, 71–72, 79–80, 90; nationhood, 90, 160; necessity, 92, 100, 155, 263; power, 73, 102, 156, 220, 234, 247; religious identity, 164–65, 167, 182, 269; rite of passage, 56, 188; safety and protection, 51, 56–57, 100, 220, 270; sexuality, 72–73, 256; violence, 82, 100, 269, 272

guns: cases, 105–7; cleaning rituals, 212; competitions, 23–25, 30, 34; cultural dystopic-style, 154, 159; exchange value of, 51, 55, 270; expressions about, 3–5, 9; fetishization of, 41, 54–56, 270; as magical objects, 240, 246, 255–56, 269; maintenance of, 177, 191, 211–23; and male youths, 41–42, 45, 49, 51, 56–57, 75; online debates about, 223–24, 229–32, 234; online discourse about, 221–23, 227–28; racks for, 263; reloading, 27, 187–88, 197–98; respect for, 188, 212–13; selfies with, 66, 69, 82; semi-automatic, 8–9, 49–50, 171; and sex, 51, 54, 72, 79, 256; sexualized images of women with, 30, *31*, 52–53, 63, 71–72; symbolism of, 42, 49, 164–65;

and visual culture, 64, 69, 72, 90, 94, 105–8
Guns and Ammo Forum, 222
gunshot fatalities, 44
gunsmithing, 6, 17, 102, 187, 189–95, *199*, 209, 264, 270; Bartlett, 215; culture, 186, 188–89; and industry standardization, 18, 187; and modular design, 18, 27; tools, 200, 202

Haag, Pamela, 6
Hackworth, David, 8, 11
handcrafting, 272. *See also* costume play (cosplay)
handguns, 19, 27, 45, 88, 207, 224. *See also* guns
Harcourt, Bernard E., 48–52, 55–56
historical battles, reenactments of, 26, 30, 33, 156
hobby-based gun communities, 5, 24, 26–27, 164, 278
holsters, 17, 66–67, 78–81, 136, 206
homicides, 44, 270
hunting, 18, 105–7, 247, 253–54, 267; communities, 99, 101; for food, 96, 187, 254, 264–67; for recreation, 22, 95, 102, 238, 249; for sport, 3, 22, 214, 253, 269; for subsistence, 96, 107, 263–68, 273; for trophies, 22, 94, 254
Hutchins, Halya, 12

Industrial Revolution, 6, 148
infantry weapons, 7, 157
International Defensive Pistol Association, 24

James, William, 239, 241–44
January 6 Capitol riot, 163–64, 182
Jim Crow laws, 32

Kent State, *31*, 63–66, 86
killings, 51, 214, 246–48, 252–54
"knock back power," 9–11

Korean War, 10
Ku Klux Klan, 171

Latinos and guns, 44–45
law enforcement: agencies, 225–26; folklore about, 30; local, 30, 173–74; training, 24, 28
LGBTQ+ gun groups, 32
Live Action Role Playing (LARPing), 144; steampunk, 33, 138, 150, 156, *160*

Malcolm X, *32*, 33
"mama grizzly," 81–82
mass shootings, 6, 82, 109, 272; at schools, 45, 94
McCallum, E. L., 42, 46–48, 52
McVeigh, Timothy, 165–66, 174, 182
media, 41, 60, 233. *See also* movies and TV shows; social media
memes, 8, 18, 20, 21, 94, 95, 217, 219, 233. *See also* bee meme; Glock: proverb
Menace II Society, 14
meta-folkloric digital folk art, 11, *20*, 21
M-4, 8
militaries, 7, 9, 103, 225–26, 248; industrial complexes, 88; training in, 24, 28, 180, 246. *See also* United States: military
Million Mom March, 64
Moms Demand Action, 64
Moro Rebellion, 9
motherhood, and gun advocacy, 64, 66–67, 80–82, 89
movies and TV shows, 26, 34, 71–72, 251. *See also individual titles*
M-16, 7–8
Mulford Act, 33
Mulvey, Laura, 72–73
Murrah building, 165–67. *See also* Oklahoma City bombing
mysticism, 239, 242–43

National Rifle Association (NRA), 33; alignment with political parties, 63, 164;

marketing techniques, 6, 249; "Refuse to Be a Victim" campaign, 84, 86, *87*, 88; safety rules, 13; sponsoring women's gun campaigns and organizations, 64, 86; training efforts, 11, 86
Native Americans, 129–30, 270
NATO, 7
nature and animals, respect for, 96, 211, 213–15, 266
"Negligent Discharge" (ND), 11, 116, *118*, 121
Nerf "Maverick," 136, *136*, *145*, 145–47
neuroscience, 243–44, 256
Noble, Kerry, 173–77
nuclear family, 81, 90, 164

Oakley, Annie, 63
Odinism, 171
Oklahoma City bombing, 165, 174–75, 182
Olympic games, 24
One-Eyed Jacks, 14
Order, the, 166, 174
oxytocin, 244, 256

Palin, Sarah, 63–64
"para-gun" groups, 33–34
Pietz, William, 46–47, 55
pistols, 9–10, 17, *18*, 24, *50*, 224–26. *See also* guns
percussion hammers, 128–29, 130–33, *130*, *131*, *132*. *See also* folk artistry
Pershing, John J., 9
personal defense communities, 27, 30. *See also* concealed-carry community; preppers
playfighting, 239, 248, 252–53; pretending to kill/die, 246–49, 252. *See also* gun play
plinking, 12, 23
postfeminist culture, 81, 88–89
posttraumatic stress disorder (PTSD), 248
preppers, 28. *See also* survivalists
proverbs, 3, 10, 218–21, 224–28, *233*, 271. *See also* Glock: proverb

QAnon Shaman, 163, 182

Railroad Bill, 58–59
Reagan, Ronald, 33, 63, 86
religion, 241–42; beliefs and practice, 167–69, 176–77, 238, 240, 244, 254
rifles, 8, 24, 94, *95*, 193, *205*, 249. *See also* firearms; guns
"right to bear arms," 29, 43, 64, 158, 172, 245
riots, 163, 176, 180; at Capitol building, 163–64, 182
Ruby Ridge standoff, 63, 165–67, 175
Ruger Mini 14, 94, *95*, 193
rural communities, 98–100, 263, 269
rural/urban divide, 8, 17, 268
Russian roulette, 14

safety rules, 11–13, *13*, 116, 206, 212, 235
Schlegelmilch, Herban A., 102–3
self-defense, 16, 19, 28, 234–35; for young males, 41, 45, 48–49, 51, 270; for women, 64, 67, 74, 82, 85–86, 88–89
selfies, 30, 65–70, 76, 87–90; vernacular, 30, 66, 69–70, 76, 89
shooting: bullseye, 23–24; historical, 26; practice, 27, 207, 238; "skeet," 24; sports, 23–24, 30; target, 18, 23–24, 97, 205, 214; "trap," 24
shotguns, 24, *104*, 199, 208
side-grip, 14–15
sighting jig, 201–2, *203*
Sitting Bull, 25
Slater, Morris, 58–59
Smith and Wesson 500, 10, 50
social media, 31–32, 69–70, 86, 140, 220, 222–28; bee meme, 217–18, *219*; copypasta, 83, 118; digital folklore, 21, 69, 121, 220; online forums, 29, 33, 110, 122, 142, 221–22
Stagolee, 58–60, 271
standoffs, 165–66, 169
Star Wars, 252
Steele, Valerie, 54
subsistence communities, 96, 107, 263–64, 266–68, 273

suicides, 44, 83, 262
survivalists, 163, 172, 176–77

"tacti-cool," 19
terror-management theory, 247–48
toy guns, 34, 247–49, *250*, 252, 269
Trump, Donald, 182
Turner Diaries, The, 166, 174, 182

Unites States: Capitol building, 163, 182; government, 165–66, 171–72, 182; gun ownership in, 5, 16, 32, 90, 245; military, 9, 28, 31, 157, 178, 226, 230–32, 278; pistol purchases in, 230–31
urban communities, 45, 173, 262–63. *See also* rural/urban divide
urban legends, 119–21

vernacular: authority, 168, 221, 228, 232; discourses, 69, 71, 163, 220–21, 271; documents, 165, 175, 178; performance, 164, 225; photography, 69–70, 73, 89, 230, 253, 255; practices, 168–70, 248, 255, 257; and religious experiences, 239–23, 246, 255–57
veterans (US), 17, 105, 256
video games, 19, 41, 117, 248, 256
Vietnam War, 7–8, 34, 170, 226
violence, domestic, 83, 166. *See also* gun violence

Waco, Texas, standoff in, 63, 165–67, 175
waiting periods, 15
Walking Dead, The, 28, 233
warriors, 9, 163–65, 175–79, 181–82
Warsaw Pact, 7
weapons, 8, 17, 50, 94, 99, 148, 218. *See also* firearms; guns
"weapons board," 110, *111*, 112–13, 120. *See also* 4chan website
White power militia movement, 170–71, 178
White supremist groups, 165–66; Aryan Nations, 171, 173–75; Aryan Republican Army, 171; CSA, 171–72, 174–78; Ku

Klux Klan, 171. *See also* Christian Identity movements
Wild West Shows, 25–26
women: and concealed-carry groups, 27, 64, 66, 73, 86; "girls with guns," 30, *31*, *68*, 72; "gun girls," 30, *31*, *68*, 68–69; and gun ownership, 64, 69, 85; gun rights, 64, *65*, 89; self-defense, 30, 74, 83, 89; self-empowerment, 67, 85, *87*, 88, 90; sexuality, 30, *31*, 72, 80
World War II, 17, 34, 105, 170, 226, 249
WROL (without rule of law), 28

Zarephath-Horeb Community Church, 172–73
Zombie apocalypse, 28, *29*